D0844750

A Jesse Stuart Reader

A Jesse Stuart Reader *Stories & poems*

selected & introduced by

JESSE STUART *with*

a Foreword by Max Bogart,

Commentary & questions

by Ella DeMers, and

An introductory note by

Jim Wayne Miller

The Jesse Stuart Foundation

Jesse Stuart Foundation
A Jesse Stuart Reader

Library of Congress Cataloging-in-Publication Data

Stuart, Jesse, date
    A Jesse Stuart reader : stories & poems / selected & introduced by
Jesse Stuart ; with a foreword by Max Bogart ; commentary &
questions by Ella DeMers ; and an introductory note by Jim Wayne
Miller.
        p.   cm.
    ISBN 0-945084-05-6 : $20.00.
    1. Kentucky--Literary collections.   I. Title.
PS3537.T92516A6   1993
818' .5209--dc20   93-21193
                                                           CIP
                                                           AC

Published By:
The Jesse Stuart Foundation
P.O. Box 391
Ashland, KY 41114
1993

To Ethel McBrayer,
a devoted educator,
a true friend to the
Stuart family, and a
member of the Board of
Directors of The Jesse
Stuart Foundation.

AN INTRODUCTORY NOTE ON
THE JESSE STUART FOUNDATION

Incorporated in 1979 for public, charitable, and educational purposes, the Jesse Stuart Foundation is devoted to preserving both Jesse Stuart's literary legacy and W-Hollow, the eastern Kentucky valley which became a part of America's literary landscape as a result of Stuart's writings. The Foundation, which controls rights to Stuart's published and unpublished literary works, is currently reprinting many of his best out-of-print books, along with other books which focus on Kentucky and Southern Appalachia.

When Stuart transferred his 730-acre farm in W-Hollow, exclusive of the home place, to the Commonwealth of Kentucky in 1980, the farm was designated the Jesse Stuart Nature Preserve and made part of the Kentucky Nature Preserves System. The Jesse Stuart Foundation cooperates with the Nature Preserve to ensure the preservation of W- Hollow.

With control of Jesse Stuart's literary estate—including all papers, manuscripts, and memorabilia—the Foundation promotes a number of cultural, recreational, and educational programs at W-Hollow and throughout Kentucky. It encourages the study of Jesse Stuart's works, and of related material, especially the history, culture, and literature of the Appalachian region.

As Kentucky's most prolific writer, and one of the country's best-known and best-loved authors, Jesse Stuart was a great American and a true ambassador of good will for his Appalachian homeland. In more than sixty published volumes, he describes his native land, its people, and their traditions and values—

such as hard work, love of the land, belief in education, devotion to country, and love of family. The Jesse Stuart Foundation is dedicated to promoting Jesse Stuart's literary achievements and to sharing his values with future generations.

Stuart also taught and lectured extensively. His teaching experience ranged from the one-room schoolhouses of his youth in eastern Kentucky to the American University in Cairo, Egypt, and embraced years of service as school superintendent, high-school teacher, and high-school principal. "First, last, always," said Jesse Stuart, "I am a teacher . . . . Good teaching is forever and the teacher is immortal."

In keeping with Stuart's devotion to teaching, the Jesse Stuart Foundation is working hard to publish materials that supplement the educational system at all levels. For example, the Foundation has reprinted seven of Stuart's junior books (for grades 3-6), and a Teacher's Guide to assist with their classroom use. The Foundation has also published many books that would be appropriate for grades 6-12, including Stuart's <u>Hie to the Hunters</u>, Thomas D. Clark's <u>Simon Kenton, Kentucky Scout</u>, and Billy C. Clark's <u>A Long Row To Hoe</u>. Other JSF publications range from books for adult literacy students to college history texts, and from cookbooks to novels. More information about JSF projects and publications may be obtained by writing the Jesse Stuart Foundation, P.O. Box 391, Ashland, KY 41114 or calling (606) 329-5233.

Jim Wayne Miller
Bowling Green, Kentucky
August 1993

FOREWORD

You enter the world of Jesse Stuart. The scene is eastern Kentucky, the hills, the mountains, the forests, the rivers, a land of primitive beauty. You meet the people of this land. Who are these people? They are determined pioneers, bold frontiersmen, feuding clansmen, brave settlers, and all of them are fierce fighters. And they are tender too. They are Jesse Stuart's people, the key to his world.

Though the scene is Kentucky, Jesse Stuart's people share the conditions of people everywhere. The themes of Jesse Stuart expose the foundations of human emotion. He has brought the humble, independent people of his land into the world of literature, where they are not Kentuckians, Californians, or New Yorkers but human beings yielding to their fate or mastering it. The result is literature with a universal appeal.

The world of Jesse Stuart, then, is people. What are they like? They are proud and loyal and tough "like the muscles of a hickory sprout." They are individuals, and one of their most cherished traditions is the sacredness of that individuality. They live with a fierce and deep-rooted love of the land. Jesse Stuart describes the closeness between the people and the land in many of his poems, essays, and stories.

> "Our roots are deep, for we are part of this land—and it is part of us.

"Land to us, to men whose ancestors fought and died for it and whose people have lived on it over a century, is a dear possession. Those who are forced to leave it never feel the same."

This land and its people are his raw material. How does Jesse Stuart use the treasury of material that is his in the Kentucky mountains? Several ways. For example, he selects an ordinary occurrence from the daily life of one of his Kentucky people, and then with a kind of magic he creates a story that fascinates thousands of readers. Take Hester King, the 135-pound weakling in the story called "No Hero." He is quite an ordinary fellow. All he wants is to be a good farmer and to make a living for his wife and children. But when crops fail and Hester is desperate for money, he agrees to go into the ring against a 386-pound wrestler. Hester becomes at that moment quite extraordinary. The Jesse Stuart storytelling magic has been applied to Hester King, and he emerges as the hero of "No Hero."

Jesse Stuart also uses folk material of his land to create a story. Take Pappie in "Rain in Tanyard Hollow." Pappie wants rain because his crops are burning up in the heat. For weeks Pappie has been trying the only cure for drought he knows: he has been killing black snakes and hanging them on the fence. He believes this will do the trick. Many of his neighbors believe it too. But somehow it is not working for Pappie. He resorts to prayer, something he had never tried for rainmaking. The results are fantastic. Jesse Stuart has woven a folk superstition into a kind of folk comedy.

All Jesse Stuart's work is filled with characters like Hester and Pappie. He has created a gallery of memorable portraits: an Indian named Cherokee Bill who modestly admitted he was "great"; Grandpa Powderjay, who had no book learning but was an "educated man"; Buck, the fighting dog in "Fight Number Twenty-five," who managed to avoid the fate of the twenty-four dogs before him; Miss Anna, who taught first grade for fifty years. Stuart's genius as a storyteller is his uncanny ability to reveal a personality in one or two paragraphs as in this one from "No Petty Thief":

> "and I watched the buggies, hug-me-tights, and the fancy express wagons.... It was fun to watch the wheels roll. I'd stand and watch them for hours, and what I wanted most in the world was to own something with wheels. Whether I could find level ground enough around our house or not for wheels to roll, if I just had something with wheels I could have sat and looked at it for hours, admiring the wheels and machinery."

Even absurd and exaggerated characters like Ezra Alcorn, who became moon-maddened in April, appear credible because of the art of Jesse Stuart.

The physical world of Jesse Stuart, its sights, sounds, and smells, comes alive in his descriptions of mountains, valleys, woodlands, and rivers. These passages are inspirational, creating a radiant and ethereal mood, lifting us out of the humdrum and heightening our sensitivity to the beautiful in nature. For example, as Stuart fondles a handful of sassafras leaves, he thinks: "I held beauty within my hand."

As he narrates the early pioneers' efforts to build new communities in the wilderness and the feuds between individuals and families, he treats the reader to the folklore of the Kentucky mountain regions.

When the major portion of an author's literary work pertains to a particular geographic region or territory, critics and historians label the writer a regionalist, or local-colorist. Generally, regional literature is literature which presents the physical landscape, the dominant features and peculiarities of a locale and its inhabitants, including the dialect, beliefs and attitudes, and folkways and customs. This literary form usually focuses upon local history, often stressing the glories and virtues of past generations in backcountry America. Hamlin Garland wrote that regional literature has "... such quality of texture and background that it could not have been written in any other place or by anyone else than a native."

All too often, however, this literary label is applied in a negative and restrictive sense. To many readers it suggests that the author's outlook is limited and that he has little knowledge of the world beyond this region.

Because a writer chooses to limit his stories and poems to a region, this does not necessarily mean that his work lacks universal implications. Jesse Stuart is a regional writer in the same way that Mark Twain, William Faulkner, and Robert Frost may be cataloged as regionalists. After all, many of Mark Twain's novels are limited to life along the Mississippi River; Faulkner's stories, with rare exceptions, are set in a mythical county in northern Mississippi; and many poems by Frost deal with northern New England and its inhabitants. Each has created a cosmos, using the geographic area as the symbol.

Readers will find the study of the language of Jesse Stuart's world a source of interest and delight. As a regionalist he has a predilection for dialect, colloquialisms, and the rhythms of frontier speech which give the English language a colorful and sprightly flavor. By including picturesque mountain expressions which are gradually becoming obsolete, Jesse preserves the country-folk vocabulary and presents realistic dialogue. Often the language is reminiscent of the sweet music of a folk song. In terms of language alone, Stuart's stories are a fine achievement, for they appeal to the ear as well as the eye.

The world of Jesse Stuart is one of conflicting currents. Generally, the main current is tenderness versus violence, but the variations are abundant. The contrasts are incessant and interwoven in Jesse Stuart's stories: compassion and kindness toward man and animal life contrasted with cruelty and meanness; the goodness of mountain people confronted with the corruption of urban influences; seemingly simple Kentucky people behaving in complex ways; deep-seated, violent conflicts between families versus peaceful coexistence; the hardships of the tenant farmer when crops fail, followed by happy days when yields are successful; a narrow provincialism balanced with a worldly outlook; primitive versus highly civilized behavior; the sneers of mountain people toward the educated person, yet the fostering of education for their children; the beauty of natural phenomena and the ugliness of particular human behavior; birth and death on the same page, occurring at the same instant; and the tragic response to death, but acceptance of it as a segment of the life cycle.

Yet in the midst of the pathos in these serious and tragic tales, he sprinkles a unique brand of frontier humor, causing the reader to laugh at many passages. A rich vein of humor and satire not unlike Mark Twain's runs through Jesse Stuart's work.

Jesse Stuart elicits the enthusiasm of readers because they quickly discover that his stories and poems are connected to their own experiences—and they respond emotionally and intellectually. In particular, his writing provides escape from daily routine, vicarious adventures into the Kentucky hills, and for all enjoyment, first and last.

In all probability Stuart's novels, short stories, and poems could not have been written in any other place or at any other time—and the depicted way of life, which we cannot forget, has all but disappeared from the American scene. It is preserved in Jesse Stuart's art, and we relive it each time we read one of his books, for his people and his world are not exclusively his. His people, and the people like him, made this country, and so they belong to all of us. The world of Jesse Stuart is, in a very real sense, your world.

Max Bogart
Princeton, New Jersey

ACKNOWLEDGMENTS

The author acknowledges with gratitude the cooperation of the publishers and publications in whose volumes the materials herein first appeared. "Nest Egg," copyright 1944 by The Atlantic Monthly Company; "The Thing You Love," *The University of Kansas City Review*, Spring, 1959; "Uncle Jeff Had a Way," *Southwest Review*; "Rain on Tanyard Hollow," reprinted by permission of Esquire, Inc., © (1941) by Esquire, Inc.; "Battle with the Bees," *Tomorrow*; "Ezra Alcorn and April," *Georgia Review*; "Wild Plums," *Household*; "The Great Cherokee Bill," *Educational Forum*; "The Moon Child from Wolfe Creek," The Curtis Publishing Company; "This Farm for Sale," *The Progressive Farmer*; "As Ye Sow, So Shall Ye Reap," from *Senior Scholastic*, copyright 1946 by Scholastic Magazines, Inc., reprinted by permission; "No Petty Thief," reprinted by permission of Esquire, Inc., © (1946) by Esquire, Inc.; "Miss Anna's Asleep," *The Land*; "Old Op and the Devil," *The Good Spirit of Laurel Ridge*, McGraw-Hill Book Company, Inc.; "A Ribbon for Baldy," reprinted by permission of Esquire, Inc., © (1956) by Esquire, Inc.; "Tradelast," *The Progressive Farmer*; "Fight Number Twenty-five," Crowell-Collier Publishing Co.; selections from *God's Oddling*, McGraw-Hill Book Company, Inc.; selections from *The Thread That Runs So True*, reprinted with the permission of Charles Scribner's Sons from *The Thread That Runs So True*, pages 11–15, 95–101, by Jesse Stuart; selections from *The Year of My Rebirth*, McGraw-Hill Book Company, Inc.; poems from *Man with a Bull-tongue Plow*, from the book *Man with a Bull-tongue Plow* by Jesse Stuart, copyright 1934, 1959 by Jesse Stuart, Dutton Paperback Edition, reprinted by permission of E. P. Dutton & Co., Inc.; poems from *Hold April*, McGraw-Hill Book Company, Inc.; "Land Where the Honey-Colored Wind Is Fair," The Curtis Publishing Company; "Our Heritage," *The Packet*, a Heath Service Bulletin for Elementary Teachers, Vol. 10, Nos. 20–21, Copyright © 1955 by D. C. Heath and Company.

CONTENTS

Jesse Stuart,
Short-Story
Writer

Nest Egg

Author's Introduction

When I look back over the years to the days when I was very young, I remember first of all going to the fields with my father. Even at six years old, I had chores to do to help him and I was proud of them. I carried drinking water for him, and I walked along behind him when he was plowing to uncover the corn that had been buried by dirt from the plow. When I got tired, I'd go to sleep under a shade tree.

Another early memory of my childhood is gathering eggs on our farm for the market in Greenup. Since we hardly ever had much cash money in those days, we had to use butter and eggs for barter in Greenup to get the things that we couldn't make or raise on the farm, things like salt, pepper, coffee, and sugar. Every Saturday my father and I would walk the 5 miles to Greenup; it seemed like a great journey to me. And it was all the more exciting to me because I had gathered the eggs we were carrying.

One afternoon when I was hunting for the hens who had made nests away from the chicken house, I came upon a hen setting on her nest in the pawpaw grove where she was sure I wouldn't find her. When the hen saw me, she jumped off her nest and I counted twenty-two eggs. The hen ran away, clucking. When I told my mother about the nest I had found, she said: "Jesse, gather those eggs before that hen sits long enough to spoil them." When I went back, the hen was setting

3

again, and again she jumped off and ran away. I took all the eggs. I stood thoughtfully a moment. I hated to rob this hen of all her eggs. I put one egg back so she would find it when she returned to the nest. But I never dreamed what a remarkable chicken this hen would hatch and raise. And I never dreamed at that moment that this chicken would become the hero of the first short story I'd ever write.

However, when I wrote "Nest Egg," I didn't know it was a short story; it was written as a theme for English class at Greenup High School. I had just passed my sixteenth birthday. It was the beginning of my sophomore year in high school. Before I entered Greenup High School, I had had about twenty-three months of rural education in a one-room country school, Plum Grove, where the teacher taught fifty classes in six hours, from the first grade to the eighth. Despite my limited education, I liked to write themes in English class. We wrote themes one day a week.

Since our teacher Mrs. R. E. Hatton said we would write better about the things we knew, she let us choose our own subject. So I wrote about animals and birds and events that happened on our farm and in our neighborhood among the hills of eastern Kentucky. That was my world. One of the themes I wrote in Mrs. Hatton's class was about my rooster that I had named Nest Egg. Mrs. Hatton said it was a wonderful theme; I got an A for it.

After I finished high school, I left Greenup. In the only suitcase I had, I packed many of the themes I had written for Mrs. Hatton. I first worked for a street carnival. But I lost my job for giving away rides on the Merry Mix-up. I then went to Fort Knox, Kentucky, and spent time in Army military training. Then I worked for eleven months in the steel mills. During all this time, I was trying to save money to go to college. I still carried my high school themes in my suitcase. "Nest Egg" was among them.

I left the steel mills to go in search of a college where I could work and go to school at the same time. I could not pay my way through. I had $30 to my name. Three colleges turned me down before I was accepted at Lincoln Memorial University at Harrogate, Tennessee. I worked a half day in the kitchen cleaning pots and pans and the other half of the day I went to classes. After working in the steel mills, college seemed an easy and wonderful life.

For one of the theme-writing assignments in freshman English I used "Nest Egg," my old theme from Mrs. Hatton's English class at Greenup High School. Again it got an A. In later years, at another college and in graduate work at another university, I used "Nest Egg" twice more. It always made A's. The only reason I tell this is because I believe that all the teachers who gave "Nest Egg" an A were right.

Many years later, after I had had five books published, a book of poems, two collections of short stories, an autobiography, and a novel, I was going through stacks of material I had written, and I found "Nest Egg." The copy was so old that the paper had yellowed and become brittle. I remembered that it had always got an A. I sent it off to the Atlantic Monthly. It got A there too. The money I got from the publication of "Nest Egg" would have paid for a whole year of Lincoln Memorial University. It was hard to believe that an almost-forgotten theme from high school days about my childhood on the farm would now be published as a short story in the Atlantic Monthly.

"**S**HAN, I DON'T WANT to tell you the second time to break that hen from sittin' on a nest egg," Mom said. "I don't have enough hens to spare to let one sit on a nest egg."

"Why don't you put more eggs under her, Mom?" I asked. "I never saw a hen that wants to sit on a nest like she does."

"It's too late in summer," Mom said. "She'd hatch off a gang of little chickens in dog days and they'd die. Now you go take that nest egg from her nest."

"All right, Mom," I said.

The wilted grass was hot beneath my bare feet as I walked across the carpet of wilted crab grass to a patch of pawpaw sprouts. I followed a little path into the pawpaw sprouts where the white agate sun had wilted the pawpaw leaves until they hung in wilted clusters. When I approached the nest, the old Sebright hen raised her wings and clucked. I thought she was tryin' to tell me to stay away. And when I started to put my hand back under her to get the egg, she pecked my arm in three places faster than I could wink my eyes. Each place she pecked me, my arm bled.

I don't blame her for sittin' in this cool place, I thought. I don't blame her for fightin' over the egg. She laid the egg.

Since Mom had asked me to take the nest egg from the nest, I ran my hand under her and got the egg and put it beside the nest. And when she started rollin' it back under her with her long hooked bill, I left the pawpaw patch.

"Did you take the egg out'n that nest?" Mom asked me soon as I reached the house.

"I took it out this time, Mom," I said. "Look at my arm!"

"That hen's a mean old hussy," Mom said.

That week hadn't passed when Mom called her chickens around the corncrib and fed them shelled corn. Since we lived in the woods and our closest neighbor lived a mile away, hawks, hoot owls, and varmints often caught our chickens. Once a week Mom called them to the corncrib to feed and count them.

"Shan, the old Sebright hen's not here," Mom said. Mom knew her chickens since we had such a variety of mixed chickens there were hardly any two with the same color of feathers.

"I guess something's caught 'er," I said.

"With her bright feathers she's a flowerpot for a hoot owl," Mom said.

Twenty-one days had passed when I saw this old Sebright hen goin' up the hill toward the woods with one little chicken. The nest egg had hatched. I didn't tell Mom what I had seen. I'd let her find out for herself. The old Sebright never came to the corncrib when Mom called our chickens to the house to feed and count them. She lived alone in the woods with her one chicken.

August passed and September came. The leaves had started to turn brown on the trees. I was out huntin' for a hen's nest when I heard a hen cackle, and I looked in time to see our old Sebright hen and her one chicken that was growin' tall and well-feathered disappear into the brush. I was glad to know that they were still alive and I wondered when they would come to the house. And this was a secret I kept from Mom and Pa.

It was in early October that Pa had finished cuttin' our late corn. He had come across the ridge and followed the path down the point to our house. When he reached the house, Mom was callin' our chickens to the corncrib to feed and count them.

"Sal, this reminds me of something," Pa said. "It must've been two miles back on the ridge, I either saw a Sebright hen with a young chicken with her 'r I saw a pheasant and a young one. They flew through the brush like wild quails before I could get close!"

"Did you take that egg from under that old hen that day?" Mom turned around and asked me.

"I did, Mom," I said.

"I don't want you to lie to me," Mom said.

"I'm tellin' you the truth," I said.

"I guess I saw a couple of pheasants," Pa said.

It was in late November, when the worms and bugs had gone into the ground for the winter, that the old Sebright hen came to the corncrib when Mom called the chickens. Hunger had forced her to come down from the high hills with her young rooster. She was very proud of him; though he was nearly as tall as she was, she clucked to him as if he were still a tiny chicken that had just come from the egg. When one of the hens came close to him, she flogged the hen.

Mom looked at Pa and Pa looked at Mom. They didn't say anything at first, but each stood there lookin' at the old hen and young rooster and then they looked at me.

"But, Mom, I did take the egg from her nest," I said.

"Where did you put the egg?" Mom asked.

"Over in the grass beside the nest."

"Didn't you know an old sittin' hen will roll an egg ten feet to get it back in the nest?"

"No," I said.

"There'll be bad luck among our chickens," Pa said.

"We're havin' enough bad luck already," Mom said. "I can't raise chickens as fast as something catches 'em. I missed eight in September and eleven in October. Since the trees lost their leaves so the hoot owls could see the chickens, I've lost seventeen this month."

"We'll lose more now," Pa said. "I'd put that young gentleman in the skillet and fry 'im if he wasn't sich a fine-lookin' young rooster."

"Don't do it, Pa," I said. "She's had a hard time raisin' 'im."

"Pap had this same thing to happen when I was a little boy," Pa said. "Before the year was over he lost every chicken he had with the cholera. They died in piles."

I didn't want to say anything to Pa, but I didn't see why a hen's sittin' on a nest egg and hatchin' it and raisin' her chicken had anything to do with the cholera. I wanted to beg him to keep this young rooster that I called Nest Egg. Pa must've forgot about killin' 'im and fryin' 'im, for November and December came and passed and Nest Egg still ran with his mother.

Nest Egg wasn't six months old when he started crowin'. Now he was much larger than his mother. He was tall and he had big legs and little straight spurs that looked like long locust thorns. His mother still ran with him and clucked to him, but he didn't pay his mother much attention. He would often stand lookin' at the spring sun and never bat his eyes. He had a mean-lookin' eye and a long crooked bill that looked like a chicken hawk's bill. He didn't look like his mother. Pa said that he was a cross between a Sebright and a black game. He had almost every variety of colors. I thought he was a mongrel rooster—a mixture of many breeds.

We had five roosters at our house; all five of them ran Nest Egg. They'd run him and flog him. Once our black game rooster, War Hawk, just missed Nest Egg's hawk-shaped head with his long, straight spur that had killed four of our roosters. But Nest Egg outran War Hawk. He took to the brush cacklin'.

"He won't always be a-runnin' you, Nest Egg," I said while War Hawk boasted to the big flock of hens around 'im.

Durin' the spring months we seldom saw Nest Egg. He kept a safe distance away from the house. He stayed away from the five old roosters who fought him every time he got near one's flock of hens. But once Mom was huntin' a hen's nest in the woods and she saw a chicken hawk swoop low to catch a hen. She saw Nest Egg hit the hawk with all the power he had. Mom said he tore a small wind-puff of feathers from the hawk. Mom told Pa about Nest Egg's fight with the hawk.

"He's a-goin' to make a powerful fightin' rooster," Pa said.

"Any rooster that's game enough to hit a hawk has good metal."

And Pa was right in his prediction about Nest Egg. In early June we saw him a-runnin' Big Bill, our gray game rooster. In late July he whipped Red Ranger, our red game rooster. In July he whipped Lightnin', our black Minorca rooster. Three days later, he whipped our "scrub" rooster that was mixed with many breeds of chickens. We called him Mongrel. He had whipped all the roosters but War Hawk.

"If Nest Egg can stay out'n the way of War Hawk's spurs," Pa said, "he'll whip old War Hawk. He's a young rooster that's run over the hills and scratched for a livin' and he's got better wind."

It was in the middle of August when Nest Egg came down to the barn. He tiptoed, flapped his wings, and crowed in the barn lot. This was War Hawk's territory. It was the choice territory War Hawk had taken for his flocks of hens. Not one of our roosters had dared to venture on War Hawk's territory. Maybe, Nest Egg had come down from the hills to challenge War Hawk's supremacy. Since he had whipped Big Bill, Red Ranger, Lightnin', and Mongrel he wouldn't be chased by War Hawk. He was a year old now and he felt his youth. He was ready to fight. And when War Hawk heard another rooster crowin' on his territory, he came runnin' with a flock of hens following 'im. He challenged young Nest Egg for a fight.

At first War Hawk and Nest Egg sparred at each other. War Hawk had fought many fights and maybe he was feelin' out his young opponent. They stuck their heads out at each other and pecked, then they came together with all their might and the feathers flew. Nest Egg hit War Hawk so hard that he knocked him backwards.

Again they struck and again, again, again. Each time the feathers flew lazily away with the August wind. Then War Hawk leaped high into the air and spurred at Nest Egg's head. His spur cut a place in Nest Egg's red comb. That seemed to make Nest Egg madder than ever. He rushed in and grabbed

War Hawk by the comb and pushed his head against the ground while he flogged him with wings and feet. When Nest Egg's bill-hold gave away, he left a gap in War Hawk's battered comb.

War Hawk was gettin' weaker. But he leaped high into the air and spurred at Nest Egg's head; Nest Egg dodged and the spur missed his head. That must have given Nest Egg an idea, for he leaped high in the air and War Hawk leaped high to meet him. War Hawk caught Nest Egg's spur in his craw, which ripped it open. War Hawk fell on the barn lot where he had seen others fall. As War Hawk lay dyin', Nest Egg stood above him on his tiptoes and crowed. He was the new king of our barn lot.

Nest Egg's victory over War Hawk spread among our neighbors and many of them asked to bring their roosters to fight Nest Egg.

"He's not the fightin' stock," Pa told them. "He's only a scrub rooster. I don't like to fight chickens, but if it's a pleasure to you, bring your roosters around."

In September he killed Warfield Flaughtery's great Hercules game rooster that had never lost one fight in fifty-three fights. Hercules had whipped War Hawk. Two weeks later he killed Warfield Flaughtery's young game rooster, Napoleon. In early October he killed Eif Nippert's red game rooster, Red Devil; two days later he spurred Ennis Sneed's gray game rooster, Big Bee Martin, blind in both eyes. Later that month he pecked a hole in a hoot owl's head that had caught one of our hens. Before January he had killed nineteen roosters and one hoot owl.

"He's some rooster," Pa said. "But he's sure to bring us bad luck."

Pa was offered fifty dollars for Nest Egg by a man from a showboat on the Ohio River. He watched Nest Egg kill his twenty-fifth rooster before he offered Pa the money.

"He's bad among my other roosters here," Pa said. "They

used to make him live in the woods; now he makes them live in the woods. But I don't want to sell him."

"That's a big price, Mick," Mom said. "You'd better take it."

But Pa wouldn't sell him. Finally, the man from the show-boat offered Pa seventy-five dollars. Then he said he wouldn't offer him another dime. He started back toward town, turned around, and came back and offered Pa a hundred-dollar bill, the first hundred-dollar bill that any of us had ever seen.

"I still won't sell 'im," Pa said.

Then the man went away and Mom was mad.

"Hundred dollars is a lot of money, Mick."

"I like that rooster," Pa said. "I'm not a-sellin' 'im."

Anybody would like Nest Egg if he could've seen him strut about the barn lot with fifty hens around him. He had nearly half the flock followin' him. When Nest Egg wanted one of our other roosters' hens, he just said something to her in his language and she followed 'im. And now when Mom called our chickens to the corncrib to feed and count them, she found that our flock was gradually growin'. This was the first time since we had had chickens that our flock had increased without our raisin' chickens or buyin' them. Mom couldn't understand how the number had grown. She saw several different-colored hens among our flock.

In February our flock increased seven; in March it increased twelve; in April it increased twenty-seven; in May it had increased thirty-two. In the meantime, Nest Egg had fought seven more fights and had killed six of the roosters; the seventh finally recovered.

In May, Warfield Flaughtery came to our house with his mule and express wagon.

"Mick, have you got some extra hens in your flock?" he asked Pa.

"Think we have, Warfield," Pa said. "How many did you lose?"

"About sixty," he told Pa.

"Would you know your hens?" Pa asked.

"Shore would," he said. "Call your hens to the corncrib."

"You're not right sure the hawks, hoot owls, and varmints didn't take some of them?" Pa asked.

"I'm sure they didn't," he said. "A two-legged varmint got 'em."

"Do you mean I stole your chickens?" Pa said.

"Not exactly," he grunted.

"They must've come to my rooster," Pa said.

"They didn't do that," Warfield said as Pa called the chickens and they came runnin'. "They wouldn't follow that scrub rooster."

Warfield and Pa were mad. Mom heard them talkin' and hurried to the corncrib.

"Then take your hens," Pa said. "Here's a coop. Catch 'em and put 'em in it."

Mom stood by and didn't say anything until Warfield got Nest Egg's mother. Mom made him put her down.

"You're a-takin' hens that I've raised," Mom said.

But Warfield insisted that he wasn't and kept takin' our hens until he had sixty. Then he hauled them away on his express wagon. He must have told others about our havin' his chickens. Jake Hix came and claimed thirty of our hens. And Pa let 'im have 'em. And then Cy Pennix came and wanted fourteen. We knew that Cy didn't even raise chickens and Pa wouldn't let 'im have 'em. Pa and Cy almost had a fight, but Pa told 'im to climb on his express-wagon seat and get outten the hollow fast as his mule could take him. Wiley Blevins, Ott Jervis, and Jot Seagraves came and claimed our chickens. "Who do you think I am," Pa asked them, "a chicken thief?" Pa showed them the way back down the hollow and they told Pa that he would be sorry.

"That rooster's a-bringin' us bad luck," Pa said. "These

men live from one to three miles from us. Nest Egg is goin'
back into the hills now since worms are scarce here. And he
meets with other roosters and their flocks and he steals the
hens. God knows I'm not a chicken thief. It's that good-lookin'
rooster Nest Egg that the hens all take to. He tolls the hens
here."

In June the four neighbors that Pa had chased away had
indicted Pa for stealin' their chickens. Pa was branded as a
chicken thief, for it was printed in the *Greenwood County News*
about his bein' indicted by four men. And before the trial was
called in August, Warfield Flaughtery came back with his
express wagon and hauled away forty-six more hens; Jake Hix
came and claimed seventy. He said all his hens had left, and
Mom said our flock had increased more than a hundred. Warfield Flaughtery and Jake Hix had always been good neighbors
to us, but Warfield's roosters had aways killed our roosters before, and now Nest Egg had killed two of his best games and he
was sore at us over it. Pa asked him if he'd been summoned for
a witness in the trial, and he told Pa that he and Jake both had.

Pa was tried on the indictment made by Cy Pennix. The
courthouse was filled with people to see how the trial ended
since there'd been much chicken stealin' in our county. We
proved that Cy Pennix didn't even have any chickens—that he
had just claimed our chickens but did not get them. And Pa
came clear. Then Wiley Blevin's indictment was next to be
tried. And when Wiley said that he would swear to his chickens'
feathers, Judge Whittlecomb threw the case out of court. Since
Warfield Flaughtery and Jake Hix had claimed and had taken
their hens, saying they knew them by the colors, they got scared
at the decision made by Judge Whittlecomb and they hauled
the chickens they had taken from us back before sunset.

"That Nest Egg's a wonder," Pa said. "Our flock has doubled
and he's killed fifty-one roosters. He's just a little past two years
old."

But boys threatened me when I went to the store. They threatened me because Nest Egg had killed their roosters. And neighborhood men threatened Pa over our rooster. Once Pa got a letter that didn't have a name signed to it and in it was a threat to burn our barn. He got another letter and the man said he was a little man, that he would meet Pa sometime in the dark. He said a bullet would sink into a chicken thief in the dark same as it would in the daytime.

"I didn't know as little a thing as a rooster could get people riled like that," Pa said. "I didn't know a rooster could turn a whole community of people against a man."

Cy Pennix shook his fist at Pa and dared him to step across the line fence onto his land. And Warfield Flaughtery wouldn't speak to Pa. Tim Flaughtery hit me with a rock and ran. And often Pa would get up in the night and put on his clothes and walk over to our barn. He was afraid somebody would slip in to burn it.

"I feel something's a-goin' to happen soon," Pa told me one day in September. "This can't go on. Our flock is increasin' day by day. Look at the chickens about this place!"

There were chickens every place. Even our old roosters had increased their flocks with hens that Nest Egg had tolled to our house—hens that could not join Nest Egg's ever increasin' flock. When we gathered eggs, two of us took bushel baskets. We found hens' nests under the ferns, under the rock-cliffs, under the smokehouse corncrib, in hollow logs and stumps— and once I found a hen's nest with twenty-two eggs in it on top of our kitchen behind the flue. An egg rolled off and smashed on Pa's hat is how come us to find the nest. We had to haul eggs to town four times a week now.

One early October mornin' when Mom called our chickens to the corncrib to feed them, Nest Egg didn't come steppin' proudly on his tiptoes. And that mornin' he hadn't awakened Pa at four o'clock by his six lusty crows. I missed my first day of school to help Pa hunt for Nest Egg. We looked around the barn. We scoured the steep hill slopes, lookin' under each green-briar cluster and in each sprout thicket. We looked every place in Nest Egg's territory and were about to give up the hunt when we walked under the white-oak chicken roost between the barn and house. We found Nest Egg sprawled on the ground beneath the roost with several hens gathered around him cacklin'. A tiny screech owl was sittin' on Nest Egg's back, peckin' a small hole in his head.

"Think of that," Pa said. "A rooster game and powerful as Nest Egg would be killed by a little screech owl no bigger than my fist. A hundred-dollar rooster killed in his prime by a worthless screech owl."

Pa reached down and grabbed the owl by the head and wrung its neck. "I can't stand to see it take another bit from Nest Egg's head," he said.

I stood over Nest Egg and cried.

"No ust to cry, Shan," Pa said. "Nest Egg's dead. That owl fouled 'im. It flew into the chicken roost and lit on his back when he was asleep. It pecked his head until it finished 'im."

"But I haf to cry," I said, watchin' Pa take his bandanna from his pocket to wipe the tears from his eyes.

The Thing You Love

Author's Introduction

Most everyone likes animals. Many of you have a pet cat, dog, or bird. Some of you may have tamed a wild creature such as a raccoon, ground hog, squirrel, fox, or deer. However, there are certain animals that cannot be tamed. One of these is the possum. My brother and I used to try though. We caught them, put them in a large pen where they had a quiet place to live and beds of leaves to sleep on, and we fed them the foods they liked until they became very fat. We treated them very kindly, and yet we could never safely touch one. However, the majority of the species of wild animals, birds, and a few reptiles will become very friendly with us, if they know we aren't going to hurt them.

In my childhood one of my greatest enjoyments was the many pets we had on the farm. No other family in our area ever loved domestic and wild animals, poultry and wild birds more than my parents, sisters, my brother, and I. Once I even had a pet black snake that I called Old Ben. At first my mother and sisters didn't like him much, but later when he became a placid old fellow, they did. All of the children in the neighborhood played with Old Ben as if he were a toy.

My mother and father named all of our domestic animals. At one time on our farm we had two teams of mules, one team of large horses, eighteen cows and fifty head of livestock, and over five hundred sheep. Everyone had a name except the sheep, and there were too many of these to name.

The reason I have told you all of this is to prepare you for the story you are about to read. This will give you a better understanding about our family's affection for our animals and pets. If you ever have many pets, you know that they sometimes can be disagreeable to each other. Sometimes they will forget they are pets and will return to a natural enmity. The pet cat will try to catch the pet bird. And the friendly, loyal dog you love will try to kill the cat or the rabbit.

"The Thing You Love" is the story of such an enmity. It tells of a conflict between two animals whose forebears have been enemies for centuries, and of the inevitable conclusion of that conflict. "The Thing You Love" was suggested to me by an incident that happened to my brother and me.

"SHAN, DON'T you hear a cat mewing?" Finn asked as he leaned on his hoe handle and cupped his hand over his ear to catch the sound. "I can hear it."

I stopped hoeing my row of sweet potatoes in the Shinglemill Creek bottom to listen. "Seems like I can hear a cat mewing," I said.

We dropped our hoes and ran up the dark Shinglemill Hollow where the sun creeps in only at midday. The pines towered high on each side of the steep bluffs. Big, tough-butted white oaks grew among the pines and the yellow poplars. The poplars were filled with wild grapevines that towered high above the oaks and pines. Under these trees were great masses of horseweeds, ragweeds, saw-briers, greenbriers, blackberry briers, wild raspberry briers, and black shoe-makes. It was a deep mass of living green where only the wind wiggled through and stirred the hot smelly weeds, briers, and leaves. Finn and I followed a fox path up this deep gorge along a little creek that lost its way in this thick mass of vegetation.

"Listen now, and let's see if we can hear it," Finn said. We stood perfectly still. We strained to catch a sound above the beating of our hearts.

"It's the sound of a cat, all right," Finn whispered to me. We listened but we could not hear it again.

"It might be a wildcat caught in a trap," Finn said. "You know Eddie Wellman killed a wildcat out here only a few nights ago."

"Finn, we don't have time to waste hunting for this cat. We've got to get back to the potatoes. It will take us the rest of today and tomorrow to finish that patch. The ragweeds and horseweeds will whip the potatoes unless we help them."

We turned and went back to the potato patch. We hoed potatoes until dark. When we went to the house Finn said, "Pa, you know we've been hearing a cat up Shinglemill near the potato patch."

"When the wind blows down to the cornfield where I'm plowing, I catch the same sound," Pa said. "I've been hearing it for over a week. It has me worried—some nights I can't sleep ... I hate to think of anything in a trap. I heard it last night as plain as a whippoorwill."

We ate and after supper stood out in the yard. The night was perfectly still save for the hollering of a hoot owl on the hill above the house, the beetles in the yard grass, and the katydids in the corn. The stars were bright in the high, blue sky. The moon was low and thin as a sickle near the potato patch. Finn and I went up the path to Shinglemill Hollow. We stopped and listened as the night wind rustled the leaves. We heard it again: "Me-ow—me-ow."

All was quiet again save the rustling of the leaves, the beetles in the dewy grass and the katydids down in the cornfield. The big owl upon the hill said: "Who-whoo-who-are-you?" It sounded like a roar of thunder among the other sounds of night.

"Looks like the cat would get scared when the owl hollers, and stop mewing," Finn said.

"It's either a wildcat," I said, "or a cat gone wild. Let's be real quiet for a while and get the direction."

We sat quietly side by side. Finn held to my shirt sleeves when the big owl hollered. On a hill far away, we heard the faint answer of another owl. Then the whippoorwills began hollering. We heard music on every hillside. Finally we heard, "Me-ow, me-ow, mee-ow."

"There it is again, Shan," Finn said to me.

"Be quiet, Finn!" I whispered. "You'd never make a possum hunter. Let's locate the best place, then start crawling toward the sound. You crawl behind me."

"What about snakes?"

"Forget about snakes."

We were quiet again. "Me-ow, Me-ow."

"Let's go to the house and get Black Boy," Finn whispered. "Then I won't be afraid of a copperhead."

"Get Black Boy and he'll kill the cat. Let's get it alive."

We started crawling under the bushes toward the sound, Finn following me. We could hear the faint mews. They sounded very weak. We crawled slowly toward these sounds, the briers and weeds scratching our bare feet, faces, and hands. Sometimes we could look up and see a star from under the roof of briers and weeds. Sometimes we couldn't see anything from the dark green tunnel. I could tell if we were going through a patch of saw-briers by the sweet smell of the leaves. I could tell when we crawled over ragweeds or horseweeds by their smells. We kept on crawling toward the sound, on and on through a tunnel that I pulled out with my hands and butted through with my head. It was hot, and the sweat poured from my face. Finn followed at my heels. We stopped again to catch the sound.

"Me-ow. Me-ow." It was right above us on the hill. We had crawled to an open place where we could stand up and get a breath of fresh night air.

We looked up at the moon and stars in the sky. We were in a place where the big trees had smothered the briers and weeds out. We sat down to rest. Holding our breath, we listened again; we must be close to the cat. Then it mewed. It was right above us in one of the tall trees.

"It's not in a trap, Finn," I said. "It's fastened some way in one of these trees. Look for two bright lights up in the dark treetops."

"I see two little balls of fire, Shan." We had found the cat. It was up in a giant sweet-gum tree. The big rough scales of sweet-gum bark chipped off when I took hold of them. The tree was thicker through the middle, than I was tall. It was almost six feet thick. The eyes of the cat shone down on us like blazes of fire from two stars. The cat meowed to us. We talked beneath the tree now. It was not in a trap for it could walk from limb to limb.

"Kitty, kitty, kitty," Finn said.

"No use to call," I said. "If that cat could come down, it would have been down long ago. If Pa's right, it's been up there nine days."

"Can you climb the tree, Shan?"

"There's not a limb on it until you get up sixty feet," I said. "The big hunks of bark won't hold. Look. See how easy they come off! I know what we can do to end its suffering."

"You're not going to kill it, Shan? You're not going to get a gun and shoot it? Let it starve first!"

"Why not take a rifle and put it out of its misery?"

"You're not going to kill it!"

Finn wept.

The weak cries of the cat ran through my body. Just think how long it had been in the tree. We couldn't cut the tree. It would take all night to cut it down, and it was not our tree to cut. It was a big fine tree for saw-timber. It belonged to the Seaton tract of land.

"Wait until morning and let's cut the tree," Finn said. "Do anything, but don't kill the poor thing!"

"When we come to finish hoeing the potatoes in the morning, we'll slip back to this tree," I said.

We crawled back through the hole we had made in the brush, and slipped quietly down to the house where Pa was sitting in the yard.

"I went to bed but I couldn't sleep for that cat," he said. "I put the window down to keep out the sound and then it was too hot to sleep."

Finn and I got a pan of water and washed our feet. The brier scratches smarted when we rubbed them with lye soap to wash the dried blood and dirt off.

"We'll get the cat in the morning Shan."

Dew covered the earth for the sun was not up yet. We ate breakfast in a hurry, and we walked out into the yard and listened. We couldn't hear the cat.

"Guess it's dead, Shan," Finn said.

We started to the potato patch.

"Let's hurry and go back to that tree," Finn said.

We walked up the wet path and stopped where the tunnel started under the dew covered roof of weeds, briers, and vines. The sun was lifting the dew from the weeds. It was going up in a white stream toward the rising sun.

"Listen," Finn said.

We stopped again to listen. The morning winds were still. There wasn't a sound but dew dripping from the steaming leaves.

Then came the faint me-ow.

"Alive!" Finn shouted. "Come on! Let's get that cat."

We dove headlong into the tunnel and crawled fast. We didn't care about the wet. We rushed up to the tree. We looked up into this tall sweet gum—for about sixty feet up the tree there wasn't a limb. At this point there were three big forks. In these forks we could see the cat. It was a long bony cat and still alive. It looked down at us with eyes big, shiny and round as a hoot owl's eyes—but they were friendly eyes.

"How can we get it, Finn? Can't cut the tree and I can't ever climb it."

"We'll have to think of something," he said. "We have to get it alive."

We looked up at the cat and it looked down at us. There was not any time to lose. We called to the cat. We wanted it to jump down to us but it wouldn't jump. It just looked down at us.

Beside this sweet gum grew a big shellbark hickory. Its topmost branches almost reached the forks of the sweet gum where the cat was. I couldn't climb the shellbark hickory either, because I couldn't reach around the body of the tree. The bark pulled off and I couldn't hold to it. After about thirty feet up the shellbark hickory, I could climb on the rest of the way and bend the top of the tree over to the sweet gum.

"Look, Shan," Finn said, "there's a little hickory above the shellbark hickory. Climb this little hickory and bend it over into the shellbark above its big body. You can climb the little part. Then you can go up to the top and bend it over to the sweet gum."

"But, Finn, I'll have to have something to lay over from the top of the shellbark hickory to the top of the sweet gum so that the cat can walk over to me," I said. "It will have to be something I can carry tied to my back. It will have to be long enough for you to reach to me when I get up thirty feet on the shellbark hickory. I can't bend this little hickory and swing with a plank tied to my back."

"What about one of Mom's quilting frames?" Finn had thought of the right thing and he started running toward the green tunnel to go home.

"Bring me a thick pair of socks, a piece of raw meat, and a bucket of water, too!" I called to him.

When Finn got back he had them all. He also brought a sea-grass string from last year's bundled fodder. I put the heavy socks over my warm bare feet. My feet were tough, but this rough hickory bark was too much for them. I poured water from the bucket onto my socks. They'll stick to the tree now, I thought. I put the piece of raw meat in my pocket, and I was off up the little hickory. It was easy to climb and I climbed to the top of it. I bent the small hickory and got hold of the shell-bark above its big body. After catching hold of a limb on the big hickory, I went over into the big tree. Above me the cat went "Me-o-w." It was very weak. Below me, standing on the ground, Finn tied the three quilting frames together. He lapped their ends and wrapped the sea-grass strings around them. He lifted the long quilting frame to me. I drew it up and untied the first frame and let the other two fall back to the ground. I tied the frame to me and up the shellbark hickory I went.

"Be careful," Finn said.

I climbed and climbed up the tree. My feet got hot and my hands tired. I was afraid to look back at the ground. I kept looking up the tree. The cat was watching me. It looked like a heap of skin and bones. I said over and over to myself as I climbed, "That cat must not die."

After I climbed to the top of the big hickory, I was where the tip would bend with me. I swung like a bird's nest in a grape-vine. I was so high that I could look right over at the cat now. I didn't look back down at the earth because this was the highest I'd ever climbed. I'd climbed many a tree to get a possum or a crow's nest, but no possum could climb a tree like this unless there was a grapevine running up to it.

"Kitty, kitty, kitty," I called.

It answered, "Me-o-w." Then it wagged its tail very slow-like. I hooked my leg over a hickory limb and untied the quilting frame from around my body. I laid it over into the sweet-gum forks. The cat looked at it. I punched the end of the quilting frame under the cat. It was all brindled, with big eyes and claws.

"I don't know, Finn, whether it's a tame cat or a wildcat," I called. "Whatever it is, we are going to get it out of that tree."

The cat stood up then and stepped on the quilting frame. It went, "Sssssssssssss-hhhhhhhhhh." It ran back weakly. It wobbled as it moved away. Then, I took the meat from my pocket.

"Kitty, kitty, kitty," I called. It moved toward me, smelling the meat I was holding. This time it walked out on the quilting frame. I held the meat closer. The frame was just about three inches wide, but the cat could walk on it. The cat had about ten feet to walk with a little down grade toward me. Slowly it started walking over toward me sniffling the meat.

"Finn, I believe it's the kitten of a cat gone wild," I said as it came closer. When it took hold of the meat, I caught it by the neck, hugged it close to my body with one arm, dropped the quilting frame, and started on my way down the tree. It was too weak to try to claw me. My feet burned as I slid down. I scaled down over the big tough-butted end of the shellbark that I couldn't climb and hit the ground.

Finn took the cat. He took the meat away from it.

"I'll take you to the house and give you some milk, kitty," he said. "You poor skinny thing!"

I carried the quilting frames and water bucket. My feet hurt but I hurried along to keep up with Finn.

"Where did you get that animal?" Pa asked. "Looks like part wildcat! Look at it, Sall!"

"Look what claws," Mom said.

"It's the kitten that's been keeping you awake at night," Finn said. "It was up in the forks of a big sweet gum and Shan climbed up and got it. It's been there nine days, we know."

"Just give it warm sweet milk, a little at a time until you get it livened up," Mom said.

Finn gave it sweet milk. It cleaned the saucer up and wanted more.

"It's sure a dangerous lookin' cat," Pa said. "Bet that's what old Black Boy's been treein' up there. Every time we got to the tree it jumped out. I've been thinkin' there was a den of coons up there. It's a den of cats, and it looks to me like part wildcat. That's just a kitten or it would a had sense enough to come down the tree backwards."

"He's my cat," Finn said. "I'm going to call him Sweetgum after the tree we got him from."

Finn gave Sweetgum more milk, then a little more and a little more. He put a collar around his neck and tied him to the porch. He fixed him a bed in a box. Finn made a hole where the cat could crawl back into the box if any of the dogs tried to bother him.

Black Boy walked out in the yard and kicking up the dirt with his hind feet, he growled. His hair stood up all over his back.

Sweetgum went "Ssssssss-hhhhh," and ran back into the box. He didn't like Black Boy. Black Boy didn't like him.

"I believe they know one another," Pa said.

Sweetgum ran free about the house when summer was nearly over. He was growing to be a very big cat with brindled stripes over his body.

"He's not like a tame cat," Pa said. "Look how long those claws are gettin', will you? He could cut a dog all to pieces. He's nearly as big as Black Boy. I saw him comin' to the house the other mornin' draggin' a black snake six feet long. He had it by the neck and it was still alive. He's been huntin' over these hills like a dog. He's a dangerous lookin' cat."

Anywhere Finn went Sweetgum would follow. The cat followed him to visit Uncle Mel. If Finn started to town, Sweetgum would run along the ridge path until Finn got near the town where the houses scared him. There Sweetgum would run back into the dark woods. When Finn came back from town, Sweetgum would be at the house. He would come up to Finn and purr. Finn would then give him a bowl of sweet milk.

One morning when Finn gave Sweetgum his milk Black Boy came up and started growling. Sweetgum wouldn't leave the milk. He stood by the pan and hissed: "Ssssss-ttttt." His brindled hair stood up on his back.

Black Boy's hair stood up on his back. He went: "Ggggggg-rrrrrrr."

This was definitely a quarrel. Black Boy never quarreled with possums, coons, weasels, minks, or ground hogs. He went in and got them. He laid them out dead when he was through. He was half mountain-cur and half hound. I had known him to crush a polecat's head in his mouth at one bite. He ran in to grab the cat. Sweetgum spatted him with his paws like a man using his fists, only faster. Black Boy kept going in and pushing Sweetgum back. Finn hollered for Pa, who came running and yelling. He ran in to grab Black Boy, because Black Boy knew how to kill a wildcat! He had killed them before. He knew one's skull was thin and easily crushed.

Finn ran in and pushed Black Boy back and picked Sweetgum up and held him in his arms.

"He's hurt Black Boy," said Pa. Pa's voice trembled. "He's hurt him bad!"

"He started the fight," Finn said. "I was feeding Sweetgum and Black Boy tried to run him away."

Black Boy's lips were split as if someone had taken a knife and split them. Under his tongue there was a hole torn almost through. His ears were riddled the way a July hailstorm riddled tobacco leaves.

"I tell you he's part wildcat," Pa said. "He's hurt Black Boy more than you think. Look, Shan!"

"I don't want to see it, Pa," I said. I looked away. "I can't stand to look."

Then I turned my head. Sweetgum had ripped Black Boy's

stomach beyond repair. He had sliced our powerful hunting dog almost to pieces.

"He'll have to be killed," Pa cried, holding onto Black Boy's collar since the dog was still trying to get the cat in Finn's arms. "The dog'll never fight any more! Somebody will have to put him out of his misery!"

"It won't be me," I said. "I couldn't do it!"

"He's always liked our old single-barreled shotgun, son. Every time it cracked, game fell from the tree or on the ground in front of him. He's not afraid of our gun. Black Boy'll look at the barrel when you point it at him!"

"But I couldn't shoot that dog," I said. "I love him too much!" Warm tears ran down my cheek. I felt them leave my eyes and run warmly over my face. "I'll leave home before I shoot him!"

"If you loved him enough, you'd kill him and put him out of his misery," Pa said.

"I don't want to kill him," Finn said, still holding his cat up while Black Boy looked up at the cat and whined pitifully. "I've killed too much wild game with him."

"What are you goin' to do with that cat then?" Pa asked. "It's killed the best dog we've ever owned or ever will own!"

"I'd like to say something," I interrupted before Finn could reply. "I read in the paper where a big cat died at the Cincinnati Zoo. I wonder, couldn't you let them have Sweetgum to take its place? He'll be put in captivity but he'll be well fed!"

"No, no," Finn shouted. "Not Sweetgum! I don't want him put in captivity!"

"Yes, get rid of him," Pa shouted, interrupting Finn. "That cat's too dangerous to run loose! Put that thing in captivity!"

"Sweetgum's not that dangerous," Finn said, bending his face over toward the cat and wiping the tears that streamed down his face on its lively bristling fur. "Black Boy tried to kill him! Now, the price Sweetgum has to pay for protecting his own life is to go into captivity the rest of his days! I can't stand to see him lose his freedom. I've raised Sweetgum from a long skinny kitten. I love him! He didn't start that fight! Black Boy started it."

"Put that cat in the corncrib this minute!" Pa shouted. "He can't get out of there! We'll decide later what to do with him. He can't go free any longer! Right now, I've got to do somethin' with Black Boy. We can't save him! Death will be merciful."

"I can't do it, Pa. He'd look up at the gun with love in his eyes and he'd think we were goin' hunting," I said.

"Shut up, Shan!" Pa shouted.

Finn walked away toward the corncrib with Sweetgum in his arms.

"I can go over the hill and get Cief Hillman to do it, Pa," I told him, with words that sounded strange to my own ears. "Cief shot his own dog, Shep, after a mad dog bit him. Cief never batted an eye! I couldn't do that!"

"You're like me, Shan," Pa sighed, wiping the tears from his sun-tanned face with the back of his knotty fist.

"I'll go over the hill and get Cief," I said.

I looked at Black Boy and had to turn my head away quickly. Pa stood beside him with his head turned away, and when Black Boy whined he said soft soothing words to him.

"Have Cief bring his own gun," Pa added as I hurried away. "I don't want mine to kill him."

When I was upon the hillside path I heard my father's soft words: "Stand it a while longer, Black Boy! It won't be much longer now!"

I ran a mile over the hill and down on Tanyard, where I found Cief. I told him what had happened and why I had come.

"Sure, I'll go," he said. "I'll take my gun. I'm surprised that a house cat got Black Boy."

"Sweetgum is a strange house cat, Cief," I explained. "I believe he's a wildcat."

When we hurried over the hillpath we found Pa standing like a sentinel guarding Black Boy.

"I've never seen anything as bad as this," Cief said. "The sooner Black Boy is out of his pain, the better! It'll have to be done here!"

"Yes, I know it will," Pa said. "Give me time to get out of sight."

When Pa walked away, I followed. Black Boy whined to follow us, but I stopped both ears with my fingers so I wouldn't hear the sounds. I hurried to keep up with Pa, who was almost running.

I followed Pa down the road about two hundred yards and then we heard the report of a gun. We turned and walked slowly toward the house. When we got there Cief's gun was lying on the ground, but he and the dog were gone.

Finn had sauntered slowly around the house into the background. Tall, slender, freckle-faced, and fourteen, he was very silent. Pa and I were silent, too. We stood in our back yard waiting for Cief to return for his single-barreled shotgun. Cief was not gone very long. He came down Shinglemill Hollow wiping the sweat from his wild-plum-red face with a blue bandanna.

"Black Boy was a very heavy dog," he said, short of breath. "I put him in a burlap sack and carried him up there near the poplar by the path. You can't miss him. Thought maybe you might have a place you wanted to bury him."

"That's good of you, Cief," Pa told him. "You've done what I forgot to tell you. I want to bury him on the top of Old Baldy where he'll be above the woods he's hunted in."

Cief picked up his gun and put it across his shoulder.

"How much do I owe you?" Pa asked.

"Not a cent," he replied, and started walking away.

"A mattock and a shovel, Finn," Pa said to me. "It'll take all three of us to carry Black Boy and the tools to the top of Old Baldy."

He carried one end of the burlap sack and I carried the other, while Finn followed with the mattock and shovel. When we started up Old Baldy the sun was down and there were long shadows in the valley, but as we reached the top of this highest point of our land, the sun was still shining. Here we dug a grave under the tall pines where high winds sighed. We laid Black Boy in his grave and shoveled him under with fertile new ground-dirt. Then we laid lichen-covered rocks over the grave and turned silently away as the sun was just setting. We went on home and I went to bed, leaving Finn and Pa sitting before a small open fire in the living room.

Sometime in the night I was having a dream about being chased by wildcats when I was awakened by the shotgun blast. I jumped up in bed and looked for Finn. He'd not come to bed. Pa came running into my room in his nightshirt.

"Where's Finn?" he asked.

"He's not here, Pa!" I cried. "He's never gone to bed."

Pa looked into the living room where he kept our single-barreled gun hanging to a joist. "The gun is gone," he said, and he opened the door and ran out into the moonlight.

"Who is that shootin', Mick?" Mom asked, getting out of bed. But Pa had gone and I was getting up to follow him.

Out in the early October moonlight, my father stood in the front yard watching a tall figure coming from the corncrib with a shotgun across his shoulder. He walked past us without saying a word.

"No use to look, for Finn's a good shot," Pa said in a whisper. He shook his head sadly.

"He's killed Sweetgum," I said. "I can't believe it! He said Sweetgum should never lose his freedom!"

"It was mighty hard for him, son," Pa said in a whisper. "He wouldn't let that wildcat go into captivity. He loved him too much for that. He had to love him a lot to kill him. It's mighty hard to kill the thing you love."

Uncle Jeff Had a Way

Author's Introduction

Once my father owned a pair of long-legged mules called Dick and Dinah. They were the greatest pair of mules we ever had, but they were the meanest. Both of them kicked at people who were working them. Once Dick nearly broke my father's leg. Nevertheless, we were all fond of these mules and kept them until they grew old and died.

About the time my father traded for these mules, my Uncle Jeff came to spend a few days with us. He stayed twenty years. Uncle Jeff had been married and was the father of a large family. Now that his wife was dead, his children married, he had no place to go. My mother, who was his sister, took him in, gave him a room, bed, and food, and washed and mended his clothes. Since we needed a farm hand, Uncle Jeff worked for us. He drove Dick and Dinah hitched to the plow, wagon, mowing machine, or hayrack. He said he understood mules and they understood him.

After Uncle Jeff came to live with us, a sort of rivalry built up between him and my father about who had the most knowledge of land and farming. Uncle Jeff could do some things better than my father, such as building a fence, driving mules, or looking at a barn filled with tobacco and guessing its weight within a hundred pounds. He could look at an animal, horse, mule, cow, calf, or steer and guess its weight within 10 to 25 pounds. He could look at a tree and tell how many board feet of lumber it would make when sawed at the mill. He could estimate how many acres there were in a tract of land. He didn't even have an eighth-grade education, but he could solve difficult problems. He had more knowledge of timber cutting, cattle, mules, and farming than any man I have ever known. My father had knowledge of these too, but he was not always as accurate as Uncle Jeff.

One day Dick and Dinah got out of the pasture. Uncle Jeff only laughed at our having trouble getting them back. He said he knew a way that would be very easy for us to get them back, but my father wouldn't believe him; he wouldn't even listen to Uncle Jeff's idea. Now, read the story of what happened and how we got the mules back in the pasture.

Long after this had happened, I was telling another farmer who couldn't get his mules back in the pasture how we had managed to do it, and he said, "What a wonderful story." This man had never gone beyond the fourth grade and, perhaps, had never read a short story. But I had never thought of this experience as a story until he said those words. Then I wrote it, exactly as it happened. Details of trials, failures, and distances are described accurately.

WHEN FINN, Pa, and I stepped outside the house after breakfast, dawn was breaking. We stopped in the front yard, stretched our arms, and breathed deeply. Then Pa looked up at the sky for weather signs. He read the skies thoughtfully for a minute.

"We're changin' our plans," he said. "Shan, you go to the pasture and get Dick and Dinah. That sky is as red as the skin of a wild, ripe plum."

"Gee, the sky is beautiful this morning," I said.

"Red sky in the morning is a farmer's warning," he sighed.

The hilly surface of our earth was still dark. And just above this dark surface of upheaved earth was a red blanket ready to be spread over the big monster who dreaded waking so early in the morning.

"Shan, you hurry to the pasture and get Dick and Dinah while Finn and I feed and milk," Pa ordered me. "Bring the mules in and we'll feed and harness 'em. Then we'll harrow the tobacco ground and lay it off. It will rain tonight or tomorrow."

"But Dick and Dinah thought they were goin' to have a vacation," I told him. "It's a shame to work them today."

"But we have to go by the weather," he said. "We must have the tobacco ground ready when it rains."

I went to the corncrib and got an ear of corn. Then I went through the barn entry and got old Dick's bridle hanging on the wall. All I had to take was one bridle and one ear of corn. None of us could catch and bridle Dinah in the pasture. And the only way we could catch Dick was to bribe him with an ear of corn. Just hold up the ear and he'd come and get it; and while he ate you would slip the bridle bit into his mouth and the bridle over his head. Lead him back to the barn and old Dinah would follow anywhere we led Dick.

When I left our barn and went under the tall, leafy oaks and dark pines, a soft warm morning wind whispered something to the oak leaves and the pine needles. There was a big secret the morning wind was confiding to the oaks and pines. I hurried on to a place where I always found the mules. When I reached this field, the red morning sky reflected a beautiful glow over the lush, soft, green grass. But I didn't see Dick and Dinah in the field they loved. I looked at my watch and it was six o'clock. Pa and Finn had the feeding and milking done and were waiting.

I hurried along the paths through the woods over the two hills on the eastern boundary of our pasture. There was plenty of light now and I never left a single spot unnoticed. Then, I went to the big hill on the western boundary of our pasture. I looked at my watch and it was seven now.

I'd started back to the barn to tell Pa and Finn that I couldn't find them when I found fresh mule tracks. I followed the tracks down the little hollow below the pine woods toward the gate. When I followed the tracks across the pasture, I found the gate was wide open and the mules had gone through. Our mules were out for the first time since we had owned them. That had been nine years. I hurried back to the barn to tell Pa.

"What in the world has kept you so long?" he asked. "We ought to have been in the field two hours ago. Where are the mules?"

"Out," I said. Then I caught my breath. "The gate was left open last night."

Uncle Jeff, Mom's big brother who stayed with us, walked out the path to the barn.

"Did you say the mules were out?" he asked me.

"They certainly are," I said. "Somebody left the gate open."

"One of the mules might've opened it," he said, grinning.

"Dick and Dinah never opened a gate in their lives," Pa replied, pointing a skinny index finger at Uncle Jeff. "It's been a two-legged mule that left that gate open."

"Pa, do you reckon we could use the horses today?" Finn asked.

"Not on that steep new ground," he replied quickly. "They can't stand up there. Besides, what are we goin' to do about the mules?"

"We'll find the mules and bring 'em home," I said.

"Ah, I don't know so much about that," Uncle Jeff sighed. "I've worked Dick and Dinah a lot and you can't run 'em and get 'em excited. If you do, they'll never stop runnin'."

"Jeff, that's a lot of foolish talk," Pa told him. "I'll drive 'em into the corner of a fence or a cliff and give Dick an ear of corn. Then, I'll ease the bridle right over his head. Now, do you know a better way to catch 'em?"

"There's a much better way to catch 'em," Uncle Jeff said, smiling. "But you wouldn't believe me. I know mules. I've worked with 'em all my life. I know their natures. I know a wonderful way to fetch the mules home."

"Then tell us," Pa said. "Don't keep such a valuable secret all to yourself."

Pa's face got almost as red as the morning skies. Uncle Jeff kept Pa's face that way most of the time. He said smart things that Pa didn't like. Pa put Uncle Jeff on the go once but Mom went after him and brought him home. Pa and Mom had words over Uncle Jeff. Mom said he didn't have a place in the world to stay, not even among his ten children, and he was her brother and she wasn't going to let him down.

"No, I won't tell you, Mick," Uncle Jeff said. "You've never respected the way I take advantage of the problems I face."

"You take advantage all right," Pa told him. "Come on, boys, let's go get the mules."

We walked away and left him standing at the gate. He was leaning part of his 286 pounds on the post. He smiled as we walked down the road under the red morning skies.

"That man back there beats all men I've ever known," Pa said. "Sits at the house and keeps his head in a newspaper. He thinks he's got all the answers. I'd like to know what kind of a scheme he's got up his sleeve this time!"

Pa shook with rage when he talked about Uncle Jeff. When we reached the lower gate, we found fresh tracks.

"I'm goin' to put a lock on that gate," Pa said. "That'll break up people's leavin' my gates open. It's about like one of Jeff's tricks to leave the gate open. Look what we're in for when the clouds and the wind tell me we're going to have rain. And our tobacco ground isn't ready for a settin'.'"

We followed the tracks down the Ragweed Hollow road. When we reached the forks, where a road branched off to Fred Doore's, our mules had gone that way.

"They've heard Fred's mules," Pa said. "I'd hate for our mules to get together. There would be some kickin'. He's got two mean mules."

"Look up there!" I shouted. "There they are!"

"Now just a minute," Pa whispered. "Let me do it the easy way. I know the nature of mules too. Give me the ear of corn, Shan."

Pa held the ear of corn in front and the bridle behind him.

"Cope, cope, cope," he called softly. "Cope, Dick and Dinah."

The ear of corn in my father's hand didn't bribe Dick of his freedom. He let Pa get up close and then he wheeled around, turning his heels toward Pa. He started kicking as I'd never seen a mule kick before. Pa started running backward. Dinah took off up the road like a greyhound with Dick at her heels. They'd always been in harness hitched to a wagon pulling along this road before. Now they were free of harness and bridles and loads. They were heading for Fred Doore's barn for a visit.

Pa, Finn, and I reached the top of the hill in time to see Dick leap first and Dinah follow over a six-wire fence around Fred Doore's barn. Then, the battle started. Both of Fred's short-legged Tennessee bay mules turned their heels on Dick. Dick gave a loud squeal and started backward, kicking as he went. He was a long-legged Missouri mule. Dinah didn't get mixed up in the fray. Fred Doore started hollering and ran from the house. He picked up a tobacco stick on the way and dove under the wire. By that time, Pa, Finn, and I were there.

"Wait a minute, Fred!" Pa shouted.

"That's the kickingest long-legged mule I ever saw!" Fred shouted as he hit old Dick across the ribs. "He's goin' to kill my mules!"

"Just a minute, Fred," Pa said. "I'll get my mules while they're in your lot. Somebody left our gate open last night."

Pa dove under the wire in a hurry. Old Dick ran to the other side of the lot. Dinah followed with her head high sniffling the breeze.

"Cope, Dick, cope, cope," Pa panted.

Finn and I helped Pa herd Dick and Dinah into a corner of the lot. Then Pa went forward with the ear of corn in front and the bridle behind his back. He spoke gently and walked softly. Dick wasn't fooled. That ear of corn wasn't the price of his freedom. He raised straight up in the wind and went over the high fence without touching it. Dinah ran a few feet before she leaped over and ran after Dick.

"I believe Uncle Jeff was right," Finn said.

"I've never seen 'em as wild," Pa sighed.

"They've got their freedom, Pa," I said. "They never had it before."

They went over the hill and down to the Doore Gap. There they turned left and went down the Womack Hollow toward the Sandy River turnpike.

"They're gone now," Finn said.

We could hear them laying their feet to the ground. They were running a race with each other.

"What will we do now?" Finn asked.

"We're goin' after 'em," Pa said.

We followed and around each bend in the road we hoped to find them standing. We went all the way down the Womack Hollow but we never found Dick and Dinah. They had run all the way and their tracks showed they had gone up the Sandy River turnpike.

"They're gone," Pa sighed. "We'll go saddle our horses."

We had a long walk back home. When we got there, Uncle Jeff was sitting in a chair under the pine in our front yard. He looked at us and then turned back to his paper.

We ate our dinners and Mom asked us about the mules. But Uncle Jeff didn't say a word to us. He was too busy fighting his face. Pa was just waiting for Uncle Jeff to say something so he could tell him what he thought. After we had eaten, we bridled and saddled our horses. Pa rode Dollie and I rode Doc.

"Finn, why don't you get on the pony and go with 'em?" Uncle Jeff said as we rode past Uncle Jeff and Finn. "It's not fair to leave you."

"Why don't you get on the pony and go with 'em?" Finn replied.

"I'm almost as big as the pony," Uncle Jeff told him. "I could come as near carryin' the pony as it could me."

"Too lazy to carry anything," Pa said as we rode away. "Too lazy to feed the livestock, build a fire, or get himself a drink. He's not too lazy to read a paper. He burns me up with his smart talk."

Pa and I rode down Ragweed, across the Gap, and down the Womack Hollow road. Dollie and Doc trotted at a fast pace. Soon we reached the Sandy River turnpike and there took to one side of the road to see if the tracks turned off on one of the lane roads. We rode for miles up the turnpike and the tracks kept going on. At about four in the afternoon Pa spied Dick and Dinah eating grass beside the road.

"We'll get 'em this time if we have to run 'em down!" he shouted.

We gave our horses the rein and the whip. We went into a full gallop toward Dick and Dinah and when they heard us coming they lifted their heads from the lush green grass. They took off as fast as their long legs would carry them. They thrust their heads forward and galloped with all their might. We chased them up a road walled on one side with cliffs and on the other side was the Sandy River. We were gaining on them when we came to the Cedar Riffles road where they turned left from the turnpike. I was so close to old Dick once I could have touched him with my short quirt.

When we got on their heels, Pa shouted, "I'm goin' around 'em!"

He was trying to get in front and turn them back. But they turned right and sailed like two wild birds over the high fence into a pasture.

"That's something," Pa panted. "Did you ever see anything like that?"

They ran across the pasture and gave chase to a herd of cattle. Dick and Dinah made them scatter in all directions. But they didn't stop. They kept on going. The red skies had turned to gray skies and darkness was settling on the land. Night was coming.

"What will we do now?" I asked.

"Ride home," Pa replied.

"What will Uncle Jeff think?" I said.

"This will please him," Pa replied. "But I won't ask him anything. I'd lose these mules before I'd seek his advice."

We let our horses walk part of the way home. They were tired of carrying us and we were tired of riding in soft saddles. It was ten o'clock before we got home. We put our horses in the barn and fed them, for we knew we'd have to ride again early in the morning. Everybody had gone to bed at home but Mom. She had supper waiting for us. Then while we ate we told her what had happened.

"Jeff says he has the answer," Mom said.

"Foot on his answer!" Pa ranted.

"Give Jeff a chance, Mick," Mom said. "He wants to show you he knows something about mules."

"If he has any ideas he can keep 'em to himself," Pa said, his face getting red again.

The next morning we left before Uncle Jeff was out of bed. A soft rain was falling just like Pa said it would. Then, I realized who had the right answers at our home. It was not Uncle Jeff. But it was Pa.

"Oh, if we only had the tobacco ground ready," Pa lamented. "We're losing a lot of good time over these mules. Tobacco season is on us now and we don't know when we'll get another rain this good."

We rode straight to the Cedar Riffles country. We stopped at Ben Kant's farm. We found Ben in his barn milking his cows.

"Good morning, Ben," Pa greeted him. "Have you seen any stray mules?"

"Yessir, Mick, they were in the barnlot this morning when I got here," he said. "I tried to get 'em up and they sailed over the fence."

"My mules all right," Pa said. "Which way did they go?"

"You'll find their tracks up the road," he replied.

"Thank you, Ben," Pa said. "We'll be after 'em with fresh horses."

In a few minutes we saw Dick and Dinah. We let our horses walk and follow them.

"When we get a chance we'll run ahead and turn 'em back," Pa spoke softly. "I'll lead and you follow."

The road was narrow, cliffs on one side and river on the other. We didn't get the chance. We followed them to Put Off Ford. And here they plunged into the Sandy River and swam over. We swam our horses over after them. Now the chase was on. We tried to head them off. But they turned left and jumped over another high fence.

"We can't follow them over that," Pa said despondently. "We'll have to ride until we find a gate."

We rode along a little-used road until we came to a gate. I got down and opened the gate and Pa rode in. I fastened the gate and followed. It was late in the afternoon now and I was very hungry. Pa had complained of being hungry too. We had planned to have the mules back home by noon. We followed the bare prints of a road until we came to a small house where a short, unshaven man stepped out.

"Something you want?" he asked.

"Our mules leaped this fence and got inside." Pa told him.

"Mrs. Kinner has eight hundred acres fenced in here," he said. "I watch about trespassers, hunters, and fires. You can get your mules but you'll have to come back in the morning."

"Maybe," Pa sighed. "It will be the third time we've tried."

"We'll be back here early in the morning," I told him.

Then we turned and rode away. We didn't get home until after dark.

"Mick, when you go back tomorrow morning to get the mules, I say you'll get 'em," Uncle Jeff told him. "I'll see that you do."

"Why haven't you seen that I got them before?" Pa said, looking angrily at Uncle Jeff. "We've lost two days now and will lose the third one. If you could be of such great help, why haven't you already been?"

"You've not asked me," Uncle Jeff said. "I've waited for you to."

"I've not asked you because I don't think you have the answer," Pa said.

"But I do have the answer," he said. "I've worked more mules than you have. I've worked them in many big logging jobs."

"I've heard that before," Pa said. "I listen to your big windy tales until I get tired. We'll get the mules some way."

When we ate supper Pa and Uncle Jeff didn't speak. Pa and I were wet to the skin. The soft rain had never let up all day.

The next morning, up early, we fed and milked, and saddled our horses for the long journey. Uncle Jeff wasn't out of bed when we left. The morning skies were blue and a few stars hadn't set when we rode away.

"That Jeff is one man I'd like to run off," Pa told me. "When I ran 'im off that time I almost lost your mother. No one will keep Jeff but me. He's just that ornery. Yet, he knows all about mules."

"Pa, he might know how to get 'em home," I said.

"If he did, I could be a little nicer to Jeff," Pa admitted.

It was a bright beautiful morning in May in a world of green beneath blue skies; down winding roads and between cliffs and a river we rode until we came to Put Off Ford. There we swam our horses across and rode up the dim prints of the old road. I heard a splash and looked behind us and saw Finn on the pony, Glory. He was swimming the Sandy River behind us.

"Reckon something's wrong?" Pa was concerned.

We stopped and waited until Finn caught up with us.

"What's wrong?" Pa asked. "Why have you come?"

"To help you," Finn said. Then he grinned. "This pony is as fast as greased lightning. He'll run the mules down."

"You'd better stay out of the way on that little pony," Pa warned.

Finn opened the gate and we rode in on the Kinner farm. Finn closed the gate and followed. When we reached the little house, Dick and Dinah were standing in the yard. They sniffled and brayed as we rode up. They shied to one side like they were going to take off.

"Wait a minute," Pa whispered. "Wait 'til I get my ear of corn."

When Finn came riding up they stood perfectly still and stared. Then the small beardy-faced man came outside.

"They came up here about daylight and have been hangin' around ever since," he told us. "Now, what is the best way to catch 'em?"

"Don't bother about that corn, Pa." Finn said. "Don't bother about anything right now. We'll see if Uncle Jeff's way will work."

Finn started riding Glory out the lane. Dick thrust his head out in the direction of the pony and took off. Dinah followed.

"What's the magic secret?" the little man asked. "I'd like to know."

"I would too," Pa said as he reined and followed.

When we rode out the lane, Finn had opened the gate and was back on his pony.

"Fasten the gate!" he shouted. "We've got 'em goin'!"

Pa rode Dollie behind Dick and Dinah and I fastened the gate and followed. When Finn rode Glory into the Sandy River, Dick and Dinah plunged in and groaned and brayed with their heads thrust forward trying to keep up with the pony. When Finn went up the river bank with water dripping from the pony and himself, the mules swam out and shook themselves and took off after the pony. Pa and I swam our horses across and followed them down the Cedar Riffles road.

"Slow down, Finn!" Pa shouted. "You're about to kill the mules!"

They were getting their breath like a blowing wind.

"All right!" Finn shouted. Then we heard him laugh. "Uncle Jeff did have the answer too. He knew mules would follow a white pony!"

There was never a ride like this one. Finn on the small white pony in front, our long-legged mules in the middle with their mouths open and their tongues out, and Pa and I behind on our horses now wet all over and with a foamy lather dripping from their bellies.

"Set your pony's pace right to give 'em all they can stand!" Pa yelled to Finn. "Don't run 'em to death, though; we need those mules."

Then Pa laughed like the Sandy River water as it poured over the rocks at Cedar Riffles. Pa laughed like the rising morning wind in the tall cedars and sycamores along the river banks.

No Hero

Author's Introduction

After I graduated from Greenup High School, I went with a street carnival for a time. And I know what it is to play to different people night after night in a small town for a week's stand, work most of the night and sleep mostly in the morning hours. Sometimes we kept the carnival open in the afternoons as well as night. And during the Fourth of July and Labor Day holidays, we kept the street carnival open day and night over a holiday week end which lasted from Friday until Monday. I learned there was a lot of work, packing up after the last show in a week's stand and moving on to another town. And without rest or sleep we put our tents up and got ready for a show that night.

While I knew I would never go on working in a street carnival, I learned to have a lot of respect for the men and women who did. I learned they lived hard lives and were on the move all the time. They didn't make much money, but they were happy because they liked to be moving, seeing new places and new faces. To this day there is something magnetic about a street carnival to me. I go and I spend money and have a wonderful time.

One time a carnival with an unusual feature, one I had never seen before, came to Greenup County. It had a large caged bear which was advertised as a great wrestler. The bear's owner was offering $25 to any man who could stay in the cage with the bear for five minutes. Now, not all men are brave, not all are cowards, and not all are foolish. But there are people who are always seeking something new. And this was something new. I stood near the cage night after night and watched the performances. I saw men who tried to wrestle this bear slapped across the cage. I saw them come staggering out through the cage door, getting out as fast as they could, half stunned and often bleeding. Old Bruin was rough. The longer one wrestled with him, trying to pin his shoulders on the floor, the rougher he got. He was gentle enough at first, but if and when the wrestler slapped the bear, then the bear really slapped back. And he was plenty good at slapping. Half of the crowd at the fair gathered round the cage to see the wrestling. When the wrestling got so rough that many men were being injured, the Greenup County law officials took steps to put this street carnival out of the county.

Before the Law had ousted them and on the last night this street carnival was permitted to operate, a new kind of wrestler came to the carnival to wrestle the bear. He was a little older than the others had been. Hester King was tall, slender, and very weak physically. He didn't look like a wrestler; he wasn't a wrestler. When he went through the cage door, there were shouts and laughter. The others who had attempted to wrestle with the bear had wanted to be a hero. But Hester King didn't want to be a hero. He wanted something more than this. And now the story will tell you just what he did.

WHEN I COULD look over at the bright lights of Landsburg, I stopped to catch my breath and do some thinking. For behind me lay the dark unfruitful hills where my crops had failed. And in a shack among these hills, seven miles away, I'd left Mollie with our three little ones. "Hester, we have to have bread," was the last thing she'd said to me. "We can't go another day without some kind of relief." And when I started walking to Landsburg in the late afternoon, Mollie couldn't understand. I couldn't tell her what I had in mind.

For nature had been against me. It wasn't that I wasn't willing to work. I was willing to work. The drouth had killed my crops. I couldn't make it rain. There just wasn't anything I could do about it except see my garden truck, corn, potatoes, and tobacco wilt in the hot June and July sun. All I'd worked for was lost.

Nature was against me in another way that I couldn't help. I'd grown up tall as a beanpole and slender as a poplar sapling. In August I'd tried to get work with an extra force, when the Railway Company was needing men. The foreman took one look at me and said, "Not heavy enough for your height. The lifting of crowbars, crossties, and T-rails would break you in two." Then I tried to get a job at the Auckland Iron Works, where they needed men. They gave me an examination and then put me on the scales. "Underweight," the doctor said. "We can't use you." It was that way every place I tried to get work.

Nature was against me more ways than one. And now I had to do some more thinking about Mollie and our three little ones before I tackled what I had in mind to do. Jim Harris told me about something in Landsburg. It was something they begged a man to do. It was hard to get a man to do it. But it was great fun for the people to see. Jim said the Landsburg Law had threatened to close the place up since one man, Hawk Weaver, was sent to the hospital.

In the distance below me I could see the bright lights along the streets and I could see one real bright spot in the town. This was the spot where I was going. For this was the fairground. I could hear the shouts of happy people coming from this spot and I could hear the music of the merry-go-round. "This way, this way," I could hear a man shout. "Three balls for the little dime, ten cents. Knock down three kitties and get yourself a quarter!" But this wasn't what I was going to do. It was harder than throwing balls at the kitties. It was something all the brave boys were afraid to do. And I wasn't brave either. I just needed the money. I had to have some money. And when I thought about it, my heart went up into my mouth.

But I'll be game, I thought. I'll try it. If they'll only let me try it after they see how tall I am and almost as light as the wind.

Then I started toward the brightest spot in Landsburg. My long beanpole legs soon covered the ground when I started walking. In a few minutes I'd reached the bright spot I'd looked over from the ridgetop. The Greenwood County people and the city people of Landsburg had filled the fairground. People were almost running over each other. They were standing in line to buy baseballs to throw at the kitties. They were standing in line to buy rings to throw over pegs where knives, alarm clocks, blankets, and pans were hanging. They were waiting to ride the merry-go-round and the merry-mixup. They were standing packed like sardines in front of a tent where two women danced and where a man beat a drum. And when the drummer and the dancers went into the tent and the announcer told them the "greatest show on earth would be inside the tent" they pushed each other down trying to get tickets before the tent was filled. Money was flowing like water and everybody was happy. I wished for a little of the money I saw coming from the fat pocketbooks. But my time was coming. Not now.

For Lefty Simmons, Landsburg's local boy, stepped upon the platform in boxing trunks and sparred with Slugger Stevens.

"Ladies and gentlemen, last evening Lefty Simmons and

'Slugger' Stevens fought an even match," the announcer shouted through a megaphone, "and this evening they will fight to a finish. It's your local boy, Lefty, against the great and powerful 'Slugger' Stevens! Ladies and gentlemen, right this way to see one of the greatest fights of all times!"

When Slugger and Lefty went inside the tent, the crowd rushed for tickets. I knew that my time would come next. It would come after this fight. For the people that loved to watch a fight would love to watch what I was going to try to do. Some of them might want to see a man killed. Though I wasn't sure about that. Yet, for years afterward they would talk about seeing Hester King's body mangled at the Landsburg Fair. But I didn't want to die. I'd thought this thing through and it was the only way I could see to make some quick money. I'd heard all my life, "Wherever there's a will, there's a way." I had the will. And I'd thought of the way.

There was one more night of the Landsburg Fair. And when I waited outside for the fight to be over, I heard screams and shouts of the people inside. "Kill 'im, Lefty, kill 'im!" I could hear men and women shout and scream. It must have been some fight, and a lot of people got worked up about it. For the Landsburg marshal and two deputies had to go inside the tent. But when the manager brought the fighters back onto the platform, he held up both their hands and said it was another draw and they would fight it out to a finish tomorrow night, the last night of the Landsburg Fair. They had fought to five draws, this made.

"Your local Lefty is some fighter," the announcer said. "He's stayed with the mighty Slugger for five nights!"

A great roar of applause went up from the people. For Lefty's face looked red and beaten and there was blood on his lips and nostrils.

"Don't leave now, folks, don't leave," the announcer shouted through his megaphone. "Stand by for an important announcement!"

I knew what was coming now.

"We are looking for a man to stay with old Bruin five minutes tonight," the man shouted. "Is there a man in the crowd that will wrestle the greatest wrestler in the world! Is there a man that will take a chance wrestling this three-hundred-and-eighty-six-pound bear? If there is a man that will stay in the cage with him five minutes, he will receive twenty-five dollars! If a man will stay with him ten minutes, he will receive fifty dollars. He will receive twenty-five dollars for every five minutes he stays with old Bruin! That's a lot of money, folks! And if he wrestles Bruin," he shouted, "he will get an extra one hundred dollars."

"I'll try it, sir," I said, holding up my hand high above the crowd.

I looked around me and not another hand was up.

"That bear'll kill you, man," a big fellow said to me. "Hawk Weaver is in the hospital over a-tryin' to fight that bear! Ain't you afraid of 'im, Slim?"

"Yes, I am," I said.

"What are you a-gettin' in the cage with 'im for, then?" the man asked.

I didn't answer him. And I heard sighs go up all over the fairgrounds.

"Another victim," said a little man standing near me.

"Then come up here, Slim," the announcer said. "Let the crowd have a look at you!"

When I walked upon the platform, everybody laughed. The announcer looked me over and he laughed. Maybe he laughed at my big feet and long hands. But the whole crowd laughed, and they pushed up closer.

"How tall are you and how much do you weigh?" the announcer asked me.

"Six feet five and weigh one thirty-five," I said.

"Ever do any wrestling, Slim?" he asked me.

"Never did," I said.

"What do you do for a living?" he asked me.

"Right now I'm unemployed," I said.

Then the announcer asked me my full name and where I lived and I told him.

"This is Hester King from Buckrun Hollow back in Greenwood County," the announcer shouted to the crowd through his megaphone. "He's six feet five, weighs one thirty-five and he's never done any wrestling! And right now he's unemployed."

"He'll be employed when old Bruin gets a-hold of 'im," some man shouted from the crowd.

"Stomp old Bruin with your big number thirteens," another man laughed.

"Slap his face with your big fire-shovel hand," another man screamed.

Then everybody laughed. More people gathered in to have a look at me. It was the first time I'd ever faced a crowd like this. Everybody on the fairground was shoving closer.

"Nobody's stayed with that bear three minutes," said a big man that stood below me, resting his hand on the platform. "That's the catch. See, you don't get anything unless you stay five minutes! Hogg Morton stayed the longest. He stayed two minutes! Had the bear down once! But it liked to 've kilt old Hogg before the referee could get 'im off! It's a mint of gold for this fair!"

"Buddie Walker didn't stay ten seconds," said a man standing beside the man that had spoken of Hogg Morton. "Bear just knocked him against the cage once and that was all there was to it!"

"How long do you think you can stay with Bruin?" the announcer asked me.

"Five minutes," I said. "Maybe longer."

"Hester King says he can stay with Bruin five minutes, maybe longer," the announcer shouted gleefully.

"That's what Hester King thinks," a man shouted from the crowd. "That bear's a man-killer and shouldn't be allowed to wrestle civilized men at a street fair!"

"Then Mr. King says he'll stay with the bear five minutes or longer and you say he won't," the announcer said. "Let's see who is telling the truth! Maybe this tall man will surprise us!"

"Old Ichabod, the beanpole, will soon find out," somebody shouted from the crowd. "There won't be any draw in this wrestling match!"

"He wants to wrestle mighty bad," another man shouted. "Or he must need the money!"

"Wait until you see this man in wrestling trunks," the announcer said. "You'll see something. Worth the price of admission, folks!"

I followed the announcer from the platform down into the tent. The crowd surged up to buy tickets. When I went into a little dressing room and started taking off my clothes, I thought about Mollie, little Naomi, Sophie, and Hester, Jr. Then I thought about going into the cage with the bear. I wondered just what would happen. And what if I can stay with 'im five minutes, I thought. Ten minutes! Fifteen, twenty, twenty-five minutes! One hundred and twenty-five dollars! What a fortune!

While I put my skinny legs into the big wrestler's trunks, I heard people pouring into the tent like honeybees into a hive. Only the people made more noise. It was a louder buzzing and there was so many jumbled words that I couldn't understand what anybody was saying. I could hear the word "kill" pretty often.

When I was ready, the manager told me the referee, Johnnie Norris, who owned the bear, would see that Bruin didn't hurt me, for he could handle him. He warned me not to be too scared and to stay with Bruin two minutes if I could.

"I must stay longer than that," I said. "I must stay five minutes!"

The manager laughed as he pushed back a flap of the tent and we walked into the arena beneath the big tent where the people were crowded close to the cage. The big black bear was inside the cage, walking around, looking between the iron bars at the people. He'd hold to the iron bars with his paws as he circled the cage and looked at the crowd.

"He'd like to get among us," said a well-dressed woman. "My, if I's a man, I wouldn't want to wrestle that ugly thing!"

When I walked among the crowd, everybody screamed with laughter.

"Ichabod Crane wrestling that heavy bear!" someone screamed.

People looked at my long skinny legs and wondered how they'd hold me up. They looked at my little waist measure.

"Not any bigger around the waist than the coupling pole in a jolt wagon," a big man said as I passed him.

"But look what feet and hands," another man said.

"Bear won't care for them," said a freckled-faced man with a bow tie that went up and down with his Adam's apple as he talked.

"Hate to see that poor man get what Hawk Weaver got," I heard someone say in a low voice. For I was near the cage door.

"Timekeepers here?" the announcer asked.

"Yep, we're here," said a tall man. "Kim Kiefer of Landsburg will help me keep the time!"

"All right, Al, you and Kim start your watches," Johnnie said, as he unlocked the cage door.

I thought of Mollie and my three little ones. That was the last thought I had before I stooped nearly double to go through the cage door.

"Shake hands with Bruin," Johnnie said. "He expects it. If you do, it will be easier for you!"

Bruin knew what his duties were. For he came up to meet me and Johnnie stepped aside when he reached me his paw. I shook his paw gently. And everybody in the tent became so quiet you could have almost heard a pin drop on the dirt-packed floor outside the cage. And my shaking Bruin's paw gently didn't help matters a bit. He backed away and then he came clumsily toward me with the full force of his three-hundred-odd pounds. He pushed me against the side of the cage with a wallop. He acted like he wanted to finish me in a hurry.

"Won't be long," said the freckled-faced man with the bow tie that worked up and down on his Adam's apple. He held his face close to the cage and peeped between the bars. But he was surprised when I got back to my feet and ran in between old Bruin's outstretched forepaws. That's the spot all the wrestlers didn't want to get. Old Bruin tried squeezing on me but I was too small for him to get the full power of his powerful arms. I hugged close to Bruin and put my hands gently on his back. Then he shoved me back and slapped at me again. He knocked me against the side of the cage. But it didn't hurt me and I didn't stay long. I ran back into his arms.

"Three minutes," said Kim Kiefer. "Longest anybody has stayed yet!"

The people surged closer. They packed around the cage.

"Down in front!" I heard them yell from the far sides of the arena. "Down in front!"

"Will he stay five minutes?" I heard wrestling fans asking each other.

I have to stay five minutes, I thought. And if I can just do. . . .

But old Bruin slapped me awfully hard and I hit the bars of the cage and saw stars.

"Four minutes," Kim Kiefer said.

"Three minutes and fifty seconds," said Al, the Street Fair's timekeeper.

"You're a little off," Kim Kiefer said. "My watch is right."

I was clinched with old Bruin again and I let my hands fall

gently up and down his back like you'd rub a piece of silk on a washboard. Bruin wasn't as rambunctious with me as he had been. Johnnie Norris looked at us clinched there, and my chin down on old Bruin's head. We stood in the middle of the cage and the long lanky muscles of my beanpole legs hooved higher than they ever had before. It looked like we were each trying to throw the other on the cage floor.

"Five minutes," Kiefer shouted.

"Seconds yet," Al said.

We stood there paw-locked and arm-locked and time was fleeting. Once Johnnie Norris passed around us and he had a worried look on his face. But I watched the referee to see that he didn't prod the bear to make him try to finish me. Spectators were watching through the bars. Women were sitting upon men's shoulders so they could see into the cage. They were watching Johnnie Norris too. Hundreds of eyes were trained on him as he moved around through the cage with a mysterious air and a worried look on his face.

"Nine minutes," Kim Kiefer shouted.

Al didn't say anything.

One minute more, I thought. Just one minute more.

Then Bruin started pushing me. And I braced my feet away out from him for I was tall and I leaned like a prop. Yet, I had my chin on his head.

"Ten minutes," Kiefer said.

"Lacks ten seconds of being ten minutes," Al grunted.

Then Bruin put his red tongue out like a tired dog. I felt his hot breath sizzle past my ear. The sweat was pouring from my face and running in little streams down my body. Holding a bear up as big as Bruin wasn't an easy task.

"Has he hypnotized that bear?" someone shouted.

And just about that time, Bruin pushed me to the floor. But he didn't come down on me. I stayed down to rest a minute. He panted harder and everybody could see his long red tongue and his full set of pretty white teeth. He stood in the middle of the cage like a very tired wrestler.

"Fourteen minutes," Kim Kiefer said.

Then there were shouts that went up from the people.

"He might even wrestle old Bruin yet," the fellow said who was wearing the bow tie. He said the words so fast the bow tie jumped up and down his neck with his Adam's apple like a tree frog.

I came back to my feet and Bruin came to meet me, slapping gently with his paws. I did a little footwork around the cage until his front paws were spread apart and then I rushed in and clinched Bruin.

"Fifteen minutes," Kiefer said.

Seventy-five dollars, I thought. Give me five minutes more.

And when I put my chin back on Bruin's head and braced my feet with my big hands planted on Bruin's back, this time Bruin went down and I went down beside him. Johnnie Norris ran up to look at our shoulders. Al ran up and looked between the bars. And the crowd screamed loud enough to raise the tent.

Bruin's weight on my left arm hurt a little. But my right arm was around his neck. My chin was still on top of his head. And we lay there, stomach to stomach, side by side, in wrestling embrace.

"What's wrong here?" Johnnie Norris said to the Fair's time-keeper. "Al, you go get the boss!"

"But who will keep time with Kiefer?" Al asked.

"I will," Johnnie said, as Al started pushing his way through the crowd.

"Referee can't serve in two capacities at one time," a big man with a handlebar mustache said as he put his face against the cage bars.

Shouts went up again from the people.

"Nineteen minutes," Kiefer said.

"Ten seconds till," Johnnie Norris said.

"Who said old Ichabod Crane couldn't wrestle," said the man with the Adam's apple. "He'll ride that bear yet!"

They didn't know it, but I knew Bruin was ready for a rest on the floor even if we were in a wrestlers' clinch.

When the boss, Solway Meadows, came running into the tent, his face looked as sour as if he'd bitten a green persimmon when he looked inside the cage and saw us lying side by side.

"Twenty minutes," Kiefer shouted.

"What's wrong, Johnnie?" Solway Meadows asked.

"Old Bruin just can't ride 'im," Johnnie said.

"Now you're a-talkin'," somebody shouted. "Old Ichabod Crane will ride that bear yet! He's some wrestler!"

"Old Bruin didn't find Hawk Weaver when he got hold of old Ichabod," said the big sports fan with the handlebar mustache. He tried to stick his face between the cage bars, and he worked his mustache like a rabbit works its whiskers.

"Twenty-four minutes," Kim Kiefer shouted.

"Old Ichabod said he'd stay with old Bruin five minutes and maybe longer," the big sports fan shouted and wiggled his handlebar mustache. "He's a-doin' more than he said he would!"

"Twenty-five minutes," Kiefer shouted.

Then the bear rolled over on his back.

The loudest scream of all went up from the crowd. There were screams, shouts, and whistles.

"Look at the shoulders there, referee," the old sports fan shouted. "Let's have the count. Bruin's down! He's down!"

Bruin didn't offer to get up. His big mouth was open and you could count the white teeth in his mouth and take a look at his pretty red tongue.

"You must have played my bear foul," Johnnie Norris said.

"I did not," I panted. "You'll see Bruin's not hurt. He's tired but happy!"

"First time that bear was ever ridden," Solway Meadows said.

"First time anybody ever stayed with 'im over two minutes," Al said.

But from the screams of the people it was hard to hear another word. When Johnnie Norris got Bruin up from my arm, he found out whether he was hurt or not. Bruin gave him a lick on top the head that sent Johnnie reeling toward the other side of the cage where he staggered a few times, shook his head, and seemed to do a little dance on wobbly legs as he slumped down to the floor.

"What do you know about that?" Al said.

"You see I didn't hurt old Bruin," I said to Solway Meadows. "He's a hard bear to handle!"

"Two hundred and twenty-five dollars!" said the freckled-faced man wearing the bow tie. "Think of it! Ichabod Crane rode old Bruin!"

Solway Meadows let me through the cage door, while Al dragged Johnnie outside where he'd have a more comfortable sleep.

"Same thing old Bruin done to Hawk Weaver," a tall beardy-faced man said as the old sports fan with the big mustache and the young man with the bow tie and as many others as could gather around me lifted me upon their shoulders. They carried me out of the tent and over the Landsburg fairgrounds, shouting "Here's Ichabod Crane! He rode the bear!"

And everybody laughed and screamed and shouted. They waved their hands at me and the women and girls threw handkerchiefs toward me. I was a hero for that night. But they didn't know how I did it. They paid me the money but told me the bear wouldn't wrestle on Saturday night. I didn't tell them or anybody what a friend I'd made of Bruin. I didn't tell them I had once owned a pet bear in the upper Peninsula of Michigan when I was trying to cut cord wood, and that I knew a bear liked to be rubbed between the ears and on the tummy. I suppose it wasn't exactly fair, but Mollie and the kids had to eat. Gentling old Bruin was an easy dollar.

Rain on Tanyard Hollow

Author's Introduction

When I attended Greenup High School, one of my best friends was Oscar Sammons. We played football together, hunted together, and took the same courses. After we finished high school, he went to the University of Kentucky, where he spent seven years obtaining a B.D. degree and a degree in law. When he returned to Greenup to practice law, he brought home a wife, Ann Michael Sammons.

In the meantime, I had gone to school at Lincoln Memorial University, Harrogate, Tennessee, and Vanderbilt University, and Peabody College, Nashville, Tennessee. I returned with a B.A. degree, plus two years of graduate work. I didn't bring home a wife. My wife-to-be, Naomi Norris, was teaching in the Greenup Elementary School. She, too, had gone to Greenup High School with Oscar and me.

When Oscar came home with Ann, we were most anxious to meet her. Naomi and I visited them often. Here was a most delightful and entertaining couple. While he struggled as a young lawyer, Ann joined Naomi and me as a teacher in the Greenup County schools. And in the meantime, Oscar and Ann built themselves a small white house overlooking the broad, blue Ohio River.

Often their house was filled with a crowd of friends who came to sit and talk. Here, we all had great evenings together. What made the evenings so interesting with these fascinating friends was that, whenever we met, we told stories. We told true stories or made them up. Oscar always told his stories for true ones, but I rather suspect he created part of them in his fertile imagination. It didn't really matter because Oscar was a master storyteller.

In this circle of storytellers, where I certainly was not the best but had to work hard to keep up with the others, I had only one advantage over the others: I liked to write stories. I liked to record them while the others just liked to tell them. I don't know how many stories Oscar Sammons has told that I have written. And when I told one of my own that met with approval of those in the circle, Oscar would say, "Now, go home and write that one." And when he said these words, which pleased me very much, I went home and wrote the story. Every story that Oscar Sammons advised me to write has since been published from one to a dozen times. One little tribute I have since paid to Oscar was to dedicate one of my short-story collections, Plowshare in Heaven, to this classmate and friend.

One evening I told a very serious story which involved nature and superstition, and man's winning against both. It even involved a man's praying for something and getting more than he asked for. It was a story that had happened in our neighborhood to a family I had worked for when I was an itinerant farm worker. I knew the family and its problems. I had never thought of this as being a story. I didn't add anything to this story and I didn't subtract anything. When I

finished with this story, everybody laughed hilariously
and applauded me. "Go write it," Oscar shouted. I
did, and the story sold the first trip to a magazine.
"Rain On Tanyard Hollow" is the story. Had it not
been for my telling it to this circle of friends in the
little white house on the Ohio River bank it would
never have been written.

"DON'T KILL that snake, Sweeter," Mammie said.
"Leave it alone among the strawberry vines and it'll ketch the
groundmoles that's eatin' the roots of the strawberry plants."

Mammie raised up from pickin' strawberries and stood with
one hand in her apron pocket. Draps of sweat the size of white
soup-beans stood all over her sun-tanned face and shined like
dewdrops on the sun. Mammie looked hard at Pappie but it
didn't do any good.

"Kill that snake," Pappie shouted. "It must a thought my
knuckle was a mole. It ain't goin' to rain nohow unless I kill a
few more black snakes and hang 'em on the fence."

Pappie stood over the black snake. It was quiled and a-gettin'
ready to strike at 'im again. It looked like the twisted root of
a black-oak tree rolled-up among the half-dead strawberry plants.
It must a knowed Pappie was goin' to kill it the way it was
fightin' him back. It kept drawin' its long black-oak-root body
up tighter so it could strike harder at Pappie. It stuck its forked
tongue out at him.

"You would fight me back," Pappie shouted as he raised a big
flat rock above his head high as his arms would reach. "You
would get me foul and bite me. That's just what you've done.
Now I'm goin' to kill you and hang you on the fence and make
it rain."

Pappie let the big rock fall on the black snake. The rock's sharp edge cut the snake in two in many places. Its tail quivered against the ground and rattled the dried-up leaves on the strawberry plants. Its red blood oozed out on the dry-as-gunpowder dust. Mammie stood and looked at the pieces of snake writhin' on the gound.

"Old Adam fit with rocks," Pappie said. "They air still good things to fight with."

Pappie stood with his big hands on his hips. He looked at the dyin' black snake and laughed.

"That black snake didn't hurt your hand when it bit you," Mammie said. "Sweeter, you air a hardhearted man. You've kilt a lot of snakes and hung 'em on the fence to make it rain. They air still hangin' there. I aint heard a rain-crow croakin' yet ner felt a drap of rain. The corn is burnt up. You know it has. The corn aint goin' to git no taller. It's tasselin' and it's bumblebee corn. If you's to drap any ashes from your cigar on this strawberry patch it would set the plants on fire. They look green but they air dry as powder. Where is your rain?"

"I don't know, Lizzie," Pappie said. "You tell me where the rain is."

"It's in the sky," Mammie said, "and you won't get it unless you pray fer it to fall. It's about too late fer prayer too. And the Lord wouldn't listen to a prayer from you."

When Mammie said this she looked hard at Pappie. Pappie stood there and looked at Mammie. What she said to him about the Lord not listenin' to his prayer made Pappie wilt. His blue eyes looked down at Mammie. The hot dry wind that moved across the strawberry patch and rustled the strawberry plants, moved the beard on Pappie's face as he stood in the strawberry patch with his big brogan shoes planted like two gray stumps. His long lean body looked like a dead snag where the birds come to light and the beard on his face and the long hair that stuck down below the rim of his gone-to-seed straw hat looked like sour-vines wrapped around the snag.

"Don't stand there, Sweeter, like a skeery-crow and look at me with your cold blue-water eyes," Mammie said. "You know you air a hardhearted man and the Lord won't listen to your prayer. Look at the harmless black snakes you've kilt and have hangin' on the fence and you aint got rain yet. Sweeter, I'm lettin' the rest of these strawberries dry on the stems. I'm leavin' the strawberry patch."

Mammie slammed her bucket against the ground. She pulled her pipe from her pocket. She dipped the light-burley terbacker crumbs from her apron pocket as she walked toward the ridgetop rustlin' the dyin' strawberry plants with her long peaked-toed shoes. By the time Mammie reached the dead white-oak snag that stood on the ridgetop and marked our strawberry patch for all the crows in the country, Mammie had her pipe lit and there was a cloud of smoke followin' her as she went over the hill toward the house.

"Tracey, your Mammie talked awful pert to me."

"Yep, she did, Pappie."

"She talked like the Lord couldn't hear my prayer."

When Pappie talked about what Mammie said about the Lord not payin' any attention to his prayers, his beardy lips quivered. I could tell Pappie didn't like it. He felt insulted. He thought if the Lord listened to prayers, he ought to listen to one of his prayers.

"I'm just hard on snakes, Tracey," Pappie said. "I don't like snakes. My knuckle burned like a hornet stung me when that dad-durned black snake hid among the strawberry plants and bit me. It didn't come out in the open and bite me. Your Mammie got mad because I kilt that snake. I know the baby-handed moles air bad to nose under the roots of the strawberry plants and eat their white-hair roots and the black snakes eat the moles. But that aint no excuse fer a black snake's bitin' me on the knuckle."

"I don't blame you, Pappie," I said.

When I said this, Pappie looked at me and his face lost the

cloud that was hangin' over it. The light on Pappie's face was like the mornin' sunshine on the land.

"It's a dry time, Tracey," Pappie said as he kicked the dry strawberry plants with his big brogan shoe. The leaves that looked green fell from the stems and broke into tiny pieces. Little clouds of dust rose from among the strawberry plants where Pappie kicked.

"We don't have half a strawberry crop," I said. "And if we don't get rain we won't have a third of a corn crop."

"You air right, Tracey," Pappie answered. "We'll get rain. If it takes prayers we'll get rain. Why won't the Lord listen to me same as he will listen to Lizzie? Why won't the Lord answer my prayer same as he will answer any other man's prayer in Tanyard Hollow?"

When Pappie said this he fell to his knees among the scorched strawberry plants. Pappie come down against the dry plants with his big fire-shovel hands and at the same time he turned his face toward the high heat-glimmerin' sky. Dust flew up in tiny clouds as Pappie beat the ground.

"Lord, will you listen to my prayer?" Pappie shouted. "I don't keer who hears me astin' you fer rain. We need it, Lord! The strawberries have shriveled on the vines and the corn is turnin' yaller. It's bumblebee corn, Lord. Give us rain, Lord. I've kilt the black snakes and hung 'em on the fence and the rain don't fall. Never a croak from the rain-crow ner a drap of rain. The black snake on the fence is a false image, Lord."

Pappie beat his hands harder on the ground. He jerked up strawberry plants with his hands and tossed them back on the ground. He dug up the hard dry ground and sifted it among the strawberry plants around him. He never looked at the ground. His face was turned toward the high clouds. The sun was beamin' down on Pappie and he couldn't look at the sun with his eyes open.

"Send rain, Lord, that will wash gully-ditches in this strawberry patch big enough to bury a mule in," Pappie shouted. "Let it fall in great sheets. Wash Tanyard Hollow clean."

I didn't bother with Pappie's prayer but I thought that was too much rain. Better to let the strawberry plants burn to death than to wash them out by the roots and take all the topsoil down Tanyard Hollow too. Can't grow strawberries in Tanyard Hollow unless you've got good topsoil of dead-leaf loam on the south hill slopes.

"Give us enough rain, Lord," Pappie shouted, "to make the weak have fears and the strong tremble. Wash rocks from these hillsides that four span of mules can't pull on a jolt-wagon. Wash trees out by the roots that five yoke of cattle can't pull. Skeer everybody nearly to death. Show them Your might, Lord. Put water up in the houses—a mighty river! Put a river of yaller water out'n Tanyard Hollow that is flowin' faster than a hound dog can run. Make the people take to the high hill slopes and let their feet sink into the mud instead of specklin' their shoes and bare feet with dust!"

Pappie prayed so hard that white foam fell from his lips. It was dry foam the kind that comes from the work cattle's mouths when I feed them corn nubbins. The big flakes of white foam fell upon the green-withered strawberry plants.

"Send the thunder rollin' like tater wagons across the sky over Tanyard Hollow," Pappie prayed. "Let the Hollow grow dark. Let the chicken think that night has come and fly up in the apple trees to roost. Let the people think the end of time has come. Make the Hollow so dark a body can't see his hand before him. Let long tongues of lightnin' cut through the darkness across the Hollow and split the biggest oaks in Tanyard Hollow from the tip-tops to their butts like you'd split them with a big clapboard fro. Let pieces of hail fall big enough if ten pieces hit a man on the head they'll knock 'im cuckoo. Let him be knocked cold in one of the biggest rains that Tanyard Hollow ever had. Let the rain wash the dead-leaf loam from around the roots of the trees and let the twisted black-oak roots lie like ten million black snakes quiled at the butts of the big oaks. Lord, give us a rain in Tanyard Hollow to end this drouth! Give us a rain that we'll long remember! I'm through with the brazen images of black snakes! Amen."

Pappie got up and wiped the dry foam from his lips with his big hand.

"I ast the Lord fer a lot," Pappie said. "I meant every word I prayed to Him. I want to see one of the awfulest storms hit Tanyard Hollow that ever hit it since the beginnin' of Time. That goes way back yander. I ast fer an awful lot, and I hope by askin' fer a lot, I'll get a few things."

"Pappie, I don't want to wish you any bad luck," I said, "but I hope you don't get all you ast fer. If you get all you ast fer, there won't be anythin' left in Tanyard Hollow. We'll just haf to move out. The topsoil will all be washed away, the dirt washed from around the roots of the trees and they'll look like bundles of black snakes. The big oaks will split from their tip-tops to their butts—right down through the hearts with forked tongues of lightnin'. Trees will be rooted up and rocks washed from the hillsides that a jolt-wagon can't hold up. There won't be any corn left on the hillsides and the strawberry patch will be ruint."

"Tracey, I've ast the Lord fer it," Pappie answered, "and if the Lord is good enough to give it to me, I'll abide by what He sends. I won't be low-lifed enough to grumble about somethin' I've prayed fer. I meant every word I said. I hope I can get part of all I ast fer."

"It's time fer beans," I said. "I can step on the head of my shadder."

Pappie left the strawberry patch. I followed him as he went down the hill. He pulled a cigar from his shirt pocket and took a match from his hatband where he kept his matches so he could keep them dry. He put the cigar in his mouth . . . struck a match on a big rock beside the path and lit his cigar.

"When I was prayin' fer the rain to wash the rocks from the hillsides," Pappie said, "this is one of the rocks I had in mind. It's allus been in my way when I plowed here."

"If we get a rain that will wash this rock from this hillside," I said, "there won't be any of us left and not much of Tanyard Hollow left."

"You'd be surprised at what can happen," Pappie said. "You can turn a double-barrel shotgun loose into a covey of quails and it's a sight at 'em that'll come out alive."

Sweat run off at the ends of Pappie's beard. It dripped on the dusty path. Sweat got in my eyes and dripped from my nose. It was so hot it just seemed that I was roastin' before a big wood fire. It looked like fall-time the way the grass was dyin'. Trees were dyin' in the woods. Oak leaves were turnin' brown.

Pappie took the lead down the hill. It was so steep that we had to hold to sassafras sprouts and let ourselves down the hill. The footpath wound down the hill like a long crooked snake crawlin' on the sand. When we got to the bottom of the hill, Pappie was wet with sweat as if he'd a swum the river. I was as wet as sweat could make me and my eyes were smartin' with sweat like I had a dozen sour-gnats in my eyes.

"Whooie," Pappie sighed as he reached the foot of the mountain and he rubbed his big hand over his beard and slung a stream of sweat on the sandy path. "It's too hot fer a body to want to live. I hope the Lord will answer my prayer."

"I hope Mammie has dinner ready."

Mammie didn't have dinner ready. She was cookin' over the hot kitchen stove. Aunt Rett and Aunt Beadie were helpin' Mammie.

"Lord, I hope we'll soon get rain," Mammie said to Aunt Rett. She stood beside the stove and slung sweat from her forehead with her index finger. Where Mammie slung the sweat in the floor was a long wet streak with little wet spots from the middle of the floor to the wall.

"It's goin' to rain," I said.

"Why is it goin' to rain?" Mammie ast.

"Because Pappie got down in the strawberry patch and prayed fer the Lord to send rain and wash this Hollow out," I said.

Mammie started laughin'. Aunt Rett and Aunt Beadie laughed. They stopped cookin' and all laughed together like three women standin' at the organ singin'.

"We'll get rain," Mammie said, "because Sweeter has prayed fer rain. We'll have a washout in Tanyard Hollow fer Sweeter prayed fer a washout in Tanyard Hollow. We'll get what Sweeter prayed fer."

They begin to sing, "We'll get rain in Tanyard Hollow fer Sweeter prayed fer it."

"Just about like his hangin' the snakes over the rail fence to get rain," Mammie cackled like a pullet. "That's the way we'll get rain."

Uncle Mort Shepherd and Uncle Luster Hix sat in the front room and laughed at Pappie's prayin' fer rain. They thought it was very funny. They'd come down out'n the mountains and were livin' with us until they could find farms to rent. Uncle Mort and Aunt Rett had seven children stayin' with us and Uncle Luster and Aunt Beadie had eight children. We had a big houseful. They's Mammie's people and they didn't think Pappie had any faith. They didn't think the Lord would answer his prayer. I felt like the Lord would answer his prayer, fer Pappie was a man of much misery. Seemed like all of Mammie's people worked against 'im. They'd sit in the house and eat at Pappie's table and talk about gettin' a house and movin' out but they never done it. They'd nearly et us out'n house and home. When they come to our house it was like locust year. Just so much noise when all their youngins got to fightin' you couldn't hear your ears pop.

"It's goin' to rain this afternoon," Pappie said. "There's comin' a cloudbust. If you aint got the Faith you'd better get it."

Uncle Luster got up from the rockin' chear and went to the door. He looked at the yaller-of-an-egg sun in the clear sky. Uncle Luster started laughin'. Uncle Mort got up from his chear and knocked out his pipe on the jam-rock. He looked at the sun in the clear sky and he started laughin'.

Uncle Mort and Uncle Luster hadn't more than got back to the two rockin' chears and started restin' easy until dinner was ready, when all at once there was a jar of thunder across the sky over Tanyard Hollow. It was like a big tater wagon rollin' across the sky. Mammie drapped her fork on the kitchen floor when she heard it. Aunt Rett nearly fell to her knees. Aunt Beadie set a skillet of fried taters back on the stove. Her face got white. She acted like she was skeered.

"Thunderin' when the sky is clear," Aunt Beadie said.

Then the thunder started. Pappie was pleased but his face got white. I could tell he was skeered. He thought he was goin' to get what he'd ast the Lord to send. The thunder got so loud and it was so close that it jarred the house. 'Peared like Tanyard Hollow was a big pocket filled with hot air down among the hills and the thunder started roarin' in this pocket. It started gettin' dark. Chickens flew up in the apple trees to roost.

When Mammie saw the chickens goin' to roost at noon, she fell to her knees on the hard kitchen floor and started prayin'. Mammie thought the end of time had come. The chickens hadn't more than got on the roost until the long tongues of lightnin' started lappin' across the Hollow. When the lightnin' started splittin' the giant oak trees from their tip-tops to their butts it sounded louder than both barrels of a double-barreled shotgun.

"Just what I ast the Lord to send," Pappie shouted. Mammie jumped up and lit the lamps with a pine torch that she lit from the kitchen stove. I looked at Pappie's face. His eyes were big and they looked pleased. All Aunt Beadie's youngins were gathered around her and Uncle Luster. They were screamin'. They were screamin' louder than the chickens were cacklin' at the splittin' oak trees on the high hillsides. Uncle Mort and Aunt Rett got their youngins around them and Uncle Mort started to pray. All six of us got close to Mammie. I didn't. I stuck to Pappie. I thought about how hard he'd prayed fer a good rain to break the long spring drouth. Now the rain would soon be delivered.

Mammie, Aunt Rett and Aunt Beadie let the dinner burn on the stove. I was hungry and I could smell the bread burnin'. I didn't try to get to the kitchen. I saw the yaller water comin' from the kitchen to the front room. The front room was big and we had a big bed in each corner. When I looked through the winder and saw the big sycamores in the yard end up like you'd pull up horseweeds by the roots and throw 'em down, I turned around and saw Aunt Beadie and Uncle Luster make fer one of the beds in the corner of the room. Their youngins followed them. They were screamin' and prayin'. Uncle Mort and Aunt Rett and all their youngins made fer the bed in the other corner of the room. Mammie and my sisters and brothers made for the stairs. Mammie was prayin' as she run. I stayed at the foot of the stairs with Pappie. When he prayed in the strawberry patch, I thought he was astin' the Lord fer too much rain but I didn't say anythin'. I didn't interfere with his prayer.

The water got higher in our house. A rock too big fer a jolt-wagon to haul smashed through the door and rolled across the floor and stopped. If it had rolled another time it would have knocked the big log wall out'n our house. Uncle Mort waded the water from the bed to the stairs and carried Aunt Rett and their youngins to the stairs. When he turned one loose on the stairs he run up the stairs like a drownded chicken. Uncle Luster ferried Aunt Beadie and their youngins to the stairs and turned them loose. Pappie had to take to the stairs. I followed Pappie.

"If we get out'n this house alive," Uncle Mort prayed, "we'll stay out'n it, Lord."

Uncle Luster prayed a long prayer and ast the Lord to save his wife and family. He promised the Lord if He would save them that he would leave Tanyard forever. I never heard so much prayin' in a churchhouse at any of the big revivals at Plum Grove as I heard up our upstairs. Sometimes you couldn't hear the prayers fer the lightnin' strikin' the big oaks. You could hear trees fallin' every place.

"The Lord has answered my prayers," Pappie shouted.

"Pray for the cloudbust to stop," Mammie shouted. "Get down on your knees, Sweeter, and pray."

"Listen, Lizzie," Pappie shouted above the roar of the water and the thunder and the splittin' of the big oaks on the high slopes, "I aint two-faced enough to ast the Lord fer somethin' like a lot of people and atter I git it—turn around and ast the Lord to take it away. You said the Lord wouldn't answer my prayer. You've been prayin'! Why aint the Lord answered your prayers? You aint got the Faith. You just think you have."

When the lightnin' flashed in at our upstairs scuttlehole we had fer a winder, I could see Uncle Mort huddled with his family and Uncle Luster holdin' his family in a little circle. Mammie had all of us, but Pappie and me, over in the upstairs corner. I looked out at the scuttlehole and saw the water surgin' down Left Fork of Tanyard Hollow and down the Right Fork of Tanyard Hollow and meetin' right at our house. That's the only reason our house had stood. One swift river had kilt the other one when they met on this spot. I thought about what Pappie said.

I could see cornfields comin' off'n the slopes. I could see trees with limbs and roots on them bobbin' up and down and goin' down Tanyard Hollow faster than a hound dog could run. It was a sight to see. From my scuttlehole I told 'em what I saw until I saw a blue sky comin' over the high rim of rock cliffs in the head of Tanyard Hollow. That was the end of the storm. I never saw so many happy people when I told them about the patch of blue sky that I saw.

"This is like a dream," Uncle Mort said.

"It's more like a nightmare to me," Uncle Luster said.

"It's neither," Pappie said. "It's the fulfillment of a prayer."

"Why do you pray fer destruction, Sweeter?" Mammie ast.

"To show you the Lord will answer my prayer atter the way you talked to me in the strawberry patch," Pappie said. "And I want your brother Mort and your brother-in-law Luster to remember their promises to the Lord."

The storm was over. It was light again. The chickens flew down from the apple trees. The big yard sycamore shade trees went with the storm but the apple trees stood. There was mud two feet deep on our floor. It was all over the bedclothes. There were five big rocks on our house we couldn't move. We'd haf to take the floor up and dig holes and bury the rocks under the floor. Trees were split all over Tanyard Hollow hillside slopes. Great oak trees were splintered clean to the tops. Our corn had washed from the hill slopes. There wasn't much left but mud, washed-out trees, rocks and waste. Roots of the black-oak trees where the dead-leaf loam had washed away, looked like bundles of clean washed black snakes. The big rock upon the steep hillside that bothered Pappie when he was plowin' had washed in front of our door.

"I promised the Lord," Uncle Mort said, "if we got through this storm alive, I'd take my family and get out'n here and I meant it."

"Amen," Pappie shouted.

"Sorry we can't stay and hep you clean the place up," Uncle Luster said, "but I'm takin' my wife and youngins and gettin' out'n this Hollow."

They didn't stay and hep us bury the rocks under the floor. They got their belongin's and started wadin' the mud barefooted down Tanyard Hollow. They's glad to get goin'. Pappie looked pleased when he saw them pullin' their bare feet out'n the mud and puttin' 'em down again. Pappie didn't grumble about what he had lost. The fence where he had the black snakes hangin' washed down Tanyard Hollow. There wasn't a fence rail 'r a black snake left. The strawberry patch was gutted with gully-ditches big enough to bury a mule. Half of the plants had washed away.

"It wasn't the brazen images of snakes," Pappie said, "that done all of this. Tanyard Hollow is washed clean of most of its topsoil and lost a lot of its trees. But it got rid of a lot of its rubbish and it's a more fitten place to live."

Battle with the Bees

Author's Introduction

After I finished college, I went to visit my father's people who lived on the Big Sandy River. This was my first visit to see this uncle and my first cousins, who were older than I. I was twenty-two. During my stay I heard the story of the battle with the bees. Many years after I heard the story, I was compelled to write it. It was a story I couldn't forget.

Now these relatives that I visited didn't take a magazine or even a newspaper. Radio was just becoming a popular medium of communication. This was in the year 1929. My cousins wanted to buy a battery radio, but my uncle, who had heard one, wouldn't let them. I could see no wrong in my cousins getting a radio, and I told my uncle so. I told him I thought radio music, news, and other communications would help him and his family since they didn't read books or subscribe to newspapers and magazines.

In this area where I visited, there were no paved roads, no telephones, no radios in those days. But in my experience, I have learned that where people lack some things they make up for this lack in other ways. When we were seated around the supper table, my uncle and my cousins began telling stories that had happened in this community. I never heard such fascinating, unbelievable stories as they told at the supper table.

When my relatives saw that their stories pleased me, they kept on telling them after we had left the table and were sitting before an open woodfire, the only kind of heat they had in the house. Now they didn't talk in perfect English. They made all kinds of grammatical errors. They used words that were used in Chaucer's time in England. They used Elizabethan English. My ancestors had been in the Big Sandy River Valley since approximately 1800.

One night after many hours had passed and the clock on the mantle was ready to strike midnight, my uncle told the story of his neighbor across the hill who kept bees, and how he and his wife and children had a nearly fatal battle with them.

My uncle had probably told this story many times. He liked it and he liked to tell it. When he came to the part of the story where another man's hogs got loose and started rooting over the bee hives, he laughed loudly and slapped his knees with his big hands. And my cousins laughed and I laughed. This was one of the most delightful stories I have ever heard. But I didn't plan then to write it. Many years after I heard the story I wrote it; it was a story I couldn't forget.

"T HAT MAKES a hundred stands of bees," Pa said as we stood the sourwood bee gum on a flat rock in the corner of our yard.

"You're not a-countin' the bees we got upstairs," I said. "How many hives have we got in that press?"

"I don't know," Pa said, lookin' at the beehives lined around our yard palin's. "All I know is, we don't have a beehive too many."

I guess there was never a man so wild about honeybees as Pa. No wonder all our neighbors called Pa "Drone," Mom "Queen Bee" and my oldest sister "Honey." They called my second sister "Beeswax" and my baby sister "Little Honey." I was called "Little Drone" and my brother was called "Beebread." Not one of us had the name of Working Bee. Maybe it was because we didn't bother to farm; all we did was hunt wild honey.

"Before I die," Pa said, "I hope to have a thousand beehives around this house."

"It's dangerous now, Pa," I said. "What would it be with a thousand beehives?"

"Afraid of a bee," Pa said. "I'd be ashamed."

"Mom can't pick a flower that grows in this yard without gettin' a bee sting," I said. "We can't play in this yard without our gettin' five or six stings apiece. We have to go to the woods to play. The bees have not only the yard but part of the upstairs."

Pa lit his cigar and watched the bees we'd just brought from the woods start workin' from the sourwood beehive. It was just a cut from the sourwood tree we'd sawed out, and Pa nailed planks over the end. He'd found the tree on Toab Gilbert's farm, and we'd slipped in with our ax, crosscut saw and log-chain. We wrapped the chain around the trunk so when we sawed the tree Toab wouldn't hear us. The log-chain silenced the sound of the crosscut saw a-rippin' through the wood. These were the tools we used when we slipped onto other people's farms to cut the bee trees we'd found. Pa didn't want anybody to have bees but himself.

No wonder Pa was called "Drone"—he wouldn't work at anything but hunting bees, hiving bees, robbing bees. But I couldn't understand why I was called "Little Drone" at school and every place I went, when I had to cut wood, feed the hogs and chickens and keep the fences mended.

"All I have to do is touch a beehive with my hand," Pa bragged and puffed on his cigar, "and I have luck with the bees. All the bees in these parts know me and love me and work for me. That's why I don't have to work. That's why I can make a livin' sellin' honey, beeswax and beebread."

Pa put his big thumbs under his suspenders and pushed them out and let them fly back while he stood watchin' the bees work, and while I carried the log-chain, crosscut saw and ax to the shed. Pa was proud of that row of beehives all the way around the palin's that fenced our house on all sides. He was proud of the bees bendin' the tops of Mom's flowers all over the yard, and the lines of workin' bees flyin' to and from the beehives all over the yard.

"You'd better do something with that press upstairs, Mick," I heard Mom say just as I stepped inside the kitchen door. "I sent Lavinia upstairs to get some clothes and she got two bee stings. I think there's a leak where the bees are a-comin' through."

"I don't think so, Queen Bee," Pa said, ticklin' Mom under the chin. "I saw my bees a-workin' in and out at the auger hole bored into the press from the outside. I'll have Shan look the press over."

"It's hard to live here," Mom said. "Children can't get out'n the house. I live in misery from day to day. Somethin's a-going to happen."

"What can happen," Pa asked, "with a few hives of friendly bees around the house?"

"Plenty has already happened," Mom said. "I can't gather a bouquet of flowers and put it on the table unless I gather it at night. Young 'uns can't put on their clothes unless they turn them wrong side out and right side in."

Pa was puffin' on his cigar stub and Mom had just put a

pan of cornmeal dough in the oven when it happened. I had gone over to the Gilberts' for something, and I came back yellin' to Pa:

"All o' Toab Gilbert's hogs are out! They've come through the yard gate!"

"Get 'em out, Shan, you and Finn," Pa said. "Get 'em out in a hurry."

"Come on, Finn," I said.

Finn tried to shoo the hogs back through the gate, and I chased three brood sows and their litter of pigs along the yard palin's where we had the beehives. The sows run right along rootin' over the beehives, and clouds of bees rolled from the hives and covered the sows and their pigs and the few shoats that were with them. I never heard such squealin' in all my life. Sows, pigs and shoats were a-takin' off down among the rest of the beehives upendin' 'em as they went. Toab's big male hog just stood and chomped his long mouth while the slobbers flew. He was a-tryin' to fight the bees, but there were too many of 'em.

And now a mad cloud of bees had me covered, and I yelled for Pa. I looked for Finn and he was gone. A pig tried to break out of the yard and he couldn't find the gate so he was stuck between the palin's, and the bees were a-lettin' him have it. I tried to get to him but I couldn't. I met swarms of bees on my way; they hit me like hailstones in a storm. Then I turned back toward the house and I saw Pa a-comin' ringin' cowbells that he used to settle the bees. But they didn't pay any attention to the bells. They covered him like drops of rain in an April shower and popped their stingers into him as they were doin' to me. Mom knocked the bees off'n me as I reached the kitchen door before she let me in the house.

"Bees are riled upstairs," Mom said. "They're comin' through the press somewhere. I've had to shut the door upstairs, but the house is full of 'em. Lavinia and Lucretia are a-swattin' 'em with fly-swats."

Pa came rushin' to the kitchen door with a cowbell in each hand. He was covered with bees, and Mom beat 'em off with a broom.

I ran to the front room to look out the window while Mom let Pa inside the kitchen, slammin' the door against a swarm of bees. I saw seven pigs stuck between the palin's, and Toab Gilbert's big hog was a-standin' in the yard covered with bees, a-chompin' with white foam a'flyin' from his mouth. He wouldn't give an inch, and the bees were a-pourin' their stingers into him. The brood sows were still a-runnin' wild among the bees but not as fast as they'd run before. They took off up the road toward Gilbert's leavin' little clouds of dust behind 'em.

"Gilbert's hogs'll remember the next time they get into our yard," Pa said.

"We'll remember Gilbert's hogs a long time," Ma said.

"They've ruined me," Pa said.

"I guess your bees have ruined his hogs," I said just as I saw the big male hog keel over like he'd been shot between the eyes. The pigs that were stuck between the palin's weren't a-movin' either.

"I don't care if my bees kill his hogs," Pa said. "Toab oughta keep his plunderin' hogs at home. I've told 'im before that we had a stock law in Kentucky."

"You don't keep your bees at home," Mom said. "Toab told you he'd keep his hogs up when you kept your bees at home."

Mom was mad for she'd been fightin' bees with a fly-swat until her arm was so tired she could hardly raise the swat; yet the bees were a-buzzin' all over the house. Mom put Little Honey in bed and laid heavy quilts over her because that was the only place she could hide her from the bees.

"Where're you a-goin', Pa?" I asked when I saw him put on his overcoat, hat, gloves, and tie a scarf around his face.

"I'm a-goin' out to try to settle my bees," Pa said.

I watched Pa from the window. He threw sand amongst the

bees and he screamed at them, but the bees wouldn't settle. I saw one of the brood sows fall over at Pa's feet. Then Pa started back to the house covered with bees and asked for his double-barreled shotgun.

I never heard such a shootin' in my life. First he fired one barrel up among them and then he fired two barrels until he shot away all the shells. But it only made the bees madder. They blackened our windows. Pa made a dash for the house, and Mom went after the bees that had crawled up under his overcoat.

"Musta been the smell o' Toab's hogs that riled 'em this way," Pa said.

"Won't they settle some time?" I asked.

"Not until night," Pa said.

Pa took the swat and I took a pillow from the bed and we tried to fight the bees.

"We can't go on a-fightin' 'em all day," I said finally.

I'd never in my life seen Pa as scared as he was then. His lips quivered. He couldn't talk.

"Mom, I've swatted bees till my arm's too tired to lift," Lavinia said.

"I can't swat any longer either, Mom," Lucretia screamed. "What'll I do? Bees are a-stingin' me to death."

"Make for the bed," Mom said. "Get under the quilts!"

"Mom," I heard Little Honey call from under the covers.

"You lay still there, Subrina," Mom said. "Don't move the quilts."

Lavinia and Lucretia ran to the bed and dove under them.

"Where's Finn?" I asked Pa.

"Here!" Finn answered from the clothespress. "But don't anybody come in. The bees are a-findin' me. They crawled up my leg and stung me five times."

"Look out the window," I said. "Toab's a-comin' after his hogs!"

"He'll haf to haul most of 'em back," Pa said as he hurried to the window with a pillow in his hand.

Toab was walkin' in a hurry toward our house. Suddenly he stopped and slapped at his face and then his leg. We watched him take off up the road and we heard his screams above the roar of the clouds of bees.

"Serves 'im right," Pa said, laughin'. But his laughin' stopped suddenly as he slapped at a bee under his pant leg.

"Oh, mercy me," Mom said, her tired arms limp at her side, "I can't do any more!"

"Mommie," I heard Little Honey call from the bed.

"You be quiet there, Subrina," Mom said.

"If it would rain and wet their wings," Pa said, "it would be a God's blessin'."

"Not a rain cloud in the sky," I said.

"I feel like a-gettin' down on my knees and prayin'." Pa said.

"Don't be a hypocrite," Mom said. "You've never prayed before and now don't ask the Lord to save you because you've got us into this mess."

"Mommie," Subrina called again from under the covers.

"You be real quiet, Subrina," Mom said. "Don't you make a move."

Finn made a break from the clothespress and a dive into the bed, with Lavinia and Lucretia.

"I can't stand it any longer, Drone," Mom said and she went to Subrina's bed.

"Mommie, Mommie," Subrina said, "tell Daddy to get the flit-gun."

"The flit-gun, Drone," Mom said.

"That's it," Pa said, "the flit-gun!" He ran to the kitchen.

"I been tryin' to tell you a long time," Subrina said, "and you wouldn't let me talk." She was only four years old, and she had thought of something none of the rest of us had thought of.

Pa came into the room as I was tryin' to lift my pillow up

to bring it down on a knot of bees that were tryin' to get under the bedquilts. Pa had the flit-gun and he was pumpin' it with all the strength he had left. It was sprayin' a sweet-smellin' cloud of fog into the room. And when this fog hit the bees, they made funny little noises and hit the floor.

"Glory, glory," Pa said, sprayin' until the room was filled with fog, "it works!"

"I don't like the smell," Finn said.

"It's better'n bee stings," I said.

Finn had got out'n just about all the fightin', I was thinkin'.

"The room's a-gettin' cleared out'n bees," Pa said. "Somebody'll haf to sweep them up before they come to life again."

"I'll sweep 'em up, Pa," I said, and I went to get a broom and I swept a roll of senseless bees across the floor.

"You think I better get up?" Mom asked.

"After I use this gun on all the rooms," Pa said. "We can't go outside until dark, though."

"We'll be after dark gettin' our work done up," I said, sweepin' the bees into a bushel basket to carry 'em outside.

And Pa used the flit-gun and I swept until we'd gone over every room in the house. Then Pa stood at the window, lookin' out as darkness was gatherin' over the land.

"Glory, glory," Pa whispered, "the night has come!"

"Glory, glory," Mom said suddenly as if she meant it. She pushed the covers back and got out of bed and shook her finger at Pa. "There'll never be any more bees around this house—and no drones either. Either I go or the bees."

"Yes, Queen," Pa said humbly.

Then I said, "Glory, glory," and I did not tell Pa I had let loose Toab Gilbert's pigs because Ma had kept telling me I had to do something to get rid o' the bees. So "glory, glory" is what I said, too.

Ezra Alcorn and April

Author's Introduction

When I was a young man, I was made principal of Mc-Kell High School in Fairlington, Greenup County, Kentucky. This is not the real name of the high school nor the village which is an incorporated town today. When I first went to Fairlington, the village was growing by leaps and bounds. However, there was no policeman there, and the only law to protect the citizens was a Greenup County deputy sheriff, who tried to keep the peace, make arrests, and jail men from the deep valleys, the ridges, and from the village. Many of these men would make the characters on television westerns seem like angels in comparison.

When I first went to Fairlington, I thought of this small village as being something like a small frontier town in the Old West. Here the bad men, those handy with fist, gun, or knife, rode into town in old automobiles over dirt roads. Very few came by horseback. And where the distances were short, say from 1 to 6 miles, they walked to Fairlington. And here they met and fought. Since only the Ohio River separated Kentucky and Ohio, many of Ohio's characters came over to join their fellow Kentuckians. And never, west, south, east, or north, did groups of more colorful characters ever get together. Men were shot and killed here and men

83

were stabbed to death. In this day and time in this part of Kentucky, people wore their pistols same as they wore their shirts. It was not until twenty years later that Kentucky passed a law to make the carrying of a concealed deadly weapon a felony instead of a misdemeanor, and this meant that by due process of the law a person could be sent to prison for carrying a concealed weapon. Too many people were getting killed and wounded. I mention this background to show you a character like Ezra Alcorn wasn't an unusual fellow in this neighborhood.

"Old Ezra" as many called him, but he wasn't old, wasn't considered in this community a bad man. People regarded him as being just a little peculiar. He had never killed anybody, but no man had ever knocked more people cold with an unexpected well-placed punch than Ezra had. Then Old Ezra, in his almost indecipherable handwriting, recorded the event in his little book. He carried this book same as others carried revolvers. Once when he was asked why he wasn't fashionable enough to carry a revolver, his reply was he didn't need one since he could knock a man out with his fist the first blow. Then he laughed at his own joke when he said while the man was lying unconscious, he could run and get away from him. He said he had knocked many out who were toting pistols. And, of course, he was telling the truth.

When I was principal of McKell High School, Old Ezra called me "Professor." He told many of my friends that he wanted to get my name in his little book. He had made the remark so many times, and I had heard about it, that I never turned my back on this man. But I had only one month, and that was April, to be on the lookout for him. I had decided when he

*started to draw his arm back to cock his fist that my
fist would be faster, and instead of his leaving me
knocked out lying on the ground, he would be lying
there and I could record this event in my diary. I told
my friends to tell Old Ezra this. Later when I got to
know him better, I told him this when we stood face
to face in April. I never ran from Ezra Alcorn. And in
my years as principal of McKell High School, he never
got my name in his little book.*

*While Ezra was living I could not write his story,
for it had no ending. However, that day when he left
this world in April, the apple, wild plums, and dogwoods, white with blossoms that rustled in the April
wind, all these made a wonderful setting for the end to
the story of Ezra Alcorn.*

THE APPLE, plum and pear trees in our big yard
and along our garden fence looked like small white rustling
clouds hovering near the green April earth. The sun was high
in the afternoon sky and birds sang as they flew back and forth
to their nests in the blooming trees. The April earth was in
a rejoicing mood. If we were in a rejoicing mood, we didn't
say anything to each other about it. This wasn't the time because we had to pay our last respects to a friend and neighbor.

"April again," Uncle Fonse said, looking first at Aunt Lillie
and then at me. "We remember a lot of Aprils don't we?"

"We certainly do," I said.

"This has been the best April I can remember in this neighborhood," Aunt Lillie said smiling. "I feel as light as that
meadow lark flying over the pasture."

"April is the right time for this to happen," Uncle Fonse chuckled as we walked along. "I've often wondered what it was about April that caused Ezra to do the things he did. The other eleven months he was a good neighbor and a good man. I've often wondered if the April moon had anything to do with his actions."

Aunt Lillie chuckled. But Uncle Fonse didn't laugh now. I knew the reason why. On an April day when we were down in the bottom planting corn, Ezra Alcorn walked slowly across the harrowed field where Uncle Fonse was riding a drill.

"Say, Fonse, you got any seed corn to sell?" Ezra asked, grinning.

"Yes, I got seed corn to sell, Ezra," he said. "Why, you need some?"

"Yep, planting the bottom over there and have just run out of corn," he said. "Would like to finish planting today."

"Go to the corncrib, shell the corn and measure it," Uncle Fonse said. "I'd like to get my corn planted today too. Might set in wet from the looks of that sky. And you know these low bottoms are so slow to dry again."

"But I wouldn't go to your crib, shell the corn and measure it without you went with me," Ezra told Uncle Fonse. "You and I have always been good neighbors, Fonse. We want to be good neighbors always. And the best way to stay good neighbors is for you to be along when I go into your corncrib."

"Come over here, Shan," Uncle Fonse said. "Watch these horses while I go to the crib with Ezra."

Uncle Fonse must have forgotten that it was April. He climbed down from the drill and I didn't have time to yell "April" and "Ezra" to Uncle Fonse. Ezra was waiting for him just as he stepped on the ground and when he was off balance, Ezra caught Uncle Fonse on the chin and he went down like a big oak sawed completely off. I was afraid to go near until Ezra took the little black book from his hip pocket and said his words as he wrote them: "April 28th in the year of our Lord, I finally got my chance to hit my good neighbor Fonse Kingston on the chin. He went down to the ground like a beef. But the plowed ground was soft as a feather bed for him to fall on and it didn't hurt him none. He is a big man and I've been waiting my chance a long time to get him. He never thought I could."

Then Ezra put the little black book back in his hip pocket and the stub of pencil behind his ear and walked slowly across the plowed field toward home. He didn't try to bother me because he never hit any man under twenty-one. But I was afraid of him in April. I ran across the field and got our water bucket from under a shade tree. Then I ran back and poured water on Uncle Fonse's face until he opened his eyes and started squirming around on the ground. Finally he came to and I helped him up. Uncle Fonse was still a little addled but he shook himself like a rooster when he comes in the hen-house after a rain.

"Well, old Ezra got me at last," were Uncle Fonse's first words. "If any other man was to do me this way, I'd follow him to the end of the earth. Did he have that little black book?"

"Yes, he did," I said. "And he wrote in it what he did to you."

"Remember when he came to my house last April and wanted to buy a pig," Uncle Fonse said, grinning, "and I told him to come back in May and I'd sell him one. I guess I forgot this was still April. If I'd remembered I'd never got down off that corn drill. I'd have reached out and give him a lash or two with my horsewhip. April moon-struck or not, he needs a horsewhip for capers like this one. In a fair fight I could whip him all over this bottom. Most every man could that he's hit."

I knew Uncle Fonse was telling the truth too. Uncle Fonse

weighed two hundred and twenty pounds. His shoulders were broad and he had the largest hands and wrists I had ever seen. His big hands hanging to his giant muscular arms looked like huge butter paddles nailed to small fence posts. And Ezra Alcorn, I thought as I watched Uncle Fonse climb back on the drill with a broad sheepish grin on his face, is a little skinny man with small hands and arms and the lower half of his skinny body tries to go faster than the top half when he walks. Old Ezra with little keen blue eyes, thin blond hair hanging down around his slouched hat, with two brown streaks of tobacco juice down the front of his faded blue work shirt where it leaks from the corners of his mouth. That's the way Ezra went about in April. All of this came back to me as I walked along with Uncle Fonse and Aunt Lillie. I knew why they were laughing and why they felt as light as two bird feathers on the April wind.

Because Aunt Lillie was setting flowers in the yard one April day when Ezra walked up to the fence, laid his hands on a post and rested his chin on his little hands. Aunt Lillie forgot that it was April too.

"Miss Lillie, I've got something to tell you," he said. "That is, if you won't say anything about it."

"What is it, Ezra?" Aunt Lillie said, leaning on her hoe handle.

"We've got bad neighbors," Ezra told her. "They are trying to do you and Fonse a lot of harm." Then, he pushed his face forward nearer to Aunt Lillie and whispered hoarsely, "The Barneys over there next to me are leading that pack of hounds they keep staked over the year to your hen-house. They're feeding their hounds on your eggs and young chickens."

Aunt Lillie was furious. She had been missing eggs and young chickens. As soon as Ezra had told her about Sweeter Barney's hounds, he slipped away on that beautiful April day to tell Mrs. Ranzy Coburn what Pinella Ousley had said about her. In April, Ezra went from neighbor to neighbor when the men were working in the fields and told one neighbor's wife what another neighbor had said about her. He always let them in on the secret by whispering over the yard fence. If they didn't have yard fences he told them by leaning against shade trees and talking softly. He never recorded these troubles he stirred up in his little black book. And always in the month of May he went around to the same neighbors, after they were at outs and fighting one another furiously, and talked calmly to them, trying to smooth out the troubles he had started.

When Uncle Fonse came in from the field that last day of April and Aunt Lillie told him about the hounds getting the eggs and young chickens, Uncle Fonse grinned and said: "Sweetheart, this is the last day of April and Ezra told you that. The man is April moon-struck or bloom-struck or something. I never believed the moon had anything to do with a man's thinking until I lived by Ezra Alcorn for the past thirty years. Looks like we ought to know him by now."

But Ezra had told Aunt Lillie the truth this time. Only Sweeter Barney didn't bring the hounds to the hen-house. They came of their own accord when they got free from the stakes in the yard. Aunt Lillie warned Sweeter to keep his dogs up but still they came. Uncle Fonse warned him too. Then Aunt Lillie tried to get Uncle Fonse to shoot the dogs but he wouldn't kill a dog. Aunt Lillie bought herself a 410-gauge shotgun and in a few days shot four hounds dead and the fifth one crawled under Sweeter's floor and died. This caused hard feelings and no end of trouble between Uncle Fonse, Aunt Lillie and the Barneys. But it was all because of Ezra Alcorn and April that they hadn't spoken for five years.

Maybe, I thought as Aunt Lillie skipped along the road like a little girl with ribbons on her hair, Aunt Lillie's face won't be so happy if Mr. and Mrs. Sweeter Barney are there. April won't be so light and gay when neighbors meet who have quarreled, fought and pulled hair over Ezra Alcorn and April.

When we reached the end of our lane that junctioned with

the river turnpike, I looked down the road and saw Mr. and Mrs. Sweeter Barney. They were dressed in their Sunday clothes too, holding hands as they had done in their youth.

"Wait a minute, Fonse," Sweeter spoke for the first time in five years.

Uncle Fonse and Aunt Lillie stopped and looked at each other strangely.

"I think we're going to the same place," Sweeter said. "Let's all go together."

"Wonderful," Uncle Fonse stammered.

Aunt Lillie must have been thinking of Sweeter's hounds she had shot. She didn't speak until they came up and everybody shook hands, greeted each other and smiled. The old family troubles were not mentioned. The soft April wind blew over and the white blossoms wafted on every wind. I looked back and saw more well-dressed neighbors coming up the road. I saw little Brad Timberlake holding his wife Essie's hand. Their seven sons were walking with them up the turnpike. They were in their Sunday clothes too. Brad was wearing a big bow tie and a straw hat. I thought he was forcing the season but it was all right on this day.

Brad was our barber down in the village of Fairlington. He worked hard and long hours and had managed to accumulate enough, besides keeping his big family, to own his home and buy two pieces of additional property. He was getting along fine until one day in April, Ezra walked slowly down to his closest neighbor, John Cantwell, and stood beneath a blooming April tree, leaned over the yard fence, and whispered to Mrs. Arizona Cantwell:

"Something I want to warn you about, Arizona. You and I growed up together and I think I ought to tell you if you want to raise your seven daughters up in decency and order you had better move away from here. Brad and Essie Timberlake's boys are peeping in your windows. Bad stuff in them Timberlakes. I've known Brad since he was a baby. Nothing there only he can cut hair. Better watch. I'm tellin' you right."

Then the Timberlakes and Cantwells, who didn't get along too well anyhow, forgot about April, blooming trees, moonlight and sunlight and soft winds and Ezra Alcorn. When Arizona told John Cantwell about it, John warned Brad about his sons. Essie Timberlake met Arizona Cantwell halfway and they pulled hair. John Cantwell said he lived there first and Brad would have to move. In May Ezra went back and tried to iron out the trouble but he couldn't. It was in the hands of attorneys.

Since Brad wouldn't move, John Cantwell constructed a board fence ten feet high between the lots. Brad Timberlake and Essie said the tall fence damaged their property and wouldn't let the morning sun on their flowers and garden. They asked the Cantwells to move it. They wouldn't, and the Timberlakes sued the Cantwells. Brad used all his savings to pay the lawyers the first year it was in court. John Cantwell won the suit after the first four tries. But April came again, and Ezra went back and told Arizona the Timberlake boys were peeping through the knotholes in the planks in the board fence. This started another round of lawsuits and Brad sold his two pieces of property to pay lawyer fees. The second rounds of lawsuits were in court four years.

I wondered when I saw Brad and his family coming, if the Cantwells would be there too. I wondered if John Cantwell's seven daughters and Brad Timberlake's seven sons would greet each other. And if Arizona and Essie would smile and shake hands after nine years of trouble.

We walked up the turnpike a quarter of a mile, all of us laughing and talking, and then we turned on a little lane that took us straight toward Ezra Alcorn's little cottage. When we arrived in sight of the cottage, we could see the yard filled with people. And people were walking along paths from three directions toward the yard. They were well-dressed, talking and laughing as if they were going to a basket dinner. The cottage had been freshly painted white as if for this occasion. The apple, pear and plum trees that surrounded Ezra's cottage on all sides were like so many white clouds hovering near the earth, shaken by April winds. Ezra had more blooming trees around his home than anybody in our neighborhood.

"I wonder if it could have been white blossoms in April that did something to Ezra," Uncle Fonse chuckled as he looked at the trees. "Maybe it was April blossoms instead of the sun or moon that affected him."

Sweeter and Ruhamah Barney and Aunt Lillie didn't try to suppress their laughter.

When we went inside the gate to the yard where our neighbors had gathered, we greeted them and they greeted us. John and Arizona Cantwell and their seven daughters were there, and Brad and Essie Timberlake were coming up the lane now with their seven sons. We would soon see what happened to them. Everybody was eyeing each group to see what would take place. When Brad came through the gate with a lighted cigar and a cloud of smoke wafting on the April breeze behind him, he tipped his hat and spoke to this one and that one. Essie greeted old neighbors with a smile too. The seven sons were rather quiet in this large crowd of friendly neighbors who had gathered to pay last respects to Ezra.

Brad looked first at John. John smiled and the two men walked toward each other.

"Well, John," Brad said, extending his hand. "We've got something in common."

"Yes, we're both in Ezra's little black book," John said, as everybody stopped talking long enough to watch.

"And we have something in common too," Arizona said, walking over to greet Essie. "Ezra leaned over the fence in April and whispered to you and he leaned over the fence and whispered to me."

Then the seven Timberlake boys looked toward the seven

blue-eyed Cantwell girls with smiles on their faces and sparkles in their brown eyes. These were the last of our neighbors with "bad blood" between them and Ezra Alcorn and April.

"Think of seein' you here, Tom," Uncle Fonse said to Tom Pennix. Tom Pennix had once carried a pistol for Ezra.

"Fonse, I'm in that little black book," he said, smiling. "If anybody had ever told me I'd have come to this occasion a month ago, I would have called him a *liar* to his face. But here I am."

"What makes us all come back?" said Ike Harris.

"Because every man here is in that little black book of Ezra's," Sam McConnell interrupted. "That's what ties us together. That's why we are all here today and friendlier than we've ever been with one another. Think of the fights and hair pullings that's happened among us in this neighborhood in the last twenty Aprils!"

"If we could have only remembered April and Ezra," Ike said, smiling. "But we'd get caught off guard and forget."

"I'll never forget April as long as I live," Uncle Fonse said. "I'll never see an April moon either in the years to come as long as I live I won't think of Ezra. I'll think of him when the trees bloom in April too."

"Something funny about it," Brad Timberlake said, walking up to join the group. "I've lost a fortune over Ezra and April. Lost my neighbors too but I'm a happy man today. We're all back neighbors again."

"Be quiet, Brad," Uncle Fonse whispered. "Here's Tim, Ezra's boy."

"Oh, they know it in the house too," Brad said, taking his hand from his pocket. "I've just been in to see Ezra. His family knows how he acted. They're surprised but happy to see all of us here. They don't mind us talking. They know how we feel," he said as Tim Alcorn walked past us. "They're good people. It was just Ezra and April.

"I'd like to know what they'll do with that book with all

our names in it," Ike Harris said. Brad said nothing but patted his pocket as Ike continued. "It was April seven years ago and I was talking to Ezra in Sam Robert's store never thinking a thing. When I woke up, he had recorded my name in his little book and left the store."

"He got me in my own barbershop," Brad said. "After I'd given him a nice haircut and shave, perfumed him and give him a free tonic on his hair to make his wife love him. When I woke up, the barbershop was full of men wanting shaves and haircuts. My oldest boy, Adger, who shines shoes and sweeps up, was holding smelling salts to my nose. I'd forgot it was April 'r I wouldn't have cut his hair. I'd do it in March or May afterwards and all the other months but never in April any more after he hit me."

"Well, we'd better go in the house, Shan," Uncle Fonse said with a little smile and a twinkle in his eye. "I'll get Lillie, Sweeter and Ruhamah."

While Uncle Fonse got our little group together, I walked among the crowd and everywhere I heard our neighbors speaking of April, that little black book, moonlight, blossoms and Ezra Alcorn.

When we walked quietly upon the porch and into the house, Aunt Lillie and Ruhamah entered first, then Sweeter and I followed Uncle Fonse. Mollie Alcorn was sitting quietly in a big rocking chair. Her eyes were dry and her daughter, Arabella, looked once toward Ezra and then toward the white sprays of pear blossoms that swished against the window pane. I wondered if she were thinking about her father and April too. Denbo, their youngest son, came from another room and sat down near his mother. His eyes were dry. Not anybody was shedding a tear.

As we filed past the long white coffin blanked with sprays of apple, cherry and plum blossoms, I looked at Ezra. He was so dressed up that he didn't look natural. But there was that same little smile on his lips like he had just before he hit Uncle Fonse. And this did look natural.

Aunt Lillie and Ruhamah walked by to pay their last respects. Sweeter hurried along. I wondered what they were thinking.

As we started back to join our neighbors, Mollie Alcorn walked over to the door and gave Uncle Fonse and Sweetei a little piece of paper.

"Ezra's first wish was to die in April," she said calmly. "His second wish was for each of you to have your page from his little black book."

Uncle Fonse and Sweeter were quick to put the little slips of paper in their pockets and hurry through the door. I wondered if Ezra had gone into another land where there was an April like we had now and if he would find friends and neighbors like us and if he would start another little book.

Wild Plums

Author's Introduction

"Wild Plums" is an April story. I've written a lot of stories about April, and I've published a book of poems called Hold April. It's my favorite month; to me there is no month as fascinating for everyone. Everything seems young in April, and especially in Kentucky.

The particular day in this story was filled with the romance of April, with the dogwoods, redbuds, wild crab apples and plums all white and pink blossoms blown by the wind in the valleys and on the slopes of the high Kentucky hills. I was twenty-six years old, and I was principal of McKell High School. I was happy to be a high school principal; I liked all the teachers on my faculty, and I was proud of our school. I liked the teen-agers in the school, and I enjoyed working with them. I always have, for young people are a challenge and an education.

But this day was so beautiful it was hard to think of anything except the hills outside my office window. I wanted more than anything else in the world to be outdoors. And I found a good excuse to get away; forty-one students were absent that day. They couldn't all be sick. That would be too much of a coincidence. I knew why those forty-one students were absent: they were playing hooky from school. They hadn't been able to resist the invitation of that April day to be outside to see the glory of the blossoms and to smell the fragrance. I decided to go out looking for the truants. I didn't have to do that but it was a handy way to get out of that office.

So I was playing hooky too. As soon as I was out of sight of the school, I headed straight for the wild plum grove by the Tygart River—one of the most beautiful wild plum groves I had ever seen. I thought to myself that grove is a good place for a student to hide from the principal, and also a good place for a principal to hide from a student.

When I got to the grove, I found a student all right. I ran right smack into him after I had crawled on my hands and knees to get under low-hanging branches. He was very embarrassed. He thought someone had told me where to find him. I didn't tell him that no one had told me. I let him think that I had come to get him. But my reason for coming was the same as his: to be out in that April day.

Now when you read the story, you will meet that student and find out what happened to him and all the other students who played hooky that day.

I liked writing "Wild Plums" as much as any story I've ever written. It is great to write about young people in the springtime of their lives, and when the year is in its springtime season too. But writing this story was not half as much fun as living it myself.

"THIS MORNING is too beautiful for one to stay in a schoolroom," thinks Principal Jason Stringer. "April has come again. The green is getting back to the hills. Men are plowing in the fields. I want to get out of the schoolroom. I want to see the tender green leaves on the water birches by the Tygart River. I want to smell the percoon blossoms. I want to see the wild plums blooming by the Tygart."

Jason Stringer fumbles the papers on the desk in his office. He checks the absentee lists of students sent from the home rooms in the Mason High School. After Jason checks the papers over again, he places them on his desk. He walks to the window. He looks at the water birches down by the Tygart River. He sees a redbird sitting on a water-birch twig. "Tea-kettle, tea-kettle, thirt, thirt, thirt," are the words he thinks it sings over and over. Soon he sees the redbird's mate fly from a Tygart bottom with a straw in her bill. She alights beside her mate. Her body is not as red as her mate's body. She sits beside him and listens to his song.

"Eustacia, we have a lot of absentees this morning," says Principal Jason Stringer. "I want you to make me out a list of all the couples that you think are playing truant together. You know more about the love affairs of these high-school students than I do. I know it's strange that there's the same number of girls absent today that there are boys. Couple them together the best you can and let me have the list."

"All right, Mr. Stringer," she says, "but don't you tell the students that I did this. I don't want them to know. They will get mad at me if they find this out."

"I'll not tell where I got my information," says Jason Stringer. "I just want to stop this playing truant. Young couples are out strolling around over these hills when they should be in school. What kind of a high school will the parents of this district think we have here? They will think we have a courting high school."

"Mr. Stringer," says Eustacia with a smile, "you remember this happened last spring. It happened spring before last. When April comes the students do their best to slip out."

"And by twos," snaps Jason Stringer. "Students that make

the best grades in Mason High School, slip out when April comes to these Kentucky hills."

"When a day is as pretty as today, you can't blame them much," says Eustacia. "As I came to school this morning, I stopped by the Tygart bridge and listened to a redbird sing. I was almost late for school. The redbird was sitting there and sang until his mate flew to the top of the water-birch tree and sat beside him with a straw in her bill. I just thought it was strange how the rooster redbird did the singing while his mate built the nest."

Eustacia looks over the absentee sheets. Jason Stringer stands by the office window and looks toward the Tygart River. He can see a green streak of timber along its winding banks. The high rocky bluffs above the Tygart are covered with budding oaks. Jason can see white spots on these bluffs that look like patches of late March snow the sun hasn't melted yet. These are patches of percoon in bloom among the rock cliffs on the coves.

"Mr. Stringer," says Eustacia, "there are forty-one absent. There are twenty girls and twenty-one boys."

"Who is the odd boy, Eustacia?" Jason asks.

"Dick Martin," she says. "He never goes with a girl."

"That's right," says Jason Stringer, "but you can't tell about what he will do. He's one of the best athletes this school has ever had. He's the best track man we've got but his grades are none too good. We have a track meet with Manchester and Dick will be ineligible. Do you think he is the boy that isn't paired off with a girl?"

"I know he is," says Eustacia. "I've got a lot of confidence in Dick."

"Now you be sure to arrange these couples, Eustacia," says Principal Jason Stringer, "and leave the list in the drawer of my table. You answer all telephone calls. You take care of this office. Don't tell anybody where I am. I'm going to go out and look around. These students should know what the penalty is for playing hooky in this school. First offense it is three days' suspension. Second offense it is three weeks' suspension and—"

"Third offense," Eustacia continues, "you expel them from school—oh, we know that, Mr. Stringer."

"But the sad thing about it," Jason emphasizes, "you students know about it; yet, you continue to play truant from Mason High School every April. I think many names on that list have played truant twice and a few have played truant three times."

Jason leaves Eustacia at the desk putting this boy's name by that girl's name. He leaves her arranging the names by twos. "It will be hard on their grades," thinks Jason as he walks out of the schoolhouse. "It will be hard on me as a high-school principal when the patrons of this district find out that forty-one students out of an enrolment of 310 are out gallivanting. I'll just have to do something about it. What will the Greenwood County Superintendent of Schools and the five members of the Greenwood County School Board say to me?"

Jason bends over when he walks around the front side of the school building so that the students and the teachers can't see him from the windows. He slips behind the schoolhouse and behind the gymnasium. Now he walks erect. He is out of danger. The students and the teachers can't see him. He walks toward the wild plum grove beside the Tygart River. "I can understand why the students feel the way they do," thinks Jason as he watches the honey bees flying from one white cluster of wild plum blossoms to another. "This is a terrible time to have to stay inside of four brick walls and study books. This is the time to be alive—the time to be awake! Spring is here! Spring has come to Kentucky's deep valleys. Spring has come to these fair hills!"

Jason stands beneath the plum trees and looks at their boughs. They look as if they were weighted with snow. But it is not snow. The warm April sun beams down from a deep-blue sky to make the plum blossoms look whiter than snow. The bees are alive with sounds as they work among the plum blossoms. The redbirds sing on almost every bough. Jason watches them carrying sticks in their bills. Just as Eustacia said, the rooster birds do the singing while the hen birds work. Jason tries to catch a honey bee by the wing. It escapes him. He tries to catch a polkadot-winged butterfly from the plum blossom. He brushes its wings with his hands but the butterfly sees the shadow of his hand before he grabs for it.

"This is a great time to be out," thinks Jason. "No wonder the students don't want to be in school today. I can see why they want to slip away from the four walls of a house that encloses them and their dreams. Here I am, a man out acting like a small boy. I am playing hooky, too. I am doing the same thing that forty-one students are doing today. I am leaving the high-school office to Eustacia. I'm leaving the teaching to the teachers. Their Principal is out under the wild plum trees—crawling on his hands and knees—trying to catch butterflies and bees. He, too, hates the schoolroom today. He can't lie about it. He has to be honest. He has to tell what is in his heart."

Jason takes a notebook from his pocket. He jots down lines of poetry. The smell of the earth revives him. He sees the beauty in the snow-white clusters of the wild plum blossoms. He hears music in the songs of the birds and the hum of the bees. He feels that the earth beneath him is alive with the white-hair roots of April and the trees above him are filled with the growing green-hair of April. He feels that the earth is alive with music, beauty, and song. This stirs him until he tries to put it down in words. He tries to make the words be alive much as the April about him is alive with growth, beauty, and smell.

The wild plum grove spreads over the east bank of the Tygart River. There is an old road that leads to a farmhouse on the west side of the wild plum grove. Jason crawls toward this old road. He straightens his body and breathes the clean air of April deep into his lungs.

Jason stops as he walks toward the thin tender-leafed water birches and sycamores along the banks of the river. Jason hears a voice down among the water birches. He can hear a voice saying over and over:

"She is as pretty as a percoon flower."

Jason walks toward the sound. He sees a boy sitting at the foot of a water birch. He is looking at the percoon patches on the other side of the river. He has a pencil in his hand and a notebook on his lap. He is thinking. Jason walks closer.

"I have found you, Dick," says Jason. "What are you doing here?"

"Oh, Mr. Stringer," says Dick Martin, "how did you know I was here? Somebody has squealed on me. This is the first time I ever played hooky in my life."

"Are you here alone?" Jason asks.

"I am," says Dick.

Dick is sitting with his back against the water-birch sapling. His feet are propped upon a log.

"Was that you I heard talking to yourself, Dick?" Jason asks.

"I guess it was," says Dick shamefully.

"You were saying, 'She is as pretty as a percoon flower,' weren't you?"

"I was," says Dick. "Look over across the Tygart at the percoon on the bluffs, Mr. Stringer! I can't say that I think a lot about flowers but just somehow they look good to me today. And don't say anything about it—but I'm trying to write a poem, Mr. Stringer. Gee, but she is as pretty as a percoon flower. This is the first poem I've ever tried to write and I can't get the right word to rhyme with flower."

Dick gets up from behind the water-birch sapling. He crumples the piece of paper in his hand. He throws it on the ground. He picks up his books at the foot of the tree. He puts his pencil in his pocket.

"Your grades are low, Dick," says Jason. "If I suspend you three days from school, you won't be eligible for the Manchester track meet."

"Mr. Stringer, you know that I'm not boasting when I say Mason High School will need me on that day," says Dick. "You know what I'm going to do to Manchester on the dashes. I plan to take five first places in that track meet. You know Big Nick won't take the 440."

"Track meet or no track meet," says Jason Stringer, "I have caught you here, Dick. I have come straight to your hiding place. You can't play hooky and get by with it at Mason High School. You are old enough and big enough to know better."

"Mr. Stringer, don't make it too hard on me," Dick begs. "Just give me a chance to beat Manchester."

"What is all that noise, Dick?" Jason asks.

"Mr. Stringer, you needn't ask me," says Dick. "You know it's time for school to be out and the children are leaving."

"I didn't know," says Jason. "I left my watch at home this morning. This day has slipped by like a shadow."

"It's slipped by for me, too," says Dick.

"I'd better be getting toward the schoolhouse," says Jason.

Dick Martin and Principal Jason Stringer walk up the Tygart River bank. They walk up the old road that leads from the farmhouse. They walk up the road to the tiny path that leads under the thicket of wild plum trees. Jason Stringer gets down on his knees and crawls under the trees. He follows the tiny path. "I have played hooky all day," thinks Jason. "It doesn't seem like it has been three hours since I left the schoolhouse this morning."

"You write poetry, don't you, Mr. Stringer?" Dick asks as they crawl on their hands and knees under the thick mass of wild plum trees.

"It's been a long time since I've written poetry," says Jason. Jason looks at the roof above him. He cannot see the sun through the thick roof of plumtree leaves and the mass of snow-white clusters of wild plum blossoms. "I'll tell you though, Dick," says Jason, "these wild plum blossoms are enough to make a man want to write poetry."

"I'll tell you, Mr. Stringer," says Dick, "I always laughed at students trying to write poetry until this morning. The notion just struck me all of a sudden to go to these woods. Spring had come and something got into my blood. I didn't think you'd find me. I thought I was in a good hiding place."

"I wouldn't have found you," says Jason, "but I heard you trying to write your poem."

"Don't tell that on me," says Dick. "What will the students think of me? They will think I'm a softie. You know I'm not."

"I know you're not, Dick," says Jason Stringer. "You are a good boy in school, Dick. You don't drink, smoke, or chew tobacco. You've always told me the truth. That's why I'm going to make this easy for you."

"Did you every play hooky, Mr. Stringer?" Dick asks.

"Yes, Dick, I have," says Jason ruefully. "I have played truant many times."

"Then you know how I feel about it."

"Yes."

Dick Martin and Jason Stringer move slowly along under the massive grove of wild plum trees. They keep their heads bent low to miss the wild plum thorns above. Jason leads the way on his hands and knees. Slowly they move under the massive clouds of green and white. Jason crawls from under the wild plum thicket into the open space first. Dick follows him. They stand and brush the dirt from their hands and knees.

"That path is like a rabbit hole," says Dick.

"Yes, it is," says Jason. "You caused me a lot of trouble, Dick. But I found you. You were out writing poetry for a girl. Who was the girl, Dick?"

"Eustacia Pratt," says Dick. "Now don't say anything about that."

"I won't," says Jason.

"Did you ever write poetry for a girl?" Dick asks.

"Yes, for many girls," says Jason.

"And you're not a sissy, Mr. Stringer," says Dick.

"I hope not," says Jason. "What is wrong with writing poetry for your true love in the spring?"

"I don't guess there's anything," says Dick, "but I'll be ineligible for the Manchester track meet now."

"I'll tell you what I'll do, Dick," says Jason. "You gather me enough of these wild plum blossoms to make twenty-one bouquets and bring them to the office. I'll go on to the office now. You bring them to the office. I'll let that be your punishment."

"Gee, Mr. Stringer," says Dick. "I'll be glad to do it. That is great! Then you're not going to suspend me three days!"

"No, I'm not," says Jason.

"I'll never play hooky again," says Dick.

"Now don't say that," says Jason. "You don't know what you will do or you won't do. If April comes again and you're in this high school, you are likely to play hooky again if the day is as pretty as this day has been. This has been a wonderful day."

Eustacia is still waiting in the office when Jason Stringer arrives.

"Mr. Stringer, I've had an awful time today," says Eustacia. "The Superintendent was here to see you. We've telephoned everywhere for you. Several students have been sent to the office. You were not here. I had to send them back. They have gone home now. Mr. Bascom found Kathleen out on the hillside gathering percoon with John Hart. He brought her back to school. I told him you were out hunting students. I didn't know where you were. Professor MacKinney and Miss Burkhardt wanted to see you. I told them you were out and that you said you'd be gone only a short time."

"I'm sorry, Eustacia, that I've caused you waiting all this time," says Jason Stringer. "I haven't been far."

"But I didn't know where to find you," says Eustacia.

"I know you didn't," says Jason. "You couldn't have found me. I was away a million miles from this schoolhouse. I was among the songs of the birds, the lapping of the water, the blowing of the wind, and the smell of wild plum blossoms. I was out among growing things and I forgot about the school. I think I've played hooky today."

"You said you weren't far away from the schoolhouse and then you said you were a million miles away," says Eustacia.

"The Tygart River bank is a million miles away from here today," says Jason. "Eustacia, you take a pair of scissors and cut out each couple's name on a small slip of paper."

Eustacia takes the scissors and cuts each couple's name from the big sheet of paper. Jason looks over the teachers' reports while Eustacia gets the names ready. Before Jason gets the reports checked, before Eustacia gets the names ready, Dick Martin walks before the office window with an armload of wild plum blossoms.

"Here they are, Mr. Stringer," says Dick as he enters the office door. "I have enough for twenty bouquets all right."

Dick's face colors when he looks down at Principal Jason Stringer's desk and sees Eustacia Pratt at work. He lays the plum blossoms on the office desk. Dick does not talk any more. He looks at Eustacia Pratt.

"Dick, you make twenty-one bouquets out of that armload of wild plum blossoms," Jason says. "Eustacia, you put a couple's name on each bouquet as long as the names last."

Dick separates the wild plum blossoms into bouquets. Eustacia smiles as she puts a couple's name on each bouquet. Jason Stringer holds the poetry he has written in the wild plum grove down on his reports.

"We have this done now, Mr. Stringer," says Eustacia. "Is there anything else you want me to do before I leave?"

"Just don't say anything about this," says Jason. "Don't either one of you mention this outside of the school. I'll tell you what I'm going to do. From now on, you students in Mason High School are going to get a spring vacation. It's something we have never had here. We'll have a week's spring vacation about the time the wild plums are in bloom. To-morrow, I'm going to surprise each couple that played truant. This will be one time when I'm not going to suspend students. I'm going to present each couple with a bouquet. I'll ask the boy to wear it all day with his and his sweetheart's name on it. That will be all the punishment that the students will get."

"Gee, Mr. Stringer," says Dick, "that will hurt them worse than if you'd suspend them from school."

"It won't hurt their grades more, I'm sure," says Jason.

"What do you want done with this extra bouquet, Mr. Stringer?" Eustacia asks.

"That's for Dick," says Jason. "You and Dick are excused now. I have a lot of work I want to stay here to do."

Jason Stringer sits at his desk. He watches Dick and Eustacia leave the school yard. Dick is carrying the bouquet. He watches them as they walk over the hill toward the country road. He watches the young couple until they are out of sight down the long winding road.

The Great Cherokee Bill

Author's Introduction

I never really planned to write about the Great Cherokee Bill. But as the years passed, and I was no longer
principal of McKell High School, and had returned to
W-Hollow to help my father farm his land and mine, I
couldn't forget him and the show he put on in an assembly program at my school. It was the most remarkable program we ever had.

I couldn't forget the way he walked into my office
one day and told me that he was the Great Cherokee
Bill. When he said that he was great, I doubted him.
But he was right.

Five years after that day he had fascinated us all at
McKell High School, I wrote an article about him. I
sent it to a magazine which bought only factual articles.
The editor didn't buy it because he thought it was a
short story. He wouldn't believe it was true. The next
magazine I sent it to turned it down for the same reason. Finally I sent it to a short-story magazine, and it
was accepted immediately.

One night years later, I was at the movies one evening with my wife Naomi. Between the comedy and
the feature an extra picture flashed on the screen, The
Great Cherokee Bill. "That's him," I shouted suddenly. Everybody started looking toward me.

"That's who?" Naomi whispered.

"That Indian," I said. "That's the Great Cherokee Bill."

"You mean there was a real Cherokee Bill?" she asked.

"Sure, there was a real one," I whispered softly, since everybody around us was getting curious. Several people gave me hard looks to keep quiet. "There he is right up there on the screen. And that is part of the program he gave in McKell High School assembly. Somebody in Hollywood realized that he was 'The Great' Cherokee Bill and that he was no fake Indian."

Naomi had read the story, but I had failed to tell her it was real. She, like the editor who had accepted the story for publication, had thought this was a product of my imagination when actually I had merely recorded in words what had transpired in our most delightful assembly program.

Now we listened to the enthusiastic reception of that movie audience, young and old, as the Great Cherokee Bill performed on the screen. I sat back and relaxed and enjoyed again the Great Cherokee Bill's delightful show. It hadn't changed much for the Great Cherokee Bill was a very determined man. He knew what he could do and he had to do what he did his own way. As I watched happily I could not help thinking what if all the people in this theater could have had the privilege to have seen "The Great" Cherokee Bill in person as we had seen him years ago in our McKell High School assembly.

I believe this story catches some of the spirit of this great performer and individualist. I believe you will find the Great Cherokee Bill a most colorful character.

HE WALKED into my office, a tall, olive-complexioned man of about thirty-five. His moist jet-black hair didn't reach his shoulders. His teeth were white, strong-looking and far apart. The green and black checked loose fitting lumberjacket gave his shoulders a broad appearance; the rattlesnake skin belt girdled tightly made his waist look small. His riding pants encasing his hips and legs made them look small. His boots were deeply scarred. My office secretary ran from the office before the man spoke; she was afraid of him.

"Mr. Stringer," the stranger said without the slightest accent in his voice, "I'm the Great Cherokee Bill. I'm three parts Indian and one part white man. I've come to see you about putting on a show for your high school."

"Nothing doing, Cherokee Bill," I said, looking him over. "I wouldn't have another Indian program here under any consideration!"

"What's the matter?" he asked, gesturing with his hands as he spoke, "don't you like Indians?"

"I like Indians all right. But we've had two Indian programs here this year and they've both been fakes."

"I'll tell you I'm no fake," he yelled. "I'm the Great Cherokee Bill." His black eyes looked straight into my eyes and his lips quivered.

"Look at this!" he said, reaching me a sheaf of recommendations.

There were two hundred at least. Many were written by teachers in Tennessee, men and women I'd gone to the University with; I knew it didn't pay to question one of their recommendations. There was a fine recommendation from Willis Abernathy, Superintendent of Maitland High School, Maitland, Tennessee. In my four years in the University with Willis, I'd never heard him say a good word for anybody; yet he'd warmly recommended Cherokee Bill as the greatest entertainer that had ever given a program at the Maitland High School since he had been Superintendent. I read Willis Abernathy's letter carefully.

"Day before yesterday, we had an Indian here," I said. "The students went to sleep in chapel."

"They'll never go to sleep on the Great Cherokee Bill," the Indian said. "I'll keep 'em awake!"

"We're having chapel in just a few minutes," I told him. "Would you mind going to chapel with me and entertain them for a minute or two to show them you are a real Indian? If you can hold them, we'll give you tomorrow's chapel program!"

"I want to show them what I can do," he said, angrily. "The Great Cherokee Bill has never been treated like this!"

"Sorry, Cherokee Bill," I said, "but we're not having any more fake Indian shows."

When the bell rang, Cherokee Bill and I followed the students into the auditorium. When they saw the strange looking man, a great laugh went up from the students. They were more interested in the personal appearance of Cherokee Bill than they had been in White Cloud's.

"Our regular program, students, will be temporarily postponed," I said. "We have a man with us who says he's three parts Indian and one part pale face. He doesn't claim to be a full-blooded Indian as did our White Cloud!"

"Old faker, White Cloud," some student said in an undertone so everybody could hear. Everybody laughed.

"I want to introduce to you, Cherokee Bill," I said, "and he will entertain you for a few minutes!"

Many of the students sighed.

"Some bad boys out there, Mr. Stringer," Cherokee Bill said. "I need my whip. Excuse me till I run to the car and get it!"

Like a flash the Indian shot out from the auditorium, his oily black hair floating on the wind behind him, while the students roared. Each boy kidded the boy beside him, saying, "You're Cherokee Bill's bad boy!" I wondered if he could pick the boys who had given the teachers trouble.

Cherokee Bill ran into the auditorium full speed and stopped suddenly like a car locking four wheels. Over his shoulder he carried a long whip.

"You back there," he pointed to Tim Sparks.

Everybody in chapel roared. Cherokee Bill hadn't missed his guess on Tim Sparks. Students called him "Sparkie."

"Come up here, young man!" Cherokee Bill commanded.

"I ain't comin'," Sparkie said twisting in his seat.

"But you will come," Cherokee Bill said. "I'll give you ten seconds and if you don't come, I'll bring you up here."

There was silence while Cherokee Bill looked at his wrist-watch.

"Are you coming?"

"No."

Cherokee Bill threw his arm back across his shoulder; gripping the giant whipstalk, he brought the whip over his shoulder, over the rows of students in front of him. The approximately sixteen-foot long whip cracked like a rifle above Sparkie's head, its long cracker wrapping around his neck. Then Cherokee Bill drew on the whip like one drawing a bucket of water from a well with a rope line. Everybody roared as Cherokee Bill drew Sparkie to the front. When Sparkie walked, the whip around his neck didn't choke him; when he balked, the whip drew closer around his neck and pushed his tongue out. Everybody wondered how he had lassoed Sparkie with a whip without hitting one of the boys around him. But he had.

"Poor Sparkie," Bill Hilton said, laughing.

"Sparkie, you stand right here," Cherokee Bill said. "Two more boys I've got spotted. They're not good boys in school. I'm picking out three bad boys!"

"Come up here," Cherokee Bill commanded, pointing to

James "Pewee" Fox. "You are a bad boy. You won't get your lessons!"

James Fox hadn't passed a single course in three months of high school work. Every student and teacher laughed when Cherokee Bill threw his whip over the heads of the students and lassoed Pewee. When Pewee balked his tongue came out. The students screamed with laughter.

"You don't fool the Great Cherokee Bill when you're a bad boy," the Indian said as he drew Pewee up front.

Mrs. Burton, Pewee's home room teacher laughed hysterically when Pewee stood beside Sparkie and Cherokee Bill and faced the laughing students.

"Why don't you fetch one of the girls up here, Cherokee Bill?" Sparkie asked.

"Girls are never bad," he answered him looking over the chapel for the third boy.

"Come," Cherokee Bill said, pointing to Henry "Custardpie" Jordon.

"He's found all three of the bad boys," Lucy Bowling spoke from the front row. There was a thunderclap of laughter as Cherokee Bill raised his whip and Custardpie started ducking down but the boys sitting beside him pushed him up straight. Cherokee Bill had picked the third boy all right. Custardpie had spent seven years in high school and hadn't finished yet. He had often left a cafeteria window unlocked, slipped back to the cafeteria at night and made way with the pies. The only way he had ever been caught was, a pie was doped and he got it. He was out of school a couple of weeks. Thereafter, he was called "Custardpie" Jordon.

When Cherokee Bill drew Custardpie up front the students arose from their seats and laughed. Never had they seen such entertainment.

"Did I get your bad boys?" Cherokee Bill turned to me and said.

I didn't say anything but a voice in unison went up from the student body.

"Y–E–S!"

"I'm no fake Indian," Cherokee Bill told the student body. "I am the Great Cherokee Bill. Now if you want me to come tomorrow for chapel, tell me!"

"WE WANT YOU CHEROKEE BILL!" the students' voices applauded!

"Then you can have our chapel period tomorrow, Cherokee Bill," I said.

"Tomorrow, I'll show you what I can do with my whip," he said. "I'll show you how I can shoot chalk from the students' mouths! Tell your parents to come for chapel tomorrow. Tell them I'm the Great Cherokee Bill!"

"We'll tell 'em, Cherokee Bill!" a student yelled.

"And bring your rifles," he said, "so I can show you that I'm not a fake!"

Cherokee Bill had taken all of our chapel time with his free entertainment. Now that he had proven himself not to be a fake but a real entertainer, the students talked the rest of the day about Cherokee Bill. They could hardly wait for the chapel program next day. The boys he had pulled from the audience with his whip were a little peeved at him but he asked my permission to talk with them awhile. I told him to talk with them long as he wanted to. He took a walk over the school yard with them.

Next day school busses were loaded almost beyond capacity. It seemed to me the whole county had turned out to see the Great Cherokee Bill after the students had gone home and advertised him. Hill men with lean beardy faces and long rifles came to the high school. My office was packed with their rifles until it looked like an arsenal. Men that could bark a squirrel with every shot, with long lantern jaws bulging with home-grown quids of burley tobacco came—first time many had ever been inside a high school. Men who had preached that education was a fake and that it was ruining the country came to watch the Indian shoot. Men, who secretly believed that they were better shots than any Indian, came. Women, young girls who had never gone to school, mothers of students and mothers carrying young breast-nursing babies, came. I had never seen such crowds at the high school not even for commencement exercises as had packed the schoolhouse and the yard. I knew we couldn't have school that day if we waited for the chapel period. I called the teachers together and we made arrangements for chapel the first period since Cherokee Bill was already there.

Then we called the special first period chapel. And our chapel receipts set a record! Money for Cherokee Bill and money for Maxwell High School! Even Cherokee Bill was pleasantly surprised when I told him his part would be over two hundred dollars!

"I'll show 'em what the Great Cherokee Bill can do," he said seriously.

Every seat in the auditorium was taken. The bleachers were filled; there wasn't standing room in the aisles. Only the stage was free for Cherokee Bill to show the audience he was the Great Cherokee Bill. When he walked onto the stage, Custardpie, Sparkie and Pewee were with him. There was a great cry went up from the student body; but the lean hill men with the beardy jaws stood in the aisles unmoved. And the hill women didn't show any signs of emotion. They remained true to their hill blood; they had to be shown.

"I'll show you mothers how to use a whip on your bad boys," Cherokee Bill said.

A smile spread over their sun-tanned broken faces.

Custardpie stood on one side of the stage holding a sheet of notebook paper stretched between his hands. He held it about eighteen inches in front of him. Cherokee Bill stood back at the far side of the stage, pulled the long whip over his shoulder and struck at the paper. The cracker split the paper as near the center as if one had measured and cut it with a knife. The audience was so still when he slashed with the whip, they could hear it cut the paper. Custardpie turned to the audience and showed them the paper split in halves. A great roar of voices then came from the audience.

"Hold that half up, Custardpie," Cherokee Bill said.

Cherokee Bill split the half into equal quarters. Custardpie held the quarter piece between his hands and Cherokee Bill split it into eighths. An eighth of the sheet was very small. The audience sat spell-bound.

"Hold that piece for me," Cherokee Bill commanded Custardpie.

"I'm afraid," he said, his hands trembling.

"Hold it, Pewee!"

"All right, Cherokee Bill!"

Pewee stood holding the narrow piece of paper before the audience, his hands were steady as steel. Cherokee Bill drew back with his great whip, his black eyes engulfing the paper as if he were aiming with a rifle. He came over, the whip made a ripping noise between Pewee's hands. Pewee turned to the audience with the paper split into sixteenths. A great applause went up from the audience.

"He could shore whop a youngin," one hill woman said to another.

"Hold it again," he commanded.

"Not me," Pewee said. "That whip was too close to my fingers!"

"I'll hold it," Sparkie said.

Sparkie held the paper while Cherokee Bill measured the strip with the width of his whip cracker.

"Mighty close but I can do it," he said.

The audience waited breathlessly while he aimed and came

over with the whip. There was a rip between Sparkie's hands. Sparkie turned with strips of paper almost razor-blade thinness. His hands were quivering. Cherokee Bill had done it.

"Did I hit your hands, Sparkie?"

"No, but it was awful close."

Great cheers came from the audience.

While Cherokee Bill rested from his whipping act, he asked the boys on the stage if they had money in their pockets. They told him they had. He told them it wasn't good money and they said it was. He asked to see a nickel. Pewee gave him a nickel. He put it between two of his front teeth, bent it double and gave it back to Pewee. "I told you it was no good," he said. Custardpie let him have a dime. He not only bent it but almost put a hole through it with his teeth. He bent a penny double. Then he took a quarter from his pocket, bent it double, and threw it back among the gawking beardy-jawed men in the aisle. Each examined it; then passed it to the next man.

"Wuz thar a trick to that whip stuff?" a long lean hill man pushed his way up front and asked. "Didn't the boys jerk the paper apart?"

"What do you think?" Cherokee Bill asked.

"I think thar wuz," he said.

Cherokee Bill drew his whip back as the high school students screamed with laughter. The whip cracked like a twenty-two rifle as it reached out—the cracker wrapping around the man's long unshaven neck.

"Was it a fake?" Cherokee Bill asked.

"Yes, I believe—"

Cherokee Bill drew the whip until the man's tongue shot out from his mouth as he pulled him close to the stage.

"Was it a fake?"

He shook his head "no" and Cherokee Bill released his whip. The man took back through the audience while the rest of the hill men laughed more than the students had ever laughed.

Then Cherokee Bill stepped off the stage. Pewee came with him. There was a long ladder, approximately fifteen feet, leaned against the wall. Pewee climbed up the ladder to the last rung. He locked his legs around the rung and held with his hands for dear life as Cherokee Bill lifted the ladder with one hand toward the high auditorium ceiling. A great applause went up and the beardy hill men craned their long leather necks as Cherokee Bill's face, flushed red as a sliced beet, held the ladder trembled in the air—up, up, he lifted it—placing the bottom rung on his chin—walking beneath it—swaying back and forward—holding it balanced on his chin while Pewee reached up and touched the ceiling. There was a great applause as Cherokee Bill brought Pewee back safely to the floor.

"Injuns must be a powerful lot," an old snaggled tooth squirrel hunter said.

Cherokee Bill leaped upon the high stage; Pewee climbed up the steps.

"Men, women, boys and girls," Cherokee Bill said, his breath a little short, "I will show you now how the Great Cherokee Bill can shoot!"

There was silence in the auditorium while Cherokee Bill placed a lead dish upon the stage wall to catch the cartridge balls. He arranged it to suit himself; then he placed Custardpie within four feet of it with a piece of chalk in his mouth. He put a blindfold over Custardpie's eyes and told him to stand still. He took his own rifle, stood at the far side of the stage, aimed the rifle, fired. "Ting" the battered bullet hit the lead dish and dropped on the floor approximately the same time half the stick of chalk fell. Half of the stick was in Custardpie's mouth. Custardpie trembled.

"Stand still, Custardpie," Cherokee Bill said, "I'm not goin' to hit you, I could cut that off with my whip and never touch your nose!"

He stood still while Cherokee Bill turned his rifle upside

down and clipped the chalk even with his mouth. A great applause went up but Custardpie jerked the blindfold from over his eye and said someone else could have it since he felt the wind from the bullet. Then everybody laughed. The old squirrel hunters laughed, slapped each other on the shoulders and jabbed each other in the ribs with their boney hands. This was what they had come to see and this was what they liked. Two boys carried the rifles from the office to the stage floor. There was a tag on each rifle with the owner's name on it to keep from getting the rifles mixed.

"Men, the Great Cherokee Bill will try your rifles," the Indian said.

When he took a rifle from the stack, he shot it first at the lead plate on the wall; then he looked through the barrel. If the rifle suited him, he shot a piece of chalk from Sparkie's mouth. Many of the rifles he wouldn't use. He told the owners they weren't good—that the rifles in the barrel were too well worn or that he didn't like the sight adjustments. Many of the rifles he bragged on and this pleased the owners—men who loved the feel of a rifle—men attached to their rifles more than anything they possessed.

Just before he closed his program, he put a wheel rigged so a boy could stand at the side and turn it. It had twenty-one pieces of chalk placed around it. With a rifle that shot twenty-one times, he got ready for his last most difficult feat. He arranged the wheel in front of the lead plate, so when he shot, the plate would catch the bullets. He showed Pewee how fast to turn the wheel. While he got himself in position, there was silence again. The men stood with their mouths open when the rifle began barking and the pieces of chalk, one by one started falling as the wheel revolved past the lead plate. The bullets hit the lead plate, dropping to the stage floor like heavy grains of corn shelled from a cob. He broke the entire twenty-one. Everybody went wild with applause. The program was over. Men rushed up front to get their rifles. The chapel had lasted almost all morning. Cherokee Bill was a hero at Maxwell High School and more than a hero with the men from the hills. They wanted to shake his hand, invite him to their homes to squirrel hunt with them. And the high school students wanted him back for another program.

"The Great Cherokee Bill must go on to new places," he told them.

While I penned a letter of recommendation to the principals of neighboring high schools for the Great Cherokee Bill, one of our teachers gave him his share of the chapel receipts. I tried to make it a letter of recommendation better than any I had read among the great sheaf of recommendations he was carrying. I tried to make it even better than the letter Willis Abernathy had written for him.

The Moon Child from Wolfe Creek

Author's Introduction

When I wrote my book about my years as a teacher, The Thread That Runs So True, the incident about the "moon child" was a chapter in that book. However, before I sent the manuscript to the publisher, I removed that chapter. The reason is that I was sure no one would believe the story of a boy who was afraid of a schoolhouse.

Sometime later, after the book was published, I was talking with several teachers, all of whom had taught for many years. As we shared our classroom experiences, I happened to tell about the moon child. I then asked if any of them had ever had a pupil who was afraid of a schoolhouse. They told me of no less than six similar cases. One elderly, retired teacher told me of the case of the pupil who was "wild as a fox." This teacher said this boy walked toward school with the other children until he got within sight of the building and then turned and started running in the opposite direction. The teacher then sent every boy in the school after him —they ran after that boy like a pack of hounds, to catch him and bring him back to school. I then learned that this boy, even though he was punished for running away from school, and even though his parents did

121

everything they could to keep him in school, never adjusted to the classroom and schoolwork.

Other teachers told me stories of how they had tried to deal with the problem of the student who was so frightened of school he wouldn't even come inside.

I was interested in what these teachers had done because when I was teaching, I had such a pupil. I didn't punish that pupil; I sought another solution. Now read the story to see if you agree that I was right.

"I DON'T WANT to tell on anybody," Vennie Mc-Coy whispered to me, "but I think you ought to know Don Crump didn't come all the way to school. He started with us but he didn't get here."

"Where did he go?" I asked. Vennie stood beside me and moved his left bare foot on the pine-board floor of the Lonesome Valley schoolhouse. "Is he playing hooky?"

"He's up there on the mountaintop," Vennie said. "Go to the door and look toward the sky and you'll see 'im."

"What's he doing up there?" I asked in low tones. My Lonesome Valley pupils looked at one another and then at me as they listened to our conversation. "Why doesn't he come on down to school?"

"He's afraid, Mr. Stuart," Vennie whispered.

I walked to the door and looked toward the peak.

"See 'im yander," Vennie said. He pointed to a tall boy who was walking across a clearing. Just above him on the ridgeline a flock of white clouds floated on a sea of July blue. I watched this tall, slender boy walk back and forth across the little clearing. He would walk first to the tall timber on one side and then he would walk back to the other. His long, lean, restless body was etched against the white clouds. This was hard for me to understand, since it was my first day of teaching in Lonesome Valley.

"Where does Don Crump live?" I asked Vennie as I stood wondering what to do.

"He lives on Wolfe Creek."

"Any other family live near him?"

"Nope."

"How long is Wolfe Creek?"

"Five or six miles long."

"What does Don do at home?"

"He helps his pappy with the croppin' during the season," Vennie explained. "All winter long he hunts and traps. That's the way the Crumps make some money. They sell hides. Don is a good hunter. He can put his nose down to a dirt hole and tell if there's anything in it. And if there's something in the hole he can tell you what it is."

"Are you sure he can do that?" I laughed.

"Oh, yes he can, Mr. Stuart," said Birch Caudill, a small redheaded fifth-grade pupil. "I've seen him do it. Once I saw him lay flat on his stummick and put his face in a water-seap hole and he sniffed and sniffed like a hound-dog, and he says to me when he took his head out of the hole: 'Birch, he's back there. It's a possum.' And we started diggin.' We followed the water-seap hole, a-diggin' through rocks and roots until we come to a big possum a-layin' there asleep in a dry bed of leaves. I'd as soon trust Don Crump as I would the best hound-dog in these parts."

Several of the boys and girls looked at one another and smiled as I, their seventeen-year-old teacher, stood in the door watching the restless figure walk back and forth like a trapped animal in a cage. I wondered why he didn't walk under the tall timber and hide. I wondered if he looked down toward the Little Lonesome schoolhouse, deep down in the narrow-gauged valley, and saw me standing in the door watching him. I tried to reason what to do with him. I wondered why he didn't walk up the steep slope to the ridgetop and into one of the white clouds that were floating lazily along the calm sky. While I stood there, I wondered why a boy of his wild restless nature, afraid of people and of school, would let the tall timber and the white clouds fence him within the semicircle of clearing where somebody pastured cattle and sheep.

"You want us to get 'im for you, Mr. Stuart?" Vennie asked.

"How would you get 'im?" I asked.

"Run 'im down and tie his hands and feet and fetch 'im to you," Vennie replied.

"Maybe you could do that," I said.

"He's fast as a rabbit but we could do it," Vennie bragged. "We've played fox and dog with him and he's faster than any of us, but if enough of us go after 'im and go up every side of the mountain and surround him, he can't get away."

"Yep, we can ketch 'im for you, Mr. Stuart," said Tom Adams, a blue-eyed shaggy-haired seventh-grade pupil. "We can go up the mountain in different directions and hide in the green timber all around the clearin'. Then somebody can give a signal and we can run out into the clearin' and ketch Don. I could almost slip up on 'im myself. I've slipped up on rabbits a-settin' and ketched 'em with my bare hands. I once ketched a ground hog that way. Nabbed 'im by the neck so he couldn't bite me."

Then all of the pupils laughed. Don Crump's being up there on the mountain had disturbed all of us. Everybody who had started to school had come but Don. And one of the first decisions I had to make in my teaching career was what to do with him. *If they run him down and tie his hands and feet and bring him down here,* I thought, *that won't tame him. That will make him wilder than ever.*

Another thought flashed through my mind. I remembered how my father had tamed cattle when they went wild in our big pasture. When we put them on grass in late March and left them alone, except for occasional visits to salt and count them, many went wild. My father finally tamed the wild ones until he had them licking salt out of his hand.

"Want us to go after 'im?" Vennie was impatient. "We'll fetch 'im in."

"Shore will," Tom Adams said.

They're wanting to get out too, I thought.

"No, leave him alone," I said. "If he likes it up there that's quite all right with me. I don't believe in roping a boy hand and foot and carrying him inside a schoolhouse. You can tell him when you see him again the school here is a fine place. Tell him we have a good time playing and that you believe he will like it. Tell him to come on down. Tell him we don't have anything here that will hurt him."

Many of my pupils looked quietly at each other and smiled. I took my last look at Don, who was still walking around in the clearing, up near the white clouds. I turned and walked back down the aisle with Vennie.

At the first recess, when my pupils played The Needle's Eye, I looked up to the high hill in the clearing and I didn't see Don Crump. Not at first. But I finally located Don sitting on a stump looking down in the valley toward the school. He was watching the pupils play. Don Crump sat there on the stump during the fifteen-minute recess (we let it run a little overtime) and looked on. Not one of my pupils paid any attention to him now. They were too busy playing. I did pay attention to him but he didn't know it. I didn't want Don to know I wanted him in school.

At the noon hour we, teacher and pupils, sat on the crumpled roots of the giant sycamores that grew all around the schoolhouse and ate our lunches. These sycamores with their massive canopy of leaves stood betwixt us and the hot July sun. My pupils hurried to eat their lunches so they could play The

Needle's Eye. Just as they were choosing sides to play, I looked toward the clearing to see if I could see Don Crump. He walked from the tall timber on the east side.

During the noon hour, I played The Needle's Eye with my pupils. Often, I looked up. Don was back on the stump where he had sat that morning. When Vennie McCoy saw him, before the noon hour was over, he came to me and wanted to get all of the boys in the school and chase him. But I wouldn't let him. I told him to leave Don alone. If Don wanted to come to school that was all right. If he didn't he could stay away. This was hard for Vennie McCoy, Tom Adams, Ova Salyers and Guy Hawkins to understand. They couldn't understand why they were in school and Don Crump was sitting on a stump, high upon the mountainside in the clearing, watching us play.

On the second day of school, Don Crump, in the early hours, walked back and forth in the clearing shade. This was before recess. During recess he sat on the same stump and watched us. At the noon hour he came from the tall timber on the east side of the clearing and watched us playing in the valley below. In the afternoon he disappeared again. At the afternoon recess he emerged from the shade of the tall timber to watch us. He had a little world of his own up on the mountainside. He had found something to interest him. That was watching us. And I was watching him too.

"Don brings his dinner in a lard bucket," Vennie told me on the third day. "His pappy thinks he comes to school. But he goes to the woods, as you know, Mr. Stuart. You want me to go to Wolfe Creek and tell his pappy what he's doin'?"

"No, whatever you do, don't tell his father anything," I said. "Leave Don Crump alone. When he wants to come to school, he'll come."

Takes a long time to tame cattle with salt, I thought. *Maybe Don will finally get here. He's a little closer now.*

For on this third day Don had moved down the mountain-side by a hundred yards or more. He was getting closer, where he could see us better from the new stump he'd found. He could hear us sing and shout as we played The Needle's Eye. He could see us better as we ran foot races and played "anti-over the schoolhouse," with a twine ball.

On the last day of the first week, Don came still closer. He was, perhaps, within a quarter of a mile of the schoolhouse now. But he was getting closer, and that pleased me. There was something about the place where the pupils played and had a good time that attracted Don. There was life, laughter and play among us. He must have realized that he was on the outside of all this. He must have craved association, play and laughter with us.

In the second week of school he moved down to a wild blackberry patch where there was a big rock covered with gray lichen moss. He sat on this big rock and watched us.

"I was tellin' Pappy and Mammy about Don Crump," said Tom Adams, as he walked over and stood beside me on the noon hour of the first day in the second week. "Pappy said he was teched. Mammy said he was a moon child."

I stood and looked at Tom.

"What is a moon child?" I asked.

"Born when the moon is tilted in the sky," he explained. "All people are strange that are born when the moon is tilted. Funny in some way or another, so Mammy and Pappy say."

"There's not anything wrong with Don," I said. "He is just not ready to come to school."

"Funny he don't like school," Tom said. "It's a wonderful place. Wouldn't miss it for nothin'."

Then Tom raced back and joined the circle playing The Needle's Eye.

During the second week, Don Crump moved from rock to stump and shade to shade until he was within one hundred yards of the schoolhouse. I warned my pupils not to talk to him, or about him, or even notice him. I told them to go ahead with their play as if Don Crump were not near the schoolhouse, and they did. Don was close enough now to see everything. He could hear the wild, high laughter of my pupils. He could watch the two teams, that had been chosen in the game of The Needle's Eye, pull against each other. He could see one team outpull the other and the pupils spill on the schoolyard and get up and brush the dust from their clothes. He could hear them laugh louder than the wild wind he had so often heard in the lonely treetops. Don sat upon the slope and smiled. This play fascinated him. On the last day of the second week, he walked onto the schoolyard, though he stood a safe distance away from the pupils. He kept a good distance away from me.

In the beginning of the third week, Don Crump walked down the little, narrow, winding valley road with the pupils. Then I got my first good look at this tall, blue-eyed, handsome, intelligent-looking boy. His hair, blond as frost-bitten crab grass, came about to his shoulders. He came onto the school-yard but he wouldn't come inside the schoolhouse. I never tried to get him inside. He sat on a gnarled root in the sycamore shade while school went on inside the house. He must have listened to what we said inside. When I had the chance, at re-cesses and noon, I looked at him and smiled, though I never approached him. My pupils left him alone too. For during the beginning of this third week, he stood nearby and watched the pupils at play. He stood and watched and clapped his hands and laughed loudly at times. He kept getting closer to the circle of pupils marching around and around singing The Needle's Eye. Before the week was over, he joined the circle and played with the pupils. But, never once did he venture inside the schoolhouse.

While the rest of us were inside, Don Crump played around

the schoolhouse. Often he sat on the sycamore root and whistled. He whistled a tune like the wind was playing in the sycamore leaves above. Ova Salyers told me once that he had whistled like the wind so much, while he was alone in the woods, that he could whistle the tune of any wind. This was hard for me to believe, until once I walked outside the schoolhouse and listened to Don's whistling on the sycamore root below, the tune of the wind in the sycamore leaves above him. He was whistling the tune of the wind all right. But, to leave this boy outside the schoolroom, while the rest of us were inside, caused considerable talk among the school patrons of my district. Many of the patrons accused me of having a "pet," one I let do as he pleased. Of course, many of my pupils didn't understand what I was trying to do and they went home and told their parents about Don Crump and what I had told them about leaving him alone. Several of the parents dismissed Don Crump and said he should not be allowed to go to school, since he was a moon child. A few of the parents thought I was afraid of him.

But on Monday afternoon, of my first month at Lonesome Valley, Don Crump came inside the schoolhouse. He walked inside, looked quickly at all the pupils, at the windows, then at the door. He held a cap in his hand when he sat down on a back seat. He acted as if he were ready to run. My pupils were naturally excited when he came inside, and started looking at him. I motioned for them to look toward my desk and to keep quiet and pay no attention to Don Crump. The stray one had finally come because of his hunger and thirst. His was the eternal hunger and thirst of youth for laughter, play, recreation, association and enjoyment upon this earth. Don had come to us. We hadn't run him down, tied his hands and feet and brought him to us either. He had come of his own accord.

This Farm for Sale

Author's Introduction

Like most post offices in small towns, the Riverton Post Office not only handled mail, it was a general store. And also like most small-town post offices, it was a wonderful place to go to get the news of the county and to listen to the men who sat around just talking.

In the Riverton Post Office I first met Melvin Spencer, the real estate salesman in "This Farm for Sale." He was already an old man, but no one, not even Melvin himself, knew his age because he was born in the deep mountains of Kentucky, long before births were officially recorded. When he died, some people said he was well over a hundred; others said he was only ninety-eight. But his age doesn't matter. What does matter is that Melvin Spencer was a poet. The poetry in Melvin Spencer came out in the language of the real estate ads he wrote for the small hill farms he had been authorized to sell. His write-ups of properties for sale were so attractive that they became a feature of our county's weekly. People looked for his write-ups in each issue, not to find out what farm was for sale but to give themselves the treat of reading Melvin Spencer's way with words. Sometimes his poetic gifts backfired on him and cost him a sale. This happened when a farmer who wanted to sell a farm read Melvin Spencer's ad about the property and was so moved by the glowing description of his own farm that he saw his place with new eyes and decided not to sell after all.

The farm for sale in this story is the Stone farm. I knew the Stones well, and I had been over their farm many times. When I decided to write this story, I felt that the telling of it would be more effective if it were told firsthand rather than from an onlooker's point of view. Thus I used the device of the first person singular in the character of Shan, who spends his summers with Uncle Dick and Aunt Emma and his cousins.

I remember hearing my friend Carl Brown say at the Riverton Post Office that the story of Melvin Spencer illustrates the old saying that the grass always looks greener on the other side of the fence. And I remember thinking to myself that Melvin Spencer is a man who has had the privilege of teaching many people to appreciate and love what they already have. "This is a story," I thought. And so I had to write it to put down what I knew of Melvin Spencer, real estate salesman and hill poet.

"THIS TIME we're goin' to sell this farm," Uncle Dick said to Aunt Emma. "I've just learned how to sell a farm. Funny, I never thought of it myself."

My cousins—Olive, Helen, Oliver, and Little Dick—all stopped eating and looked at one another and then looked at Uncle Dick and Aunt Emma. When Aunt Emma smiled, they smiled, too. Everybody seemed happy because Uncle Dick, who had just come from Blakesburg, had found a way to sell the farm. Everybody was happy but me. I was sorry Uncle Dick was going to sell the farm.

"This farm is just as good as sold!" Uncle Dick talked on. "I've got a real estate man, my old friend Melvin Spencer, coming here tomorrow to look the place over. He's goin' to sell it for me."

"I'd like to get enough for it to make a big payment on a fine house in Blakesburg," Aunt Emma said. "I've got the one picked out that I want. It's the beautiful Coswell house. I understand it's up for sale now and no one's livin' in it!"

"Gee, that will be wonderful," Cousin Olive said. "Right on the street and not any mud. We wouldn't have to wear galoshes all winter if we lived there!"

"I'll say it will be wonderful," Helen said, with a smile. "Daddy, I hope Mr. Spencer can sell this place."

I wanted to tell Aunt Emma the reason why no one was living in the Coswell house. Every time Big River rose to flood stage, the water got on the first floor in the house; and this was the reason why the Coswells had built a house on higher ground outside Blakesburg and had moved to it. And this was the reason why they couldn't keep a renter any longer than it took Big River to rise to flood stage. But this wasn't my business, so I didn't say anything.

"Mel Spencer will come here to look this farm over," Uncle Dick said, puffing on his cigar until he'd almost filled the dining room with smoke. "Then he'll put an ad in the *Blakesburg Gazette*."

"What will we do about the cows, horses, hogs, honeybees, hay in the barn lofts and in the stacks, and corn in the bins?" Cousin Oliver asked.

"Sell them, too," Uncle Dick said. "When we sell, let's sell everything we have but our house plunder."

It was ten o'clock the next day before Melvin Spencer came. Since he couldn't drive his car all the way to Uncle Dick's farm, he rode the mail truck to Red Hot. Red Hot is a store and post office on the Tiber River. And at Red Hot, Uncle Dick met him with an extra horse and empty saddle. So Melvin Spencer came riding up with Uncle Dick. And I'll never forget the first words he said when he climbed down from the saddle.

"Richard, it's a great experience to be in the saddle again," he said, breathing deeply of the fresh air. "All this reminds me of another day and time."

Oliver, Little Dick, and I followed Melvin Spencer and Uncle Dick as they started walking toward the Tiber bottoms.

"How many acres in this farm, Richard?" Melvin Spencer asked.

"The deed calls for three hundred, more or less," Uncle Dick said.

"How many acres of bottom land?" he asked Uncle Dick.

"I'd say about sixty-five," Uncle Dick replied.

We walked down the jolt-wagon road, where my cousins and I had often ridden Nell and Jerry to and from the field.

"What kind of land is this?" Melvin Spencer asked. He had to look up to see the bright heads of cane.

"It's limestone land," Uncle Dick bragged. "Never had to use fertilizer. My people have farmed these bottoms over a hundred years."

Then Uncle Dick showed Melvin Spencer the corn we had laid by. It was August, and our growing corn was maturing. Melvin Spencer looked at the big cornfield. He was very silent. We walked on to the five acres of tobacco, where the broad leaves crossed the balks and a man couldn't walk through. Then we went down to the river.

"My farm comes to this river," Uncle Dick said. "I've often thought what a difference it would be if we had a bridge across this river. Then I could reach the Tiber road and go east to Blakesburg and west to Darter City. But we don't have a bridge; and until we go down the river seven miles to Red Hot where we can cross to the Tiber road, we'll always be in the mud. I've heard all my life that the county would build a bridge. My father heard it, too, in his lifetime."

"You *are* shut in here," Melvin Spencer agreed, as he looked beyond the Tiber River at the road.

"Now, we'll go to the house and get some dinner," Uncle Dick said. "Then I'll take you up on the hill this afternoon and show you my timber and the rest of the farm."

When we reached the big house, Melvin Spencer stopped for a minute and looked at the house and yard.

"You know, when I sell a piece of property, I want to look it over," he told Uncle Dick. "I want to know all about it. How old is this house?"

"The date was cut on the chimney," Uncle Dick said.

Melvin Spencer looked over the big squat log house with the plank door, big stone steps, small windows, the moss-covered roof. Then we went inside, and he started looking again. That is, he did until Uncle Dick introduced him to Aunt Emma and Aunt Emma introduced him to a table that made him stand and look some more.

"I've never seen anything like this since I was a boy," Melvin Spencer said, showing more interest in the loaded table than he had in the farm.

"All of this came from our farm here," Uncle Dick said.

I never saw a man eat like Melvin Spencer. He ate like I did when I first came to Uncle Dick's and Aunt Emma's each spring when school was over. He tried to eat something of everything on the table, but he couldn't get around to it all.

"If I could sell this farm like you can prepare a meal, I'd get a whopping big price for it," he said with a chuckle as he looked at Aunt Emma.

"I hope you can," Aunt Emma said. "We're too far back here. Our children have to wade the winter mud to get to school. And we don't have electricity. We don't have the things that city people have. And I think every country woman wants them."

Melvin Spencer didn't listen to all that Aunt Emma said. He was much too busy eating. And long before he had finished, Uncle Dick pulled a cigar from his inside coat pocket, struck a match under the table, lit it, and blew a big cloud of smoke toward the ceiling in evident enjoyment.

He looked at Aunt Emma and smiled.

"The old place is as good as sold, Mother," Uncle Dick said with a wink. "You're a-goin' to be out of the mud. We'll let some other woman slave around here and wear galoshes all winter. We'll be on the bright, clean streets wearin' well-shined shoes—every blessed one of us. We'll have an electric washer, a radio where we won't have to have the batteries charged, a bathroom, and an electric stove. No more of this stove-wood choppin' for the boys and me."

When Uncle Dick said this, Olive and Helen looked at Aunt Emma and smiled. I looked at Oliver and Little Dick, and they were grinning. But Melvin Spencer never looked up from his plate.

When we got up from the table, Melvin Spencer thanked Aunt Emma, Cousin Olive, and Helen for the "best dinner" he'd had since he was a young man. Then he asked Aunt Emma for a picture of the house.

Aunt Emma sent Helen to get it. "If you can, just sell this place for us," Aunt Emma said to Melvin Spencer.

"I'll do my best," he promised her. "But as you ought to know, it will be a hard place to sell, located way back here and without a road."

"Are you a-goin' to put a picture of this old house in the paper?" Uncle Dick asked, as Helen came running with the picture.

"I might," Melvin Spencer said. "I never say much in an ad, since I have to make my words count. A picture means a sale sometimes. Of course, this expense will come from the sale of the property."

He said good-by to Aunt Emma, Olive, and Helen. Little Dick, Oliver, and I followed him and Uncle Dick out of the house and up the hill where the yellow poplars and the pines grow.

"Why hasn't this timber been cut long ago?" Melvin Spencer asked, looking up at the trees.

"Not any way to haul it out," Uncle Dick told him.

"That's right," Melvin Spencer said. "I'd forgot about the road. If a body doesn't have a road to his farm, Richard, he's not got much of a place."

"These old trees get hollow and blow down in storms," Uncle Dick said. "They should have been cut down a long time ago."

"Yes, they should have," Melvin Spencer agreed, as he put his hand on the bark of a yellow poplar. "We used to have trees like this in Pike County. But not any more."

While we walked under the beech grove, we came upon a drove of slender bacon hogs eating beechnuts.

"Old skinny bacon hogs," Uncle Dick said, as they scurried past us. "They feed on the mast of the beeches and oaks, on sawbrier, greenbrier, and pine-tree roots, and on mulberries, persimmons, and pawpaws."

When we climbed to the top of a hill, the land slanted in all directions.

"Show me from here what you own," Melvin Spencer said.

"It's very easy, Mel," Uncle Dick said. "The stream on the right and the one on the left are the left and right forks of Wolfe Creek. They are boundary lines. I own all the land between them. I own all the bottom land from where the forks join, down to that big bend in the Tiber. And I own down where the Tiber flows against those white limestone cliffs."

"You are fenced in by natural boundaries," Melvin Spencer

said. "They're almost impossible to cross. This place will be hard to sell, Richard."

Then we went back down the hill, and Melvin and Uncle Dick climbed into the saddles and were off down the little narrow road toward Red Hot. Their horses went away at a gallop, because Melvin Spencer had to catch the mail truck, and he was already behind schedule.

On Saturday, Uncle Dick rode to Red Hot to get the paper. Since he didn't read very well, he asked me to read what Melvin Spencer had said about his house. When I opened the paper and turned to the picture of the house, everybody gathered around.

"Think of a picture of this old house in the paper," Aunt Emma said.

"But there are pictures of other houses for sale in the paper," Uncle Dick told her. "That's not anything to crow about."

"But it's the best-looking of the four," Cousin Olive said.

"It does look better than I thought it would," Aunt Emma sighed.

"Look, here's two columns all the way down the page," I said. "The other four places advertised here have only a paragraph about them."

"Read it," Uncle Dick said. "I'd like to know what Mel said about this place. Something good, I hope."

So I read this aloud:

Yesterday, I had a unique experience when I visited the farm of Mr. and Mrs. Richard Stone, which they have asked me to sell. I cannot write an ad about this farm. I must tell you about it.

I went up a winding road on horseback. Hazelnut bushes, with clusters of green hazelnuts bending their slender stems, swished across my face. Pawpaws, heavy with green clusters of fruit, grew along this road. Persimmons with bending boughs covered one slope below the road. Here are wild fruits and nuts of Nature's cultivation for the one who possesses land like this. Not any work but just to go out and gather the fruit. How many of you city dwellers would love this?

"What about him a-mentionin' the persimmons, pawpaws, and hazelnuts!" Uncle Dick broke in. "I'd never have thought of them. They're common things!"

When we put the horses in the big barn, Mr. Stone, his two sons, his nephew, and I walked down into his Tiber-bottom farm land. And, like the soil along the Nile River, this over-flowed land, rich with limestone, never has to be fertilized. I saw cane as high as a giraffe, and as dark green as the waves of the Atlantic. It grew in long, straight rows with brown clusters of seed that looked to be up against the blue of the sky. I have never seen such dark clouds of corn grow out of the earth. Five acres of tobacco, with leaves as broad as a mountaineer's shoulders. Pleasant meadows with giant haystacks here and there. It is a land rich with fertility and abundant with crops.

"That sounds wonderful," Aunt Emma said, smiling.

This peaceful Tiber River, flowing dreamily down the valley, is a boundary to his farm. Here one can see to the bottoms of the deep holes, the water is so clear and blue. One can catch fish from the river for his next meal. Elder bushes, where they gather the berries to make the finest jelly in the world, grow along this riverbank as thick as ragweeds. The Stones have farmed this land for four generations, have lived in the same house, have gathered elderberries for their jelly along the Tiber riverbanks, and fished in its sky-blue waters that long—and yet they will sell this land.

"Just a minute, Shan," Uncle Dick said as he got up from his chair. "Stop just a minute."

Uncle Dick pulled a handkerchief from his pocket and wiped the sweat from his forehead. His face seemed a bit flushed. He walked a little circle around the living room and then sat back down in his chair. But the sweat broke out on his face again when I started reading.

The proof of what a farm produces is at the farm table. I wish that whoever reads what I have written here could have seen the table prepared by Mrs. Stone and her two daughters. Hot fluffy biscuits with light-brown tops, brown-crusted corn bread, buttermilk, sweet milk (cooled in a freestone well), wild-grape jelly, wild-crab-apple jelly, mast-fed lean bacon that melted in my mouth, fresh apple pie, wild-blackberry cobbler, honey-colored sorghum from the limestone bottoms of the Tiber, and wild honey from the beehives.

"Oh, no one ever said that about a meal I cooked before," Aunt Emma broke in.

"Just a minute, Shan," Uncle Dick said, as he got up from his chair with his handkerchief in his hand again.

This time Uncle Dick went a bit faster as he circled the living room. He wiped sweat from his face as he walked. He had a worried look on his face. I read on:

Their house, eight rooms and two halls, would be a show place if close to some of our modern cities. The house itself would be worth the price I will later quote you on this farm. Giant yellow poplar logs with twenty- to thirty-inch facings, hewed smooth with broadaxes by the mighty hands of Stone pioneers, make the sturdy walls in this termite-proof house. Two planks make the broad doors in this house that is one-hundred-and-six years old. This beautiful home of pioneer architecture is without modern conveniences, but since a power line will be constructed up the Tiber River early next spring, a few modern conveniences will be possible.

"I didn't know that!" Aunt Emma was excited. "I guess it's just talk, like about the bridge across the Tiber."

After lunch I climbed a high hill to look at the rest of this farm. I walked through a valley of virgin trees, where there were yellow poplars and pine sixty feet to the first limb. Beech trees with tops big enough to shade twenty-five head of cattle. Beechnuts streaming down like golden coins, to be gathered by the bacon hogs running wild. A farm with wild game and fowl, and a river bountiful with fish! And yet, this farm is for sale!

Uncle Dick walked over beside his chair. He looked as if he were going to fall over.

Go see for yourself roads not exploited by the county or state, where the horse's shoe makes music on the clay, where apple orchards with fruit are bending down, and barns and bins are full. Go see a way of life, a richness and fulfillment that make America great, that put solid foundation stones under America! This beautiful farm, fifty head of livestock, honeybees, crops old and new, and a home for only $22,000!

"Oh!" Aunt Emma screamed. I thought she was going to faint. "Oh, he's killed it with that price. It's unheard of, Richard! You couldn't get $6000 for it."

Uncle Dick still paced the floor.

"What's the matter, Pa?" Oliver finally asked.

"I didn't know I had so much," Uncle Dick said. "I'm a rich man and didn't know it. I'm not selling this farm!"

"Don't worry, Richard," Aunt Emma said. "You won't sell it at that price!"

I never saw such disappointed looks as there were on my cousins' faces.

"But what will you do with Mr. Spencer?" Aunt Emma asked. "You've put the farm in his hands to sell."

"Pay him for his day and what he put in the paper," Uncle Dick told her. "I know we're not goin' to sell now, for it takes two to sign the deed. I'll be willing to pay Mel Spencer a little extra because he showed me what we have."

Then I laid the paper down and walked quietly from the room. Evening was coming on. I walked toward the meadows. I wanted to share the beauty of this farm with Melvin Spencer. I was never so happy.

As Ye Sow, So Shall Ye Reap

Author's Introduction

When I was made an officer in the United States Naval Reserve in World War II, I was sent to Washington where I was attached to the Writers' Unit in the Bureau of Aeronautics. I was one of a dozen officers assigned to do special writing assignments for the United States Navy. All of us in this Writers' Unit, before enlisting in the United States Naval Reserve, had been either editors or writers. We were trained to do any writing assignment requested by the Navy.

To give you an idea of the type of men we had in our small unit, one of our group was assigned to write a manual on the types of rockets which were being developed at that time. Although this officer had never seen a rocket before, he was sent to Hawaii to study rockets for about three weeks. When he returned, he had written a rocket manual that was used by men in the service for the duration of the war and for many years after. He was told by regular duty officers about the rocket, until he understood its functions well enough to write the manual. This rocket manual was considered a minor classic in military writing. This same officer is the one who returned to his position as an associate editor of a magazine after the war. And it was he who accepted "The Moon Child from Wolfe

Creek" a few years later and published it as a story in his magazine.

Often when we finished our assignments before the end of the day, we would talk of writers and writing. One afternoon, when our work was finished, I went back into the days of my youth and told them of a time when my cousin Penny and I got very angry at a neighbor because he didn't want us to date his daughters. So Cousin Penny and I decided to get even with that man. We wanted to make him sorry for being so hostile to us. After I finished telling the story, one of my friends said:

" 'As Ye Sow, So Shall Ye Reap,' that's your title."

He had been a magazine editor before entering service.

"Do you think it's a good short story?" I asked.

"Perfect," replied another officer. He too had been a magazine editor before entering the service. "Write that one. Send it somewhere. It will be accepted." It was accepted, three years later.

I WANT YOU to know that I didn't plan it. I'd 've never thought of doing such a thing to a neighbor if it hadn't been for my cousin, Winn.... Winn Shelton.... He's the one that has idears about gettin' even with people. When anybody does 'im a wrong once, he never forgets it. He goes back after 'im if it is a year, two years, or ten years later. I'm not like that. I never was like that.

"Knucklehead," Winn said to me when we stood in the barn loft with two empty lard cans. "What's th' matter with you? Are you a-goin' to get cold feet?"

"But this ain't right, Winn!" I told 'im. "Something down deep in me tells me it's wrong!"

"That's not the way you talked when old Jeff made you play on one side the creek and Martha on the other," Winn said, showing two missin' teeth as he laughed. "He never thought enough o' you to let you go with 'er. You know that! And you know you love 'er too!"

Winn knew just what to say to make me warm under the collar. I was in love with Martha and when I went to Skinner's shack on Sundays to play with Eddie and Tom, Jeff Skinner, Martha's Pappie would get himself a chair and sit under the peach-tree shade with an open Bible on his lap. He'd pretend that he's a-readin' his Bible but all the time he'd have his eye on me. He'd make us boys play on one side the little creek that flowed down past his house. He'd make his girls play on the other side. Though Minnie and Mary were pretty, Martha was the one for me. She was so pretty, she hurt my eyes.

"Well why don't you say something?" Winn asked me as he put his lard cans down on the barn-loft floor. "You know what I got against th' Skinners! Tom and Eddie double-teamed on me and whopped me but I'll make 'em pay for it. I'll make 'em do a lot o' diggin'. I thought you'd want to get even with 'em too."

"But I tell you, I'm afraid. They've got shotguns and rifles in th' house and they're all good shots!"

"But they'll never see us," Winn said, shaking his long index finger under my nose. "They'll all be in bed asleep. You're a coward! You've got cold feet! Let Martha's Pappie push you around any old way and you don't do anything about it!"

When Winn reminded me again of the way Martha's Pappie had treated me, he didn't have to say another word. That's why I started scooping up double handfuls of mixed timothy, red-top, orchard grass, blue grass, and Johnson grass from the hay where Uncle Mel had forked it to feed his cattle.

"Now, you're a working fellow," Winn said, working to fill

his can first. But as I worked I thought about Martha and I beat Winn. Winn is right after all, I thought. I ought to get even with old Jeff Skinner. He has never been a friend to me. Long ago when Martha and I were smaller he used to invite me to come to his house and stay all night with his boys. And now that Martha is fifteen and I'm sixteen, he won't do that. But he didn't know I had my eye on Martha when I was smaller and that I've never taken it off'n her since.

Just as soon as Winn had filled his can we climbed down the barn-loft ladder and took off up the hill through the bushes and briers. But it wasn't as bad as you'd think for Winn had made a little path to Jeff Skinner's strawberry patch.

"Since they didn't invite me to their fresh strawberries this spring, I had to invite myself," Winn grunted, getting his second wind as we climbed the winding path, over the rocks, around the trees and through the briers with our loads restin' on our shoulders.

I'd never heard that anybody was a-takin' Jeff Skinner's strawberries either. When anything like this happens on the creek where I live, everybody knows about it and everybody's a-talkin' about it. One thing the people on th' creek where I live don't like and that's a thief. And I didn't know my cousin was a thief. If anybody'd a-told me that he'd a-stolen strawberries, I wouldn't 've believed 'im. And if I'd 've known it in time I wouldn't 've been headin' toward Jeff Skinner's strawberry patch with a load o' grass seeds either.

"Oh, boy, ain't this wonderful," Winn said as we broke through the trees into the big clearin' surrounded by trees. "Here's where we do th' work! A pretty berry patch ain't it? Look how pretty and clean! But in a couple o' weeks it'll be pretty grassy!"

A moon, brighter than a shined brass button and bigger than a wagon wheel, looked from a low blue sky on us. And it lighted up the berry patch until we could see the grass seeds we were broadcastin'. Each took a row of strawberries at a time, like Winn planned it.

"It'll take a lot of grass seeds to sow all this field," I whispered to Winn. "It'll take us to midnight if we sow it a row at th' time."

"We've got plenty o' seed in our barn loft," Winn said, "and we've got all night to do it. We must not leave any spot without seeds upon it."

And the strawberry patch was just right for sowin' in grass since Skinners had gone through it with their hoes and had cut th' sprouts and pulled each little sprig of grass with their hands from around their strawberries. The ground was clean around the plants as a hound dog's tooth. And it was as soft where they had used garden rakes to harrow the tiny clods as a lettuce bed. I knew that grass would come up almost overnight and sod the berry patch if Skinners didn't get down on their knees and pull it out.

And they will know the kind of grass it is too, I thought. They will know the kinds of hay Uncle Mel Shelton feeds his cattle. They will know where the seeds come from. And something Mom used to tell me went through my head: As ye sow, so shall ye reap. And when I thought of these words, I trembled as we went down the path for more grass seeds.

We'd carried eleven loads of grass seeds to Skinner's strawberry patch and had broadcast 'em row by row so as to be sure there would be enough seed on the ground. And this was enough seed the way Uncle Mel and Pa had sowed our pasture fields, to have sowed forty acres. That's what I tried to tell Winn as we went after the twelfth and last load. That would make us twenty-four lard cans of seeds sowed on less than four acres. But Winn would have it his way and I was so tired I could hardly walk.

As I climbed the hill with my twelfth lard can, my legs felt weak and trembly. And all over the country the roosters started crowin' for midnight. That's why I know it was after midnight for we'd reached the field and had just finished the little rows in the topmost corner of the field when it happened.

"It's a good job well done," Winn said as he scraped his last handful of seed from the bottom of his can and sowed 'em on a spot he'd sowed before just to be sure. "Now, I can go home and sleep in peace since I'm even with Eddie and Tom. They'll lose more sweat diggin' out this grass than I lost on them. They'll take more of a beatin' in this field than they gave me. I'll slip up here and peep from the bushes when they start diggin' up this grass and I'll laugh to myself as I watch 'em work! You'll come along too, won't you?"

"No, I don't think I will," I said, sowing my last handful. "I'll be glad to get away from here. I'll never want to see this field again; I'm tired. I want to go home and go to bed!"

"I thought you'd enjoy seeing old Jeff bend his back over his hoe handle," Winn said. "I thought you'd like to see 'im get down on his prayer bones and pull grass."

And then Winn laughed loud enough for anybody to hear 'im.

"What is that, Winn?" I asked, pointing to something white and black a-comin' into the berry patch.

"It's a dog," Winn said, partly holding his breath. "And I believe it's a mad dog. Look how it's a-comin' in an even trot not lookin' to right nor left!"

It had come up the path Winn had made to the berry patch. That is the reason I saw it. We'd started back and we were facin' th' path.

"I believe it's a mad dog too," I screamed as it came toward us. "Which way'll we go? We can't make th' path! We'll have to pass it!"

"This way," Winn screamed takin' off with the lard can a-bangin' against his leg as he went. "Follow me!"

I was right at Winn's heels with my cap in one hand and

my lard can in th' other, liftin' my feet so high my heels were a-hittin' me in the back.

"This way," Winn screamed, hurdlin' a pile of logs at the far end of the berry patch. I ran over the logs and crashed into the brush and was through it like a rabbit. I was on Winn's heels when he reached th' loggin' road that led to my house.

"Head for my house," I screamed as we sailed like two birds down the broad loggin' road that had a few low stumps just right to catch our toes. And one did catch Winn's toe before he reached the foot of the hill and he must 've scooted fifteen feet flat on his stomach, his lard can rolling ahead.

"The dog's on our heels," I screamed as Winn jumped to his feet and grabbed his lard can. "Come on!"

I passed Winn up when he fell but I didn't hold my gain long. His legs were a little longer than mine and he pulled up beside me and we ran side by side almost a half mile. Then I looked back 'r I might 've stayed beside Winn . . .

"He's behind us, Winn," I screamed. "Can we take to a tree?"

"Lord no," Winn shouted. "Let's get to your house and get a gun!"

How we did it I don't know. I was tired when we started. But you let a mad dog get after you and you see what happens! Just something in you, no matter if your legs are tired, trembly and shaky, that lifts you up and makes you almost fly. And this was a time when I wished that I was a bird with wings! My breath came hard and then it got easy again. And then it came hard again. And just as we reached a pair of drawbars, I saw Winn throw his lard can and sail over 'em like a bird, his body bent forward, his hands almost touching his toes as he went over with the seat of his pants barely missin' th' top drawbar. I turned and threw my lard can at the mad dog and then dove head foremost between two bars, hittin' th' ground on my stomach.

When I got to my feet I looked behind me and here came the mad dog. His shoulders were at an even pace and he didn't look to th' left nor th' right.

"Come, Shan!" Winn screamed. "Maybe we can make it!"

"You'll make it," I yelled. "But he's about to get me!"

Winn shouted to me. "Save your breath. You can do it!"

We had one more pair of bars and then we had to cross over a little gap where the road went over from the hollow to our house. I don't know how I did it but I laid my hand on the top drawbar just as Winn had done seconds before. I hand-sprung th' drawbars and hit runnin' with all the breath I had left and all the strength in my body, for we'd run nearly two miles. The mad dog was twenty feet or less behind me as I climbed the grade between the cliffs in the gap and coasted down the other side to our house. Winn beat me and hit our door like a ton of rocks.

"Mad dog!" he screamed. "Mad dog! Uncle Mick, fetch the gun!"

Winn held to the doorknob to stand up and I pitched headlong on the grass, scootin' on my stomach over the wet grass up to where my head hit the log wall of our house and it jarred me all over. Pa come out o' th' house in his nightshirt with a double-barreled shotgun in his hand.

"Where is he?" Pa shouted.

"We've barely escaped 'im," I grunted from where I lay on the grass. "He come nigh t' a-bitin' both o' us!"

Just then we heard Black Boy start growlin' and Pa took off barefooted around th' house.

"Be keerful, Uncle," Winn grunted with a half breath.

"But I'll get 'im," Pa said. "And in a hurry too!"

We waited in silence for him to shoot.

"Behave yourself, Black Boy," we heard 'im say.

And then the two dogs stopped growlin'.

"What color was that dog?" Pa asked as he came back

around the corner with th' double barrel across his shoulder and a disappointed look on his face.

"White and black," I said.

"That's Jeff Skinner's dog," Pa said. "He's around there a-arguin' with Black Boy over a bone! He's not mad! Mad dogs don't eat! They don't fuss over a bone! They bite!"

"Why did he run us if he wasn't mad?" Winn asked.

"Skinners don't have a dog like that," I said.

"Oh, yes they do," Pa said. "I was over there Wednesday and Jeff showed me his new dog. He's a trained dog for thieves and somebody's been a-gettin' into Jeff's berries."

I got up to my feet and looked at Winn. He stopped leanin' against th' house and looked at me.

"He's trained, so Jeff told me, just to run people," Pa said. "And if one tries to make a tree he really works on 'im as he goes up th' tree. Or if he stops on the road he'll mighty nigh take a leg off. I suppose Jeff and his boys 're a-comin' somewhere along th' road behind him now!"

Winn didn't speak and I didn't speak but I heard his heart poundin' and I know he heard mine poundin' faster than it did when the dog was behind me.

"Don't suppose you boys were in his berry patch?"

I didn't answer for the words wouldn't come. They choked in my gullet. Winn looked down at the ground. I looked at Pa but I didn't see him. I could see Winn in front with his long-handled goose-neck hoe as he went up the path toward the berry patch. And I could feel my hoe handle in my hand as I followed 'im. I could see the green meadow before us we would have to hoe, weed, and clean while Jeff Skinner came to the field each day to see if we were doin' it right. And I could see Eddie and Tom sittin' in the shade and I could hear 'em laughin' at Winn down on his prayer bones. Martha, I could see her too. So pretty she hurt my eyes. Maybe she'd know I'd done it for her.

No Petty Thief

Author's Introduction

"No Petty Thief" is another story that I wrote while I
was in the Navy in Washington during World War II.
But before I tell you how I happened to write it, I must
go back to an August day in 1939 when Uncle Jeff, Old
Op, who lived alone in a cabin on my farm, and I were
working. While we were cutting trees, hoeing tobacco,
or cutting with scythes the sprouts and briers that had
grown up on the pasture fields, Uncle Jeff told us about
a man he had known very well who stole a steam shovel
and carried it to his barn. This was a story that made
Old Op shake his head. He thought Uncle Jeff was
telling a tall tale and I thought he was, too. Uncle Jeff
was a little offended when we didn't believe him.

In 1940 when I visited the county in the eastern
Kentucky hills where my mother's people were born,
I took Uncle Jeff with me. When Uncle Jeff was talking to one of his old neighbors, he asked what had ever
become of the man who stole the steam shovel. We
learned that the man was still in prison. Then I asked
Uncle Jeff's old neighbor some questions and he told
me that same story Uncle Jeff had told Old Op and me.
Although I had written many stories and had had many
published in magazines and two collections of stories
published at this time, I decided not to write this story.
I was sure no one would believe it.

By 1944, when I was serving in the Navy Writers' Unit in Washington, I still had not written the story. However, one day I was talking to the three fellow officers who were my best friends in the Unit: Captain George Campbell, United States Navy, who not only liked to tell a story or listen to one but who wrote stories for many of America's finest publications, Colonel Mandel Jones, and Lieutenant Hudson Long of the United States Army, who had written books. We four were having lunch and, as usual, talking about books and stories. When I had finished telling about the man's stealing a steam shovel, Captain George Campbell roared with laughter.

"He was no petty thief," he said.

Hudson Long said, "That's a wonderful story!"

"Have you ever written that story?" Mandel Jones asked me. He held back his laughter. He didn't believe the story either.

"No, I've not written it," I replied.

"Why don't you?" Captain Campbell asked.

"Why write it?" I replied. "No editor will believe it."

"It's one of the funniest stories I ever heard," he said.

These three friends caused me to write "No Petty Thief." I would have never written this story if they hadn't laughed so heartily and encouraged me to write it. That afternoon I wrote the story. I let the man who stole the steam shovel tell the story, just as Uncle Jeff and his old neighbor had told it to me. After I had finished writing the story, I took it with me to let my commanding officer, Lt. Commander Larry Watkin, read it. When he finished the story, his face beamed with delight. But like all the others, he thought it was a tall tale, the manufactured product of my imagination. He laughed louder than ever when I told him the story was true.

"*Where are you going to send this story?*" *he asked.*
"*I don't know where to send it,*" *I told him.*

Then he told me where he would send it if it were his. But I didn't believe this magazine he mentioned would buy the story. Yet, I sent it to the editor. And I had the quickest reply I ever had on any manuscript. I heard from the editor in three days; he didn't write a word to me. He just sent me a check for "No Petty Thief," and to a writer, this is the nicest reply an editor can send him.

M AYBE IT was the coming of the rains that caused the thing to happen. For the rains came early that November to the mountains. They were cold rains as well as I remember, dropping from the black clouds that raced over the mountaintops like thin-bellied foxhounds. Driven by high mountain winds, they lashed at the treetops, stripping them bare long before it was time to shed their leaves. It was these early rains that stopped the work on the highway they were building through the mountains.

I guess I ought to 've been ashamed of myself, too, for it was the first road ever to be built in our county. It was a real road they were making. They were going down into the deep valleys and around the rocky-walled mountains and over the mountains. Of course we had several jolt-wagon roads, log roads, cowpaths, goat paths, fox paths, rabbit paths, and footpaths. But you couldn't drive an automobile over one of these. And if the contractors could've only finished the big road and covered it with loose gravel before November, we'd a-had a real road that people could've driven automobiles over. It would've been a real road like I've heard a few counties in the mountains already had. I've only heard about these roads. I've never seen one of 'em.

And because we didn't have automobiles in our county, nice spring wagons and hug-me-tight buggies and a lot of fancy vehicles like they had in other counties and in Edensburg, the county-seat town of our county, maybe that is what caused me to do what I did. For I'd stood in the Edensburg streets many times and watched the automobiles roll over the dirt streets and out of town a little ways as far as the turnpikes went. And I watched the buggies, hug-me-tights, and the fancy express wagons. I loved to watch their wheels roll. It was a lot better than the sleds we used, pulled by a team of skinny mules on our hilly farm. The sled slid over the ground on runners winter and summer. And it wasn't any fun watching runners slide and hearing the green dogwood runners grit on the rocks and the hard dry dirt. But it was fun to watch wheels roll. I'd stand and watch them for hours, and what I wanted most in this world was to own something with wheels. Whether I could find level ground enough around our house or not for the wheels to roll, if I had just had something with wheels I could have sat and looked at it for hours, admiring the wheels and the machinery.

Now if it wasn't the rains coming early or my love for wheels and machinery, I don't know what made me do it. I do know that I was raised in a decent home. My pa never used the word "raised" when he spoke about one of his ten young'ins. He allus said he he didn't raise young'ins but he "jerked 'em up by the hair on the head." And Pa was about right in a way. He did jerk us up by the hair on the head but he didn't use any monkey business. He was a strict man in a fashion, belonging to the Old Fashion Church, and when he jerked us up by the hair on the head, he did it in decency and order. That's why I hate what

I've done on account of Pa and Ma. They never learned us to lie, steal, gamble, cuss, smoke, and drink. And when I tell you what happened to me, I don't want you to blame Ma and Pa. They had nothing to do with it. And I'll regret what I done to my dying day just because of Ma and Pa.

As I have said, the rains came early to the mountains in that November. And before the Big Road got too muddy, the men got the machinery out. I mean they drove the dump trucks, the caterpillar tractors, and big graders back to Edensburg where they had started the road from in the first place. But one piece of machinery they didn't take back with 'em was the big steam shovel. Maybe it was because it couldn't go back over the muddy road under its own power, and maybe it was too big for a caterpillar tractor to pull. Maybe they were afraid it would bog down even if pulled under its own power and with a tractor helping it. Anyway, they left it a-settin' there lonesome-like in the November rain.

I didn't work on the road. I had too much work at home to do. For I raised light burley terbacker on the steep mountain slope, where it was too steep to plow with mules but I dug the ground up with a hoe. And every time I had a chance to leave the terbacker, say fer a few hours, I would hurry over the mountain to watch 'em build the Big Road. I liked to watch a piece of machinery working like a man and I liked to watch the wheels roll. One of the pieces of machinery I loved most of all was the big steam shovel. And when it was left alone sitting in the rain, an idear popped into my head. And I went back home to get my monkey wrench.

You may think it was a hard job. But it wasn't too hard. I started taking off the little pieces first. I started stripping it like the wind and rain was stripping a big tree of leaves. Only I had a warm feeling for the steam shovel, and the wind and the rain didn't have any feeling fer the tree. There was something about this steam shovel that I loved. It was a beautiful thing to me. I had the same love touching it that a lot of the mountain boys have fer their pistols. It was the touch of ownership; yet I knew it didn't belong to me. But it would belong to me. It would belong to me even fer a little while. I knew that it was mine. Fer I was going to take it. And I was taking it to a place where I didn't think it would ever be found. And if it was found, it would be a place that it couldn't move out under its own power plus a dozen caterpillar tractors pulling at it.

After I'd taken it apart I started carrying the little pieces over the mountain. Maybe I'd better tell you what kind of strength I have. I'm not a little weakling what you might think. I'm not what you'd call a real tall man. I just measure a bit over twelve hands high, which is a little over six feet. But I'm almost six hands across the shoulders. And my legs above my knees are about the size of tough-butted white oaks big enough for banks timbers and below my knees they are big as gnarled locust fence posts. My wrists are big as handspikes, tapering up to my arm muscles, which are pretty powerful and I'm not a-lying. When I swell my arm muscles they're nigh as big as half-a-gallon lard buckets.

If Brother John was alive today, he could tell you the time when I lifted the back end of a jolt wagon from a chughole when it was loaded with corn. Eif Porter could tell you the time when ten wood choppers, one at a time, tried to lift the butt end of a sawlog and I was the only one that could come up with it. I didn't even get red in the face lifting it, either. I ain't a-saying that I'm the biggest and the stoutest man in the hills, but I ain't a-lyin' when I tell you I'm powerful on a lift. And everybody around home could tell you that I couldn't get a pair of boots big enough to fit me. My legs wouldn't go down into 'em. Too much calf on my leg. I was pretty well fitted fer the task that I was a-going to do.

So I started carrying my steam shovel up over the mountain

and down the other side to my terbacker barn that was built on the steep slope with a high lower side and a short upper side. And I arranged my terbacker that was a-curing on terbacker sticks on the tierpoles all around the sides and the ends of the barn. I had a big open space in the middle of my barn with big brown terbacker walls all around that no human eye could see through. Right in the middle of my barn, I shoveled off a level place to set up my steam shovel.

You'd be surprised how many parts there are to a steam shovel. The best way to find this out is to start taking one apart. It's a lot of work. And it would be awfully hard if a body had to do a lot of watching out fer somebody a-trying to catch him. But I guess the road builders thought a steam shovel would be safe to leave where they had stopped working on the road. They even guarded their trucks and tractors in Edensburg, but they didn't bother to guard the steam shovel or even send anybody back to look about it. So I didn't have anybody around to bother me. And I got in some good time.

If I's to tell you how long it took me to take it down and take the parts apart, it would surprise you. I had it down in less than three days and had taken it apart. And I didn't let any dead leaves gather under my feet when I started carrying it over the mountain. I'd take a big load and I'd never set it down to wind a minute. I'd carry it right to the barn and take it back under the bright wall of terbacker to the place I'd prepared for it.

Believe it or not, I rolled the wheels, one at a time, over the mountain. A steam shovel's wheels ain't too big a thing but they are powerfully heavy. And the beam that holds the shovel is one of the pieces I couldn't carry. So I hitched my mules to it and dragged it like I's a-snakin' a big crosstie up over the mountain. I took all the parts loose from the engine I could, but the main body of the engine I hauled on my sled across the mountain. And the shovel was as big a load as any

man would want to carry, but the worst thing about it was
the durned shovel was so unhandy fer a body to get on his
back. So I hauled that over on a sled, too. I carried all of it or
rolled it but these three pieces. And I got it in the terbacker
barn by myself because I didn't want to let anybody in on the
secret. I carried so many loads over the mountain that I made
a path from where the steam shovel used to be to my barn.
My shoe heels had sunk into the earth since I carried such
heavy loads on my back. But I knew the sun would come out
and dry the leaves and the wind would blow the leaves over
the mountain again and kiver up all the trail. I knew it was
too much of a job for me to go back with a stick or a rake and
kiver up the path that I had made with my heavy brogans. So I
left it to the wind, sun, and the rain to kiver the trail of evidence I'd left behind me.

Then came the happiest hours I ever spent in my life. I was
putting my steam shovel back together. I'd laid out all the parts
careful not to get them mixed. First I put the wheels on good
foundations and got up the framework. And then I used a block
and tackle that I used at hog-killing time to swing up the beam
and the shovel. For I couldn't get up steam and let it work
under its own power in my terbacker barn. I would have set
the barn on fire and lost my terbacker crop and my steam
shovel. I had to do it myself just with the help of the block
and tackle. And I had by the end of November one of the
prettiest things in my barn that ever my eyes looked upon when
it come to machinery.

It was hard for me to believe that I had it. Sometimes it
seemed like a dream. But I would pinch myself as I went to
my barn to look at it again, again, and again to see if I were
asleep and dreaming or if I were wide awake. But I wasn't
dreaming. I was very much awake. Even my wife knew something was wrong with me, since I spent so much time at the
barn. But I told her my terbacker was in "case" and I was taking

it down and handing it off. She had allus helped me at this busy season with the terbacker, but she felt good and thought I loved her more when I told her that I would be able to take care of the terbacker this season. Since she was slender as a beanpole and I was such a mountain of a man, she had allus climbed up on the tierpoles and handed the terbacker down fer me to strip. She was allus afraid that a tierpole would come unnailed when I swung onto it a-climbin' up in the barn. But she didn't have all this worry about me now.

I would go to my barn in the morning and just stand and look at my steam shovel. And I'd think of the power it had. I'd think about the way I'd seen it bite into the dirt and rocks easier than I could sink my teeth into a piece of squirrel or possum. And how it would lift a big bite of dirt and rocks onto the trucks. How graceful the long beam would swing around just by pulling a little lever, and then there was another little lever a body pulled and it would unload its bite into the truck. And how it puffed, blew, and steamed but it never sweated no matter how much dirt and rocks it moved. All day long it worked and it never tired. I guessed it could do the work of a hundred men with picks and shovels. And after it had dug a slice of road, how it would move with huffs and puffs under its own powerful power to a new place and start work. And now I loved to put my hand onto it and I had a sense of ownership and power, a feeling that nearly lifted me to the skies.

But the November rains stopped falling. The winter sun had come out again, making the day bright and warm. Though the ground froze a little at night, it wasn't enough to have stopped my steam shovel's eating away the earth. For the bright sunlight and the crisp wind had made the weather good again for road building. And as I had expected, the road builders came back and brought their machinery. Naturally, they didn't find the steam shovel.

There was a lot of excitement. They had expected it to be

right where they left it. And the day I sauntered over where
I had dismantled the shovel, I found a crowd gathered around
and I joined them to listen to their talk. I never saw a crowd
of men so confused. Nearly every man on this road gang said
the steam shovel had to be taken off under its own power and
there wasn't any road for it to get out except going back through
Edensburg.

They had all been living in Edensburg and not one had
seen a steam shovel rolling through the streets of this little
mountain town. Besides, when it had passed through on its
way to build us a road, all the young'ins in the town had followed it. And the old people who had never seen a steam shovel
had come out to watch it, too. It was the biggest thing that
had ever gone through the town. And now the road builders
argued with each other how the shovel had ever been taken
back through the town, popular as it was among the people,
without someone a-seeing it. One man laughed, said it had
grown wings big enough to fly it over the mountain back to
"civilization." The men said a lot of foolish things like that.
But one of the old men with hard, cold, blue eyes said he
didn't think it was impossible for a man to carry it away on his
back and that was the only way he believed it could have got
away. When he said these words he looked me over. He looked
at my shoulders and my big hands, forearms, and my legs that
were cased in my overalls, stretching them like full mealsacks.
Then he pointed out that the steam shovel tracks didn't leave
the spot, and the ground had been tramped down like a floor
around where the steam shovel had once been. But when he
said these words everybody laughed and said that was impossible, but I could tell from the way this old man acted that he
believed it had been carried away.

I didn't feel comfortable any longer around these men. And
when I snuck away they were talking about bringing in an
"expert" to find the steam shovel. I didn't go back the way

I'd carried the steam shovel fer I thought they might get suspicy and come over the path to my barn. I went down another path and circled out of my way a couple of miles like a fox. Instead of going down to my barn from the north, I came in from the west. And I went in to look at my shovel again. There it was, safe, pretty, and dry. And it was in a place that I didn't think it would ever be found. Even if they had to buy a new steam shovel or stop building the road that we needed so much, I didn't care. It was a toy I loved to fondle and something I wanted to keep forever.

I guess I did neglect my wife and my two young'ins since in these last days I spent so much time at the barn. Rhoda thought my work with the terbacker was coming along mighty slow. She even tried to hurry me to get it off to the market before Christmas. But Christmas or no Christmas, I still fondled my toy. I looked at its beauty and thought of its power and forgot about Christmas although the terbacker was in case and the season was wonderful. Rhodie even threatened coming to the barn and helping me. But I told her not to mind for I had the work well under hand and that I could easily do it myself.

And I guess I would have gotten along someway if it hadn't been for the "expert" the boss-man of the road gang went out somewhere and got to help him find the shovel. And maybe it was the wind and the sun of that early December that were against me. Maybe it was the rain had failed to do its part. I could have laid it onto several things when I heard voices upon the mountain and peeped through a crack in the barn. I saw a big man in front, dressed in good clothes, whose face I'd never seen with the road builders before. He was leading the men like a pack of hounds. He was out in front on my tracks. He was following the path I had made. The rain had never erased my deep shoe prints in the dirt and if the leaves had once kivered them, the sun had dried the leaves and the wind had blown them off again, leaving my path clean as a whistle fer 'em to follow. And that old man with the cold, hard, blue eyes must have put the "expert" wise that a man could carry off a steam shovel. For they found it clean, dry, and purty in my terbacker barn.

No use to tell you more about it. Naturally I was arrested and tried in Edensburg. And people came in great droves to hear the trial. There was a lot in the papers about it. They even had my picture in the papers. And everybody wondered how I had carried away a steam shovel. Even the jurymen would hardly believe it until I told them the truth. When they swore me to God that I could tell the truth that is just what I done. I told 'em I wasn't no petty thief. I told 'em I'd never stole anything in my life before. I told them the whole story how I'd carried it all but three pieces and that I thought I could've carried two of them. Even I had a time convincing the jury against my lawyer's advice that I had done it. But I finally convinced them after the whole jury went to the spot. They followed me over the path to my barn where I showed them the shovel.

If you know the people and the laws in our state, it would've been better fer me to 've kilt a man. I would have stood a better chance of coming clear. Anyway I wouldn't have got but one or two years in the pen even if I hadn't done it in self-defense. But when you steal something, even if it's just a chicken, let alone a steam shovel, you're a gone gosling. Why they let me off with only seven years and a day was, I was honest enough to tell the truth after they found the shovel in my barn. If I'd a-tried to got outen it, I'd been given life. The road builders fit me hard, too, fer they had to build a road to my barn to get the shovel. Not a one of the whole gang was man enough to carry it back.

Miss Anna's Asleep

Author's Introduction

When our daughter Jane was six and it was time for her to begin school, my wife Naomi and I had to make a decision. Since our farm was partly in the Greenup County School District and partly in the Greenup City Independent District, we could have sent her to either elementary school. Both were about five miles from the farm so distance was no factor. We finally decided to send Jane to the Greenup Independent School; Naomi had taught second grade there. But sentiment was not the reason for our decision; the reason was Miss Addie Downes. Miss Addie Downes had taught the first grade at the Greenup Independent School for fifty years. She was a great teacher. Three generations of Greenup people had been her pupils. Many people attribute the good citizenry of the town to the influence of their schools which have been consistently good over the years. But among all the good teachers, the one greatest influence was the first-grade teacher, Miss Addie Downes.

"They got a good start with Miss Addie," everybody said. Since we wanted Jane to get a "good start," the only logical thing to do was to take Jane to Miss Addie for her first year.

One afternoon I drove very early to Greenup to get Jane. I went over to Leslie's Drug Store and bought a paper. Sam and Phil Leslie, brothers, who ran the drug store, had gone to school to Miss Addie. I didn't know the Leslie brothers' ages but their hair was gray. They spoke of her affectionately as Miss Addie. No one in the whole town, unless a newcomer had moved in, ever called her Miss Downes. Everybody referred to her as Miss Addie. After I got my paper, I drove around and parked my car in front of the schoolhouse. The time was April, and the pear, apple, and plum trees and shrubs and flowers were in bloom all over the town, particularly in yards of homes near the school. Now I thought of the days when I had gone to school here. I thought of the thousands of students who had come and gone from this small efficient school.

While I read my paper and thought over the past, I came upon an item in the paper about an elderly teacher's dying in the schoolroom. I thought, what would happen in this town if that teacher had been Miss Addie?

Then, I took a notebook from my pocket and I began to make notes. Here was a story. All I had to do was tie up the real facts of Miss Addie's life with my imaginary reactions of how her death would affect the people in Greenup.

I thought of more as I drove Jane home from school. And after I got home I wrote the story. Many magazines refused this story because it dealt with death. But, since death comes to all of us, why should the subject be taboo? Finally, I was able to give this story to a magazine of high literary value, one which had only a small circulation. Then, I sent the tear pages of this story from a copy of this magazine to the National

Education Association Journal. *However, I didn't think the editors would reprint the story. But I was wrong. They liked the story. When they reprinted it, "Miss Anna's Asleep" reached a million readers who were teachers. Often an author has to fight for one of his stories which he believes is good enough to be published. Not all stories should be of just merely entertainment value. And I felt this way about "Miss Anna's Asleep."*

WHEN MARY McEnnis asked Miss Anna if she could make figures on the blackboard, Miss Anna didn't answer her. Then Mary asked her again, and she didn't answer.

She asked Miss Anna again and again while her little classmates listened. Still there wasn't any answer while she stood there looking at her teacher.

The wind came thru the window in the second story of the Landsburg Grade-School Building and played with the stray strands of hair that escaped the knot at the back of Miss Anna's neck. The wind ruffled the lace collar at her throat. Miss Anna was fast asleep, and this was funny to all the little girls, 16 of them, with pigtails and missing teeth. It was funny to all Miss Anna's 19 boys, too.

"Miss Anna," Mary asked, "are you asleep?"

Not one of the pupils had ever seen Miss Anna go to sleep before. Not one of their mothers and fathers when they were in Miss Anna's room had ever seen her go to sleep. They had told their children what a great teacher Miss Anna was.

The fathers had told their sons not to drop marbles on the floor in Miss Anna's room. For Miss Anna had always made it a rule to throw all the marbles dropped on her floor out the window. She had done that 30 years ago. She was still throwing marbles out the window.

At recesses and noon when Miss Anna escorted her class down the steps, after the other grades had been dismissed, her boys made a mad scramble for the marbles thrown from the windows. Not any of the boys from the upper grades could get them. They were not allowed on the northwest corner of the schoolyard, where Miss Anna's children played.

This was their part of the schoolyard, so the larger pupils could not overpower them at play. Miss Anna saw to this. She protected her pupils as if she were their real mother.

She had played with the grandmothers and grandfathers of the boys and girls looking at her now and whispering to each other about her being asleep. That was before the turn of the Twentieth Century. In those days, she played with the beginners under the same elm tree in the northwest corner of the schoolyard. Only the elm tree was much smaller then.

It wasn't as tall then as the second-story window near Miss Anna's desk. This was the window where the wind was coming thru to rustle Miss Anna's soft brown hair and lace collar. Now the tree had grown higher than the bellspire of the Landsburg Graded School. Its topmost branches towered toward the sky. At least they looked that way to Miss Anna's pupils when they played under its spreading branches in the autumn when the leaves were falling and in the winter when the branches were leafless. They had played under its leafy branches in the spring when the great tree was a green canopy of shade.

"Miss Anna told me she'd shake me if I ever went to sleep again," said little Billy Reed. "Now I ought to shake Miss Anna."

Then the pupils, who whispered when Miss Anna first went to sleep, laughed and talked behind the closed door of their room. It was funny to see their teacher asleep. She looked almost as if she were awake. She was sitting erect in her chair behind her desk. She had sat here and faced so many inhabitants of the town.

She had taught hundreds and hundreds that had moved away. But of the town's population of 2300, she had taught four out of every five of those under 56. A half century had passed since Miss Anna had started teaching first grade in the Landsburg City Schools. She was then a brown-haired and brown-eyed girl of 17.

She often made silent comparisons of the pupils, contrasting daughter, mother, grandmother, and son, father, and grandfather. That was a little game Miss Anna often played, by herself, as she sat at her desk or walked over the room.

"When Miss Anna gets hold of you, she'll make a little lady out of you," a mother often told her daughter. The mother remembered Miss Anna's influence on her. The father often said much the same thing to his son.

Now the pupils of Miss Anna's fiftieth class were whispering and talking out loud about the funny thing that had happened. They had something to tell their mothers and fathers and grandpas and grandmas about Miss Anna. They had something to tell them that had never happened before.

There was disorder in Miss Anna's room. There was more disorder than the pupils had ever seen before. Many remained in their seats. A few went to the blackboard and used chalk to make letters, figures, and marks. Many of them came around Miss Anna's desk and looked at her. They whispered to each other and they smiled, for it was funny to see Miss Anna sitting up straight in her chair with her eyes partly closed and her hands crossed on the table in a position that was familiar to the children.

They had seen Miss Anna sit that way so many times with one hand lying palm down on the table and the other hand, palm down on top of the bottom hand. There was a smile on Miss Anna's lips. This was characteristic too. The pupils had seen her look this way so many times.

Miss Anna had never worn glasses in all her years of teaching. She still had her natural teeth, but they were no longer as white as the plum petals on the ancient plum tree in Zinzer's backyard.

Since this would be Miss Anna's last year of teaching because she would have to retire, the people of Landsburg were wondering who they would get to take her place. They knew she had taught two years beyond retirement age. She was 67, but everybody would have loved for her to teach the first grade 100 years instead of 50. They didn't want her to retire. But it was a rule of the state. That was why it had to be.

A few of the people of Landsburg knew Miss Anna had other ideas. They knew how she remembered every child she had taught down thru the years. They knew how she had kept up with his progress, that she knew about his life and living from the time he had left her class. They had heard her say so many times the reason she loved to teach the first grade was the beautiful, imaginative, unprejudiced minds of the little people.

When she would soon be forced to retire on her $31-a-month pension, some people knew that she planned to start a school of her own and go on teaching. Because Miss Anna didn't have a bank account. Everybody in Landsburg knew this. In her first year of teaching she had made $33 a month. She had gradually increased her salary over the years until now she received the sum of $160 a month.

While Miss Anna's pupils played in the room, laughed, and talked, little Billy Reed opened the classroom door and ventured into the corridor.

"Miss Anna's asleep," he told John Zinzer, a fifth-grade pupil who was passing by. Then he grinned sheepishly. He had told on his teacher. Miss Anna would never let one pupil tell anything on another.

"I try to make good citizens out of my pupils," Miss Anna often said. "It's very important they're started off right."

But when Billy Reed told John Zinzer that Miss Anna was asleep, John looked puzzled at Billy Reed.

"Miss Anna's not asleep either," John said. "She never went to sleep when I was in her room."

Billy walked on down the corridor sliding his hand along the slick cool wall. Then John, thoughtfully, eased the door open to Miss Anna's room. When he opened the door, the pupils were having a great time playing in the room. Billy Reed was right. John knew that he was. Miss Anna was sitting at her desk with a smile on her face. John closed the door and ran to tell Miss Bennett.

"It can't be, John," Miss Bennett said as she hurried up the hall.

"Miss Anna," Miss Bennett said, tapping her gently on the shoulder. Miss Anna didn't answer. "Miss Anna," Miss Bennett said again.

Still there was no answer. Miss Bennett's voice trembled when she dismissed Miss Anna's pupils. She told them to take their books and go home. It was the first time that Miss Anna's pupils had ever gone down the steps without her going with them and guiding them from the school building.

In a few minutes, all of the teachers of the Landsburg Graded School were gathered in Miss Anna's room. When they spoke to her, she did not awaken. She was asleep all right. Pupils in the other grades, when they heard Miss Anna had fallen asleep at her desk, came from their rooms into the corridor. They knew if Miss Anna had gone to sleep in her room, it was the first time anything like this had happened.

When they saw Dr. Torris hurry up the street to the front door, they looked strangely at each other. There was silence among them. Miss Anna had taught all of them. They had been her beginners. She had braided pigtails and tied ribbons and buttoned the little boys' clothes and washed their hands. They stood in deep silence now.

When Dr. Torris came outside her room, his face was white. He too had gone to school to Miss Anna. He always said she was the reason he was a doctor. She had inspired him by talking of helping others and of riding horseback into the hill country to minister to the sick.

When Miss Anna's pupils raced into the streets, without the usual order, telling the people Miss Anna had gone to sleep, people started rushing toward the schoolhouse as if it were on fire. In a few minutes, the news had spread until stores were closed and the schoolyard was filled with weeping people. The parents had come. The grandmothers and the grandfathers came too. White handkerchiefs among them going from their hands to their faces and back again were like the wind moving the wild plum petals in Zinzer's backyard. Only there were more handkerchiefs than there were plum petals.

In a few minutes the ambulance came. Perry Hornbuckle and Thomas Reed rushed upstairs with a stretcher. There was silence when they came down the steps with Miss Anna covered with a blanket.

The wind in the newly resurrected April blossoms on the plum tree in Zinzer's backyard mocked the movements of the handkerchiefs.

Old Op and the Devil

Author's Introduction

When I bought 252 acres of rugged hill land that joined my farm, I discovered a cabin I didn't know was there. In this cabin on a high ridge an old man lived alone. After I talked to him, I asked him to stay on. I had a deed recorded in the county court records for this land, but Old Op Acres had a deed for it in his heart. He knew and loved every foot of land, tree, and rock cliff because he had hunted over it. He had dug wild-roots to sell. In the Sandy River, in the deep valley below the ridge, Old Op caught fish and turtles for food. In spring and summer season he picked wild berries which he ate, canned, and sold. He found wild bees in trees which he cut and got their honey. In the autumn he gathered nuts, a part of which he put away for his own use, and if he needed a few dollars, he sold bushels of hickory nuts and walnuts. He had a small garden for his own use.

Here was an old man who lived like a hermit, and my land was his land. He was very fond of me, for I liked to hear the stories he told. And I was very fond of him because he was a great storyteller. He told me stories about ghosts, hunting, fishing, and about turtles and snakes. He told me how he got tired once and sat down on a log. And when the log began to move with him, he discovered he had sat down on a big snake. Then, he told me that every weed, flower, and tree was put on earth for a purpose and that the blossom, bark, and roots of these had medicinal purposes. He said the proper mixtures would cure any disease he knew about. He had remedies for everything. Old Op was a character.

Once when I was talking to my editor about this old hermit, I repeated a story he had told me about a ghost. I told my editor that I had tried to put this tale into a short story but it was too long. "Sounds like a good novel," he said.

Then, I expanded this short story by adding other stories he had told me. I told something about his life, how he doctored himself with barks, roots, and blossoms of wild flowers. I told about how he lived from the land and how he had observed the life of animals, birds, and snakes. He lived by hunting and fishing. He lived a life as free as the wind. And he enjoyed living alone.

My dog Jerry went with me to visit Op and took a liking to him. He liked him so well that he lived in the cabin with Old Op for two years. He slept with Old Op and he ate at the table with him. Op fixed him a chair which Jerry hopped up in at mealtime. In the autumn, they hunted possums. One day Op told me about the time he and Jerry had met up with the devil. Since Jerry couldn't talk and tell me his version of this story, I had to take Old Op's account. I wrote this story just as he told it to me.

When I had finished writing about Op, I sent the manuscript, The Good Spirit on Laurel Ridge, to my publisher and it was accepted. The story about the devil is one of Op's many stories which I used in this novel.

"**L**ET'S STOP here fer a few minutes, Alf." Op took the mattock from over his shoulder and held it on the ground beside him. "Somethin' happened to me here onct that I'll never ferget!"

"What was that, Op?" Alf was breathing heavily after climbing the steep slope from Sulphur Hollow to Laurel Ridge. They had added to the bulging sack some yellow root ("fer bellyache and sore mouth"), life everlasting ("good fer the asmie"), boneset, toe-each, and calmus.

"Right here is where I climbed on the Devil's back and rode 'im home," Op said.

"Oh, good Lord!" Alf stared at Op standing there with the coffee sack filled with herbs over his shoulder and the mattock in his hand. He looks like some sort of prehistoric man, Alf thought.

"I don't care whether ye believe it or not," Op told him. "I know I'm a-tellin' ye the truth. I climbed on the Devil's back right here one night and he took me home. I'll tell ye just how it happened.

"It was in October and I'd come out here a-possum-huntin' with old Jerry the night before," Op explained. "It might've been two nights before. I'd fetched along a quart of 'simmon brandy. It was a dark night when possums love to stir. There wasn't a wind to shake the dead leaves on the trees and skeer 'em. The air was hot-like and felt like rain. Jerry had treed one possum up a bull 'simmon tree. So I took an extra snort of brandy and scaled up the tree atter it. Throwed 'im down and Jerry sulled 'im. Out Laurel about another hundred yards and old Jerry treed one of the biggest possums I ever saw up a little pawpaw bush. All I had to do was shake 'im from the bush. I put 'im in the sack and I felt purty good atter gettin' that possum. Then I took a real big snort of brandy.

"The next thing I woke up right about here where we're

a-standin' and I was flat on my back and my eye sockets were filled with water. But my clothes were dry. That's the reason I say I might've come out here a couple of nights before the Devil carried me home. I might've been here that long. I know it had poured rain some time atter I'd laid down or my eye sockets wouldn't have been full of water. And that's a sign that I'd never moved till I'd woke up. The wind on this ridge had dried my clothes atter the rain. Old Jerry was a-layin' beside me when I rose up and the water run down my face. The moon was shinin' and poor Jerry looked like a mud dauber, he was so thin in the middle. The possums were a-jumpin' around in the sack. I got up on my feet, wiped the water from my eyes with my shirttail and looked up at the thin little moon above Laurel Ridge. I didn't feel bad at all. I felt purty good. Old Jerry barked and ran circles all around me when I come alive agin. I picked up this very mattock I'm a-carryin' now, put the possum sack across my shoulder and hadn't walked five steps till I met somebody. I thought he was a fox hunter at first!

" 'Howdy, Op,' he said to me. 'Where do ye think ye're a-goin'?' 'I'm goin' home,' I told him. 'Ye've not been there for three days,' he said to me. 'How do ye know?' I ast him, suspicious-like. 'Ye've not been fox huntin' that long, have you, Plack?' I thought he was old Plack Rivercomb who hunts the fox here on Laurel Ridge. 'I'm not Plack Rivercomb,' he said to me. 'Op, look me over. I've never fox-hunted in my life. Several of the fox hunters are my boys and I'm with 'em a lot. Ye know, Op, I take keer of my own. Climb on my back and I'll give ye a lift. I'll take ye home.' I wasn't a bit skeered right then. I thought he was the speret of one of the big timber cutters that had gone on before. But when I looked him over right there in the moonlight, I knowed he wasn't the speret of a man."

"How did you know?" Alf asked amiably.

"Ye never saw the speret of man with a pair of horns above his ears that come out about two feet from the side of his head and bent back like oxbows, did ye?" Op said. "I never saw such horns. How he managed to get through the brush with that pair of horns was a mystery to me. I'd thought when he first spoke to me he was wearing a dark suit of clothes that needed pressing, for the legs of his pants were like big, round, dark-black oaks. But when I looked him over more keerfully I saw he wasn't wearing a suit at all. His skin was somethin' like a bearskin, only the hair was longer. And when I looked at his feet I saw he had the cloven hoof. Whether he was wearin' steel shoes like the giant oxen on Laurel Ridge ust to wear I'll never know. But he was made in the image of man. He walked standin' up and not on his all fours. He had shoulders broader than my cabin door and a big unshaven face somethin' like a bear's. He had a full set of teeth that looked like small white handspikes. He had mule ears he could twitch in the direction of any sound.

" 'What kind of a speret are ye?' I asked, lookin' 'im over. 'I've never seen ye before on Laurel Ridge.'

" 'But I've been on Laurel Ridge many times before!' he said. 'I was on Laurel Ridge before ye were born. And I'll be here atter ye're gone. I'm a speret ye've heard more about than any other speret on Laurel Ridge. I'm the Devil. Get on my back, old Op, and let's get goin'.' 'No thank ye, I'll walk,' I said, nice and polite-like. 'No, I'll take ye home, Op,' he insisted. 'If ye don't ride on my back, ye'll be a sorry speret one of these days.' Then old Jerry, who had whined and barked, inched a little closer to smell of this giant Devil. Old Jerry must've thought he was another harmless speret like so many he'd seen when we hunted at night on Laurel Ridge. But the Devil kicked at Jerry with a mighty hoof that whistled as it cut the air, and if Jerry hadn't been quick on the dodge, he'd've kicked his head clean offen his shoulders! Jerry took off around Laurel Ridge a-runnin' and a-barkin' as I'd never heard 'im before. That's the only time he ever fersook me. And I've never held it against 'im.

" 'Get on my back, Op,' the Devil said, speakin' plain as I ever heard with a voice as big as the roar of waters in April down at Sandy Falls. 'I don't have time to fool too long with ye. I've got business to do. Ye know I'm a busy speret. I never sleep, I go day and night and have to be in a thousand places at once. I'm nowhere else tonight but right here. Ye're not a-gettin' my split personality. Ye're gettin' all the charm I can turn on one of my prospective subjects. I saw ye here sleepin' with puddles of dark rain water in yer eye sockets. Saw ye drinkin' my brew from the 'simmon. So I want to do somethin' fer one of my own.' 'But I have my mattock and my sack with two possums in it,' I said, thinkin' fast. 'That won't add too much to the load I'm able to carry on my broad shoulders,' he said. And he took my mattock in his hand big as a coal scoop, with hairy fingers big as sticks of stovewood. He took the possum sack in his other hand. I leaped upon his back like a squirrel. I took him by the horns and swung my weight up to his shoulders. Put a leg over each shoulder and a hand on each horn. And he started around Laurel Ridge with me."

"That's enough, Op," Alf said. "I don't want to hear any more."

Alf started walking around Laurel Ridge, and Op followed with the sack across his shoulder and the mattock in his hand.

"No matter what ye want to hear, I'm gonna finish. It happened right where we're a-walkin' now. This is the way we come."

"You carry these tales too far," Alf said, walking faster. "I've heard enough. It does something to me."

"What do ye think it did to me that night?" Op answered. "Don't ye think I was nervous? But I thought I'd better ride. I didn't want to take any chances. When a man's old body is planted back on this earth and his speret leaves the old clay temple and journeys on into the next world, he never knows where he's goin' to land. I had to play along with 'im, don't ye see, Alf?"

"I expect so," Alf murmured.

"Now right along here was where the Devil started trottin' with me." Op pointed at the path. "He jogged up and down so I thought he was a-tryin' to throw me off. But I locked my legs around his bull neck and gripped his big horns fer dear life while the fire streaked like lightnin' from his feet. That's the reason I've often wondered if he wore steel shoes like an oxen on his cloven hoofs. And while I held onto his horns and he trotted, there was a great rumblin' among the leaves still a-hangin' on the tough-butted white oaks. I thought all the leaves were fallin' from the trees. Then, suddenly, the Devil changed his pace. He started rackin' like one of the hosses I'd seen young men and wimmen ride around this ridge when I was a boy. 'How do you like yer ride?' said the Devil to me. 'I love the rackin',' I said. When I said this, he changed to a slow pace. And dark clouds started rollin' over Laurel Ridge and hidin' the moon and stars. It suddenly got dark as charcoal and all of Laurel Ridge began to tremble. I could feel it on the Devil's back. All of a sudden the lightnin' flashes cut the dark, thick air. They danced over the Devil's horns till I thought, onct, I'd have to let go.

" 'How do ye like it now?' the Devil ast me. 'I don't like it 't'all,' I said. And he laughed and it sounded like the thunder that was jarrin' Laurel Ridge to its foundations. I heard trees a-splinterin' on both sides of me as the Devil took off in a gallop. I thought he was a-runnin' to beat a great storm that was at our heels. I could hear the rain behind us but I couldn't look back to see. The fire was flyin' in all directions, rain fallin' behind, yet the Devil was gallopin' ahead of the storm. And I was a-ridin' as comfortably as I'd ever ridden anything in my life, with my legs locked around his bull neck and my hands ahold of his horns. He took me full speed right up in front of my cabin and stopped so suddenly his big feet skid twenty feet on the ground, and streaks of fire shot from them. Old Jerry ran from the cabin barkin' and growlin'.

" 'Get away from me, ye mongrel!' the Devil shouted as he kicked at 'im agin. 'Don't try to bite me! I'll kick yer head clean from yer shoulders.' 'If ye kick that dog, I'll dehorn ye,' I said. I would have done it too. I had my knife from my pocket and I'd've really worked on one of his horns. 'Wonderful, Op,' the Devil said. 'That's the way I like to hear ye talk, especially to anyone who has done ye a favor. Allus be that grateful and ye'll be my favorite speret someday. I'll call ye home. I've got a great need fer ye. Get down offen my back, friend!' Well, right there I climbed down offen his back. Right in my own front yard.

"And the Devil gave me my mattock and my sack of possums. He smiled, a-showin' his full set of big white teeth. He looked down at me right kindly, and fer a minute I thought he was gonna pat my head. Good thing he didn't, he'd a probably crushed it. I didn't thank the Devil fer my ride. To hell with him, I thought, that's a friendship that can't do me no good. When I got my gate opened, I looked back to see if he was still standin' there grinnin' his big horse-whinny grin. But the Devil had gone. And with him had gone the thunder, lightnin', splinterin' of trees, and the great roar of the storm among the white oak leaves. The sky was clear agin and the moon and stars were a-shinin'."

"That was some ride," Alf said, looking Op in the eye. "Don't guess you were able to do much sleeping after that.'

"I turned the hungry possums loose, went into the cabin, shelled my rags off down to my shirttail and underwear," Op said. "I went to bed and slept like a log. Got up next mornin' and thought so much about my ride on the Devil's back that atter breakfast I walked back out Laurel Ridge to see how many trees the lightnin' had struck and what the storm had done. Not a tree was split by lightnin' and the 'simmons and pawpaws were all a-standin'. And I decided to myself the Devil was a big bluff. Jist a big wind. If I ever got on his back agin, I would shore dehorn 'im!"

A Ribbon for Baldy

Author's Introduction

As I grow older, I constantly rediscover the beauty of the land where I was born and where I still live today. This valley becomes more valuable and precious to me every day. It has been and still is the source of my work as a writer.

One day as I walked over my land, I remembered that I wasn't the only writer who had explored and used his own backyard for inspiration. Emily Dickinson, Henry David Thoreau, Nathaniel Hawthorne, and Robert Frost are just four who have done so. And so I was grateful to the land for what it had given me as a human being and as a writer.

One day as I stood by the W-Hollow stream, listening to its sound, I thought of Old Baldy. Old Baldy is one of three cone-shaped hills that you can see if you stand on the ridge overlooking the valley. These three hills are independent of the other hills that enclose the valley; they are separate formations and very unusual.

The highest of these hills looked like a giant wigwam. It was part of the first fifty acres my father ever bought. Since much of his farm was pastureland, we needed to use as much land as we could for farming. We had to grow feed for our domestic animals and corn and wheat for our meal and flour. So we had to use the cone-shaped hill. We called it Old Baldy. We cleared Old Baldy from bottom to top. Then I plowed it, breaking the roots with a bull-tongue plow. I drove my team of

178

mules around and around the hill like a corkscrew until I reached the top. Then when I laid off a furrow in which to plant the corn, I began at the bottom and went around and around again all the way to the top, making one long row of corn. It was the longest row of corn in this valley, the longest row in eastern Kentucky, and maybe in the whole country.

When we were asked by our teacher in general science in Greenup High School to write about the most unusual thing we had ever done or seen, I wrote about this row of corn. And I had the most unusual paper in my class. This was one of my themes that I never kept. And now, I went back to this cone-shaped hill which we used to call Baldy and memories of high school days came back to me. Now Baldy and I had time to renew our friendship; I thought about this paper I had written. And one day I sat on a mossy stone under a poplar tree near the base of Baldy and rewrote that theme. Later, my wife Naomi gave it the title of "A Ribbon for Baldy," and I sent it to a magazine where it was accepted as a story. This factual article, which became a story, was written in a day. It was written of experiences I had lived in my association with this piece of earth while I was a student in Greenup High.

T HE DAY Professor Herbert started talking about a project for each member of our General Science class, I was more excited than I had ever been. I wanted to have an outstanding project. I wanted it to be greater, to be more unusual than those of my classmates. I wanted to do something worthwhile, and something to make them respect me.

I'd made the best grade in my class in General Science. I'd made more yardage, more tackles and carried the football across the goal line more times than any player on my team. But making good grades and playing rugged football hadn't made them forget that I rode a mule to school, that I had worn my mother's shoes the first year and that I slipped away at the noon hour so no one would see me eat fat pork between slices of corn bread.

Every day I thought about my project for the General Science class. We had to have our project by the end of the school year and it was now January.

In the classroom, in study hall and when I did odd jobs on my father's 50 acres, I thought about my project. But it wouldn't come to me like an algebra problem or memorizing a poem. I couldn't think of a project that would help my father and mother to support us. One that would be good and useful.

"If you set your mind on something and keep on thinking about it, the idea will eventually come," Professor Herbert told us when Bascom Wythe complained about how hard it was to find a project.

One morning in February I left home in a white cloud that had settled over the deep valleys. I could not see an object ten feet in front of me in this mist. I crossed the pasture into the orchard and the mist began to thin. When I reached the ridge road, the light thin air was clear of mist. I looked over the sea of rolling white clouds. The tops of the dark winter hills jutted up like little islands.

I have to ride a mule, but not one of my classmates lives in a prettier place, I thought, as I surveyed my world. Look at Little Baldy! What a pretty island in the sea of clouds. A thin ribbon of cloud seemed to envelop cone-shaped Little Baldy from bottom to top like the new rope Pa had just bought for the windlass over our well.

Then, like a flash—the idea for my project came to me. And what an idea it was! I'd not tell anybody about it! I wouldn't even tell my father, but I knew he'd be for it. Little Baldy wrapped in the white coils of mist had given me the idea for it.

I was so happy I didn't care who laughed at me, what anyone said or who watched me eat fat meat on corn bread for my lunch. I had an idea and I knew it was a wonderful one.

"I've got something to talk over with you," I told Pa when I got home. "Look over there at that broom-sedge and the scattered pines on Little Baldy. I'd like to burn the broom-sedge and briers and cut the pines and farm that this summer."

We stood in our barnlot and looked at Little Baldy.

"Yes, I've been thinkin' about clearin' that hill up someday," Pa said.

"Pa, I'll clear up all this south side and you clear up the other side," I said. "And I'll plow all of it and we'll get it in corn this year."

"Now this will be some undertakin'," he said. "I can't clear that land up and work six days a week on the railroad section. But if you will clear up the south side, I'll hire Bob Lavender to do the other side."

"That's a bargain," I said.

That night while the wind was still and the broom-sedge and leaves were dry, my father and I set fire all the way around the base. Next morning Little Baldy was a dark hill jutting high into February's cold, windy sky.

Pa hired Bob Lavender to clear one portion and I started working on the other. I worked early of mornings before I went to school. I hurried home and worked into the night.

Finn, my ten-year-old bother, was big enough to help me saw down the scattered pines with a crosscut. With a handspike I started the logs rolling and they rolled to the base of Little Baldy.

By middle March, I had my side cleared. Bob Lavender had finished his too. We burned the brush and I was ready to start plowing.

By April 15th I had plowed all of Little Baldy. My grades

in school had fallen off some. Bascom Wythe made the highest mark in General Science and he had always wanted to pass me in this subject. But I let him make the grades.

If my father had known what I was up to, he might not have let me do it. But he was going early to work on the railway section and he never got home until nearly dark. So when I laid Little Baldy off to plant him in corn, I started at the bottom and went around and around this high cone-shaped hill like a corkscrew. I was three days reaching the top. Then, with a hand planter, I planted the corn on moonlit nights.

When I showed my father what I'd done, he looked strangely at me. Then he said, "What made you do a thing like this? What's behind all of this?"

"I'm going to have the longest corn row in the world," I said. "How long do you think it is, Pa?"

"That row is over 20 miles," Pa said, laughing.

Finn and I measured the corn row with a rod pole and it was 23.5 miles long.

When it came time to report on our projects and I stood up in class and said I had a row of corn on our hill farm 23.5 miles long, everybody laughed. But when I told how I got the idea and how I had worked to accomplish my project, everybody was silent.

Professor Herbert and the General Science class hiked to my home on a Saturday in early May when the young corn was pretty and green in the long row. Two newspapermen from a neighboring town came too, and a photographer took pictures of Little Baldy and his ribbon of corn. He took pictures of me, of my home and parents and also of Professor Herbert and my classmates.

When the article and pictures were published, a few of my classmates got a little jealous of me but not one of them ever laughed at me again. And my father and mother were the proudest two parents any son could ever hope to have.

Tradelast

Author's Introduction

Perhaps you do not have such a place now, but in later years you will have a place on earth that you know so well, to which you are so strongly tied by memories that you can go there and sit and dream back over the hurried years. For me this place is the Plum Grove churchyard and cemetery on a hilltop in the Plum Grove hills. Among these rolling hills I can recall going to the one-room schoolhouse which stood across the road from the church. I can recall the friends of my boyhood with whom I shared work and play. Many of these boyhood friends are now in my stories and books. And I remember all the paths and hills and valleys of this land. This is a land that holds dreams and my early youth, and now holds my dead, for my mother and father and my two brothers sleep in the earth of this land.

Here in the Plum Grove hills, beautiful in all seasons, I have found enough stories that I learned in my youth to fill a volume, Tales from the Plum Grove Hills. And I have often come off this hilltop with the idea for poems and sometimes for an article.

One Sunday afternoon in the spring of 1952, I drove alone up to the Plum Grove hilltop and parked in the churchyard. After placing some of the wild flowers my mother had always loved on her grave and on the other graves of my people, I walked over and around the cemetery and churchyard. Many of the old dreams of my youth were revived. I thought of the time when Big Aaron had given "Old Cief" the tradelast so he, Cousin Penny, little Edd, and I could fish in his pond. And then I remembered how I had gone to see Miss Dovie Maynard and I made up a tradelast for her for the privilege of hunting on her father's large farm. All of this came back to me on this quiet hilltop where quietly slept over a thousand dead.

I was the only living person here and the sun had gone down over the Plum Grove hills in the west and left a patch of red sky behind where the sun seemed to have dropped down into oblivion. Here an eerie twilight, a strange light betwixt bright day and dark night, hovered over the green pasture hills. I could hear cowbells ringing as boys drove the cows home to be milked. Yet, I found myself in a gay mood because I remembered how our giving this older couple these false tradelasts brought courtship and marriage to two people who had known each other all their lives and had never thought of love and marriage. And, I remembered how Old Cief's life was transformed after his marriage to pleasant Miss Dovie Maynard. "This is a story," I thought. "Why haven't I written this story before?"

There was a reason why I hadn't written it. Big Aaron and Little Edd and Cousin Penny and I were afraid to tell about giving them the tradelasts that were false. We were always ashamed of this after we grew up. We never wanted Old Cief and Miss Dovie to know how we had lied to them. But now the years had passed and Old Cief was gone. He slept at Plum Grove with five generations of his ancestors. And Miss Dovie went too, a few years after the death of the man she *loved. Now they would never know. And when I drove back home, I was in a very happy mood because I thought that our tradelast, without an iota of truth or fact, had brought happy years to this couple.*

"I BELIEVE Old Cief'll let us fish in his pond," Big Aaron said. "I think what I've got to tell 'im will make him a different man!"

"It'll be the first time he's ever let us," Little Edd said. "Got the best place to fish in this county. His pond is full of fish. Got so we can't ketch many fish in Little Sandy River anymore."

"Too many people fish in the river," Cousin Penny Shelton said.

"But nobody gets to fish in Old Cief's pond," I said. "He doesn't fish himself. Just keeps the fish there and feeds 'em."

Big Aaron led the way along the winding path across the meadow toward the big, unpainted 100-year-old house where Old Cief Meadowbranch lived with his mother, the last living members of the Meadowbranch family. Cief Meadowbranch was called "Old Cief" by everybody, though Cief wasn't old. He wasn't much more than thirty. It was the way he had always acted.

He'd never had a date with a girl—not that anybody had ever heard of. He wouldn't let people hunt on his land. He wouldn't let anybody walk across his land—not even some of his closest neighbors. He had signs up every 30 feet around the border fences of his 400-acre farm—*No Hunting Allowed.* Then he had these words below: *This Means You.* He even put up signs around his big Meadowbranch Pond: *No Fishing*

Allowed. Below this sign he had in smaller words: *This Means for You to Keep Out.*

Yet we followed Big Aaron, for he was our leader in hunting, fishing, and playing baseball. He was the oldest of our gang, and when he got something in his head, we were willing to listen. He had been right too many times. He had guessed wrong only a few times. We had our fishing poles across our shoulders and cans of bait in our hands. We knew that we were running a great risk as we crossed the Sandy River bottom toward Old Cief's home. For Old Cief was considered by the men around Plum Grove as a dangerous man. He had once sprinkled Uglybird Skinner for hunting on his land. He had shot at us one night when we slipped in to fish in his pond. It was a dark night, too, and he couldn't see us; but his dog barked toward the pond, and he came out into his yard with a pump gun and started shooting. Little hard pellets fell among us, and we took off into the darkness fast as our legs would carry us.

That wasn't all about Old Cief. When the electric company men started to run an electric line up the Little Sandy River, he wouldn't let them cross his farm. Since he owned all the land from the rocky cliffs, where they couldn't put poles down for the line, to Sandy River, he had the line blocked; and all the people above him got mad because they wanted the new-fangled lights and everything that went with electricity in their homes. The telephone company was also trying to get a line beyond Old Cief's farm, but it couldn't get through either. Both lines ran to the edge of Old Cief's farm and stopped. He told company men, both electric and telephone, when either of them set a post on his farm somebody was going to die an unnatural death. And everybody knew he meant what he said.

I thought of all these things and followed Big Aaron toward the house. I gritted my teeth and prayed: "God, don't let Old Cief shoot us." I kept saying this over and over to myself. I don't know what went through Little Edd's and Cousin Penny's heads as we reached the front door. Big Aaron knocked on the door while we waited, and knocked the third time before Cief came to the door.

"What do you boys want?" he growled. "Have you come here to ask to fish in my pond?"

"Not exactly, Mr. Meadowbranch," Big Aaron said. "I got something to tell you!"

"Tell it and begone," Old Cief shouted. "I've worked today! I was eatin' my supper when you disturbed me."

"It's a tradelast, Mr. Meadowbranch," Big Aaron said. "I've known about this for a long time, but I've been afraid to tell you."

"What on earth is a 'tradelast'?" Old Cief asked.

"It's something good somebody has said about you," Big Aaron said.

"Do you mean to say somebody has said something good about me?" Old Cief looked puzzled. "I thought nobody liked me as much as I hate about everybody."

"Not so many people hate you," Big Aaron said. "I know there's one that doesn't."

I looked at Little Edd and he looked at me and we looked at Cousin Penny. We didn't know what it was all about. We didn't know anybody except Old Cief's mother cared anything about him. He has some distant cousins, we had heard, who had moved to Ohio because they'd had a gun battle with Old Cief over a line fence and he had a better gun and sprinkled them deeper than they had sprinkled him. But Old Cief had never killed anybody. He had just sprinkled a lot of people. He went to church and Sunday school every Sunday at Plum Grove Church, where five generations of his people had gone to worship.

"Well, what about this person who thinks well of me?" Old Cief asked, and it sounded kind of sarcastic to me.

"Since it's a tradelast and I'm telling you something good somebody has said about you," Big Aaron explained, "the rule is you got to tell me something good somebody has said about me."

"I don't know anything good anybody has said about anybody," Old Cief said. "If I told you something good somebody's said about you, I would have to lie. I don't do that. And no one better tell me a lie, either. I won't stand for that. I have heard you hunt on posted farms and fish where you pleased. That's not good, so I can't tell you anything."

"In a tradelast you have to do something for the person who tells you, or it's not a tradelast and not any good," Big Aaron said. "But the rule is, you could do me some favor for tellin' you and that would be all right and make the TL good! Besides," Aaron added, "I have to tell you this in secret. My friends here don't know about it."

"Then come out here in the yard," Old Cief invited Big Aaron. "I'd like to know who on earth's been saying anything good about me."

Old Cief walked down the steps and started across the yard, and Big Aaron followed. "We have to be mighty keerful about a TL, Mr. Meadowbranch, but I'll tell you," Big Aaron said. "And then you'll have to do us a favor, for if you don't, something will happen to you. The person who thinks well of you will forget about you!"

Then Big Aaron got up closer to Old Cief than I'd've wanted to be. He talked in a low whisper so that we couldn't hear.

"You don't mean to tell me *that*," Old Cief said soon as Big Aaron had finished. "I've known her since she was a little girl and have gone to Sunday school and church with her at Plum Grove, but I didn't know...."

"Sh, don't..." Big Aaron whispered. "This is a TL, remember! Don't tell it!"

"I forgot," Old Cief apologized. "That stuns me. It's hard to believe!"

"Well, it's the truth," Big Aaron said. "I got the news straight."

"Then I must do something for you," Old Cief said.

Old Cief was all excited. His face was redder than ripened redtop in the Sandy River bottoms. His mouth was like a bow upturned, the ends of the bow nearly reaching his ears.

"You fellows like to fish, don't you?" he asked Big Aaron.

"We'd like to find a place that has some fish," Big Aaron said. "We can't ketch anything anymore in Tygart and Little Sandy Rivers. We're on our way now to East Fork, and I thought I'd stop by and tell you this TL because it's been on my mind for some time, but I've been afraid to mention it to you."

"I've got the fish for you right down there in my pond," Old Cief said. "Big fish and plenty of 'em."

I just couldn't believe it. I looked at Little Edd and his mouth was like an upturned bow, too. Even Cousin Penny, who never laughed, was grinning like a possum, showing about every tooth in his head.

"It's fishing time, all right," Big Aaron said, "and we'd be much obliged to fish in your pond. This will be enough to make the TL binding on your part. My little calendar says now is the time to fish. Even this is the hour to fish. It said to fish tonight until midnight, and it tells the kind of bait to use. We've got it right here in our cans. Instead of going to East Fork, we'll go down to your pond."

"Just a minute, boys," Old Cief told us. "Wait until I go to the corn bin and get you some sacks. You'll need 'em to carry your fish."

"What about your supper?" Big Aaron asked.

"I don't mind a cold supper," Old Cief said gruffly as he led the way to the corn bin. He was a big man, with big brown arms and big calloused hands. Everything was in order in his corn bin. Loose grains swept up for the chickens. Corn nubbins separated from the big ears. This man was a farmer. This man meant business. He was a serious man. But the first time I'd ever seen him smile was when he heard the tradelast Big Aaron had traded him for our right to fish in his pond.

"Good luck, boys," Old Cief said as we started to the pond with our poles, bait, and sacks to carry the fish in.

"And good luck to you, Mr. Meadowbranch," Big Aaron said. "I hope everything turns out all right for you, and that our fishing down at your pond turns out all right for us, too."

"My pond will beat East Fork, all right," he waved to us friendlylike, and we waved back and ran toward the pond. We knew there were fish in that pond.

"Big Aaron, what on earth did you tell 'im?" I asked.

"That's my business," Big Aaron answered slyly.

"Did you tell him the truth?" Little Edd asked.

"That's my business, too," Big Aaron answered.

"You'd better tell him the truth," Cousin Penny said. "If you didn't, it will be our hides. Old Cief is a dangerous man."

"Come on, everybody," Big Aaron shouted. "We get to fish don't we?" The 20-acre pond filled with clear water, water lilies, branch willows, pussywillows, wild snowball bushes, and cat-o'-nine-tails was right before us. We ran to the water's edge, baited our hooks, and cast our lines in a hurry. Soon as my hook went into the water, I saw that Old Cief's fish were ready for some diet other than grain. I pulled up a catfish that bent my pole. Then I yanked out another catfish soon as I rebaited my hook and cast again. After that the fishing really started. We'd never seen anything like it. Fast as we put our hooks into the water we came up with a sunfish or a mud cat with long whiskers and a big mouth. We got some other fish but didn't know what they were. It was six in the evening when we reached the pond. At nine o'clock we had more than we could carry. We had to throw some back in the pond. They weren't hurt, for we'd put our sacks in the edge of the pond and tied them to a willow.

"If it only works, we'll get more of these," Big Aaron said, after we'd sweated under our loads for the nearly 4 miles home.

"What do you mean, 'if it only works'?" Cousin Penny said.

"I'll tell you now," Big Aaron said. "I want to warn you now," Big Aaron said. "I want to warn you so you can run if this fails to work. *But I told Old Cief that John Maynard's old maid girl, Miss Dovie, is in love with 'im!*"

"Oh, oh," Little Edd shouted. "Big Aaron, why did you do it? You know she's not! She never had a beau in her life!"

"We'll be sprinkled sure as the world," Cousin Penny sighed. "If he ever sidles up to her, she'll smack the fire right out of his face! You know that, Big Aaron! Why did you do it? Why did you lie like that? That fishing we enjoyed won't be any fun now. I won't sleep tonight!"

I was standing there thinking about what would happen next Sunday at Plum Grove Church if Old Cief did sidle up to Dovie Maynard, and her not knowing the facts. They'd gone to Sunday school and church together at Plum Grove all their lives, and Miss Dovie had never cast sheep's eyes at Old Cief, and he'd never noticed her. She'd been an old maid about ten years at Plum Grove. They'd never looked at one another. No young men had looked at Miss Dovie, and no girls had looked at Old Cief.

We just stood there resting ourselves, letting the fish move in the sacks at our feet, while we looked at Big Aaron and wiped sweat from our faces.

"You're a-goin' to get us killed, Big Aaron," Cousin Penny repeated. "I won't be able to eat fish for thinkin'. I don't want to be sprinkled. I want to be able to look everybody square in the eye and have a good time. That Meadowbranch Pond is troubled water from now on. We're in for something. If you had to lie to somebody, why did you have to go and lie to the most dangerous man in these parts?"

"How did such a thought ever get into your head, Big Aaron?" Little Edd asked.

"Now let me explain this to you," Big Aaron said. "You know I'm in love with Murtie Griffie. Have been for two years and expect to marry her in two more years, when I'm eighteen. How do you think I found the right girl in my life?"

We stood there in silence and waited for Big Aaron's answer to his own question.

"I've never told you this before," he talked on, "but Jack Truitt had a TL for me. I didn't have one for him. So I traded him my first baseman's glove, a baseball, and bat for the TL. When I sidled up to Murtie, thinking Jack had told me the truth, she slapped my face all right, but it was only a love lick. This makin' a start and sidlin' up to a girl is something Old Cief has never done. A man has to make a start. It ain't natural for a girl to sidle up to the man.... It worked for me, and it might work for Old Cief!"

"But Old Cief Meadowbranch ain't Jack Truitt," Cousin Penny said as we stood under the big, bright moon and heard the songs of the whippoorwills and mockingbirds. "We're fooling with fire when we fool with that man!"

"We've got one square mess of fish anyway," Little Edd laughed. "No matter if we do have trouble ahead of us."

But I thought what Big Aaron had said might work. I thought some more, too. If the tradelast worked on Big Aaron and it had worked on Old Cief, why wouldn't it work on Miss Dovie? Besides, she and her old father, John Maynard, owned hundreds of acres of timberland where there was plenty of squirrels and squirrel season was right at hand.

They'd never allowed anybody to hunt on their timbered acres. Why couldn't I go and do some trading with her? I could at least see how she felt toward Old Cief! If I could work this, I would have done as much as Big Aaron, and, besides, she couldn't any more than tell me to leave.

Monday afternoon Big Aaron had traded his good words to Old Cief, and Monday evening we were fishing in the Meadowbranch Pond. On Tuesday all of us were eating fish, and on Wednesday I was on my way to see Miss Dovie Maynard.

Miss Dovie and her father lived in a large unpainted house down on Big Lost Creek, where acres of grassland slanted up the slopes to meet the timber lines. When I walked over to her big house and knocked on the door, she came. She was tall, with blue eyes that looked straight at me, and her hair was almost as golden as corn silks just before the corn begins to ripen. I wondered why she'd never married, for she was nice-looking. She didn't look old enough to be an old maid, although I'd heard Pa and Mom say she was.

"Miss Dovie, I've got a tradelast for you," I said. "It's been bothering me for some time. Do you have one for me?"

"No, I haven't," she said with a little laugh.

"*Somebody has said something very nice about you,*" I said. "*I'll trade it to you if you'll let me hunt squirrels on your land this season!*"

"Sure I will let you," she said, laughing more than ever. "I'd've let you hunt squirrels before if you'd come and asked me. You're my neighbor, Shan, and I've seen you grow up. I know you'll be careful with a gun in the pastures where we have livestock, and that you won't build a fire and go off and leave it. So I'll let you hunt, but I would like to have the tradelast. I never got one in my life."

When I told her that Mr. Cief Meadowbranch was sweet on her, her pale face got red and her lips curved in a smile. It didn't make her mad. It made her happy.

"Well, I didn't know that," she said. "I've known 'im all my life and went to school with him, and he never looked at a girl. I've wondered why he never. I've gone to church and Sunday school with him at Plum Grove all my life, and he's never smiled at me. He has queer ways, but I'll say that he's a gentleman, and it's nice to know he does think well of me."

I just couldn't say another word for thinking how it would work the coming Sunday. Only four more days, and we'd know how this thing worked. I stood there and looked at Miss Dovie, and she looked at me and smiled. I'd never seen her, in all the years since I could remember, smile like she was smiling now.

"Yes, you can bring your friends, too, when you hunt on this land," Miss Dovie said as I went backwards, turned around, and took off toward home.

Sunday morning when I went to Sunday school, Little Edd, Big Aaron, and Cousin Penny were already there. I saw Pa, Uncle Mart Shelton, and John Howard get together under the big white oak and I overheard them talking about "fish." I looked at Big Aaron and he looked at me, and Little Edd looked at Cousin Penny and then they looked at Big Aaron and me. Our faces didn't get red then. Not until we saw Old Cief Meadowbranch drive up the hill in his old car, and it was washed and shined more than any fancy bridle I'd ever seen. Old Cief was dressed fit to kill, too. Suit was pressed and there was a red rose in his coat lapel. Mrs. Lucy Meadowbranch, his mother, was sitting beside him. Old Cief was wearing a little square straw hat, too, with a flower-colored band around it. He'd never come dressed like this before. When Pa, Uncle Mart, and John Shelton saw Old Cief, they stopped talking about fish and looked at each other.

But this was not it. Nothing had happened yet. When Miss Dovie Maynard came, driving another old car that wasn't shined at all, she was dressed as I'd never seen her before. She was wearing a pretty straw hat with a broad black band around it that crisscrossed and fell over the brim. She was dressed in white, and there was a ribbon sash around her wasplike waist. She was tall, and when she got out of the car and helped her father out, I thought Miss Dovie was one of the prettiest women I'd ever seen. Everybody looked surprised.

"Gee, what's a-goin' on here?" Big Aaron said. "I expected to see Old Cief—but look at Miss Dovie!"

Then Big Aaron smiled, and Little Edd smiled. Cousin Penny grinned like a midnight possum, and since I knew more than the other fellows, I just stood there and watched Old Cief. I never saw two people look at each other like they did. They looked at each other and spoke in soft words, and their eyes seemed to speak, too. Big Aaron jumped up in the air and cracked his brogan shoes together twice. Little Edd slapped me on the back until it hurt, and Cousin Penny grabbed Little Edd by the shoulder and spun him around and around.

This was the beginning of the talk for the whole summer at Plum Grove. Old Cief changed his place in the choir. He'd always stood among the men, between Uncle Mart Shelton and John Howard, but now he hung around the women, near Miss Dovie. And when Old Cief sang this Sunday, it was something to hear. When we were singing "Rock of Ages," I could see the big rock cliffs where the Sandy River swerved against the mountain near Old Cief's farm. When he sang, I heard a voice prettier than the voices of the mockingbirds and whippoorwills in the sycamores at nighttime.

The following Sunday Old Cief took Miss Dovie home, and everybody talked about it. Everybody thought Miss Dovie and Old Cief meant business. My Mom and Pa went so far as to wonder what Miss Dovie and Old Cief would do when they got married—if they'd go to his home or to her home, and what he'd do with his 400 acres of fine farming land, and what she'd do with her 1,000 acres of good grazing and timberland . . . wondered if they had a barn big enough to hold all their cattle when and if they put them under the same roof. It seemed funny to everyone—after all the years they'd known each other—they had fallen in love so suddenly.

One night when Big Aaron was flipping out catfish fast as he could bait his hook and throw it back in the water, he said, "We wouldn't have been able to do all this if it hadn't been for me."

"You're takin' all the credit," I said. "On Wednesday after the Monday in June that you gave your TL to Old Cief for rights for us to fish in this pond, I went to Miss Dovie with a TL from Old Cief, and she gave us rights to hunt squirrels on her 1,000 acres of timber. And that's why she was all dressed up that same Sunday Old Cief came all dressed up!"

Well, you should have heard Little Edd and Cousin Penny laugh. They slapped me on the shoulder, and they were proud. Big Aaron didn't say too much, for he always wanted to lead our gang.

"That's wonderful, Shan," Big Aaron finally admitted.

Before the end of August—just two months after the trade-last—Old Cief's mother passed away suddenly. Then Old Cief had more friends than he had ever had in his life. There was a big funeral. Since Big Aaron, Little Edd, Cousin Penny, and I had learned to like Old Cief, we went to the woods and picked armloads of wild flowers and brought them to the church while other people made big wreaths of flowers from their yards and bought them already made from the florist. When Old Cief and Miss Dovie saw the wild flowers we brought, they were deeply touched.

After the death of Mrs. Meadowbranch, Old Cief was lonely. His mother had never been very friendly, and now people began to think that she was to blame for Old Cief's peculiar disposition. He began to change even more after her death. People got to know him better. He began to take an interest in church affairs, and we heard he was giving more to the church. So no one was surprised when in early September it was announced in the church that Dovie Maynard and Cief Meadow-branch would be united in marriage on October 14.

"See what tradelasts will do, don't you?" Big Aaron whispered to me.

By the middle of September, Old Cief let the electric line go through his farm, and all the people at Argill rejoiced and wondered why he'd had such a change of heart. The manager of the telephone company, Mr. Rufus Windrow, after hearing about the electric line going through, drove his car to the Meadowbranch farm and found Old Cief plowing and singing in Big Sandy River bottom. Old Cief gave his permission to put the telephone line across his farm without cost. Old Cief had his house wired for electricity, and before he started dating Miss Dovie I heard him say once that he'd as soon have as many copperheads tied by the tails to each other and strung over his house as to have the same number of feet of electric wires. Now he even went so far as to have a telephone put in his house and to have the house painted.

Old Cief then bought a new car, and when he brought Miss Dovie to church and Sunday school on Sundays, he and Miss Dovie didn't take up as much room in the front seat as it should have taken for one. She really sat close to Old Cief, and she put her arm around his shoulder. Mr. Maynard rode in the back seat. It made Big Aaron, Little Edd, and Cousin Penny and me feel good that it had happened like this. We talked about it while we thinned the fish in Meadowbranch Pond or we hunted possum, squirrels, coons, rabbits, quail, and pheasant in the Maynard woods. Old Cief told us that we could not only fish in his pond, but we could hunt on his land as well.

By October 14, two frosts had fallen. But we knew what Old Cief and Miss Dovie would like. Big Aaron, Little Edd, Cousin Penny, and I went over the hills searching for wild flowers that the frosts hadn't nipped. We found armloads of fare-well-summers, white and purple, wild asters, goldenrod, and we gathered bright leaves and cones of ripened shoe-make berries and wild bittersweet, and we decorated the Plum Grove Church as it had never been decorated for a wedding before. Mom, Aunt Lydia Shelton, and Mrs. John Howard helped us arrange our decorations. We climbed ladders and put flower chains, wreaths, bouquets all over the place.

Where we made our mistake on the day of the wedding was going to Plum Grove Church at our usual time. Other people went earlier to get seats. Finally there wasn't even standing room. Never had any funeral or wedding or basket dinner on the ground brought this many people. The electric people and the telephone people came, too. The Argill people who had got electricity into their homes came. All the Plum Grove people came. There was just enough room at one of the windows for our four heads. It was the window closest to the altar. And we saw our first wedding. There'd been other marriages at Plum Grove, but we hadn't seen them.

"Just think—if it hadn't been for us, this wouldn't've happened," Big Aaron whispered to us.

"Shucks, I don't care so much about the weddin'," Cousin Penny whispered as they were pronounced man and wife, "but look what we got for a tradelast."

Not long after the wedding, I was going past Miss Dovie's house, and she called to me. When I went over, she said, "I never did thank you enough for that TL. When Big Aaron told me last week that you had made up the story so that you could hunt on my land, I knew it was he who was lying to me. He was just jealous of you—he didn't want you to get so much credit. But I understand and I can never thank you enough."

Her eyes were shining so, all I could say to her was that I thought tradelasts were wonderful things. And I do!

Fight Number Twenty-five

Author's Introduction

Writers get to the very heartbeat and pulse of America through our people in the country, village, small town, and the large city. I have found more colorful characters in the country, village, and small town than I have found in the large city. Perhaps I can show you what I mean.

Have you seen a vast forest where the trees are close together? They grow tall and much alike. But in fields where there are small clumps of trees, they grow up in a dozen different ways for they have more freedom in which to grow. Now, isn't this true of people?

In this story the heroes are Eddie Battlestrife and his dog Buck. Eddie told me this story, and I wrote it just as he told it to me. I cannot tell you any more about the story except that it sold to the first magazine I sent it to. Since I cannot tell you about writing this story I would like to tell you something about the man who told it to me.

Eddie is one of the most colorful men I have ever known. Eddie is from an unusual family, too. He is one of sixteen children. There were five sets of twins. Eddie is a twin. He was born on a farm in these eastern Kentucky hills. High schools didn't exist close to him. Eddie grew up working hard, with his brothers, sisters, and parents. They had to work hard to make a living.

Eddie moved to Greenup, Kentucky, in 1911 when he was a young man and established the first garage ever in this town. Maybe operating a garage for fifty years and living in a Kentucky town of 1,200 people doesn't sound very exciting to you. But Eddie found excitement because he lived it.

The first time I remember him, I was fifteen years old. I was working for a contractor who was paving the streets in this town. This was in 1921–1922. In those days we mixed our concrete in a big mixer which was run by a gasoline engine. When the engine stopped, all the workers stopped. My job was to feed the mixer cement, sack after sack. The first time it stopped, the contractor's two mechanics couldn't get it going. I said, "Get Eddie Battlestrife." After trying again to start the engine, Mr. Pancake, the contractor, sent me to get Eddie. When Eddie came, he didn't bring any tools. He smiled at everybody, then he said, "Watch her start, boys." He waved his hand over the engine. Then he gave the crank a turn. The engine sputtered, groaned, then began running like a new engine. Eddie laughed until he could be heard from one end of Main Street to the other. And everybody laughed except Mr. Pancake, who stood there shocked, looking at Eddie. Three more times I remember we got Eddie to start the concrete mixer. All he had to do was walk close by and wave his hand.

Eddie never smoked a cigarette in his life. He never took an intoxicating drink. He played baseball for the sandlot as a boy, later on the small-town team. Still later he played on city teams. He played first base, and he was also an excellent pitcher. He was a long ball hitter too. I saw him hit the longest ball I have ever seen hit. The bases were loaded too. He knocked the ball out of the diamond over a pond and the top of a tall sycamore into a green grove of trees on the Ohio River bank where wild honeysuckle grew. We couldn't measure the distance, for we couldn't find the ball. He played baseball until he was fifty years old. If big-league baseball had been then what it is today, Americans who follow sports would have known the name of Eddie Battlestrife.

Eddie has been a hunter all his life until recently. He has never owned less than a half-dozen hounds. He has hunted squirrels, rabbits, and birds, too. And Eddie's hounds have treed wildcats. And the wildcat in the story was caught on my farm.

Once in autumn one of his hounds smelled under a stump in Sulphur Spring Hollow on my farm. The hound began to dig and bark. Eddie pushed a stump over and here he captured alive two of the largest rattlesnakes ever taken, dead or alive, in this part of Kentucky. He has trained dogs and sold them over all parts of America. And this story, "Fight Number Twenty-five," is just one of the many hunting stories he has told me.

I'D JUST taken my first shipment of hides to the Greenwood express office when Hade Stableton saw me.

"Eddie—hey, you Eddie Battlestrife—just a minute," Hade hollered at me. "I want to see you!"

"Make it snappy," I yelled. "I want to get this batch of hides on Number Three."

I didn't want to fool with Hade. For every time he'd ever stopped me in his life, he wanted to borrow something from me or he wanted me to do something for him.

"Eddie, I had bad luck last night," Hade grunted soon as he reached me.

"What happened?" I asked.

"Lost my good tree dog, old Rags, and a hundred dollars to boot," he sighed. "You caused it, Eddie!"

"How did I cause it?" I asked him.

"Remember that big wildcat you catched out on Seaton Ridge?" he asked me.

"But what does that have to do with your losin' your best tree dog and a hundred dollars?" I asked. "That wildcat went to West Virginia."

"West Virginia!" Hade said. "That wildcat's right up here at Auckland in a cage. I wish that wildcat's hide was among this batch of fur you're expressin'. I'd be a lot better off."

"How'd that wildcat get to Auckland?" I said. "I sold 'im to Elmer Pratt."

"You know who's got the wildcat now?"

"No, I don't."

"Jason Radnor's got 'im," Hade told me.

"Jason Radnor?" I said.

"Yep, Jason Radnor's got 'im," Hade said, shaking his head sadly. "He's got 'im in a big cage. And you pay a dollar to get in to see the cat fight a dog. If you fight a dog against the cat, you pay five dollars! And there's plenty of betting a-goin' on. Old Jason will cover any bet that the cat will whip a dog. Now he's even giving odds. Last night bets went up to five hundred dollars. Jason covered everything that the men bet against his cat!"

"I sold that wildcat to Elmer Pratt for fifty dollars," I said. "I don't need a cat. I didn't want to keep 'im. I could get more for 'im that way than I could for his pelt."

"I know it's bad, Eddie," Hade said. "But I thought I'd tell you! I thought you ought to know about it."

"Yes, I'm glad you told me," I said, as I began thinking

about what the wildcat had done to Hade's dog. "I need to know about it. Where do they have that cage?"

"Over the hill from the slaughterhouse where we used to fight our game roosters. But listen, Eddie," Hade went on to warn me, "if you're thinkin' about a-takin' old Buck up there and fightin' that cat you'd better be keerful! I'm a-tellin' you, Eddie! It looked like easy money to me. And I went atter it. Old Scout kilt many a wildcat too. But he never fit one like this cat! He'll never fight another cat! Scout was the nineteenth dog the wildcat's kilt. Boys told me up there last night that old Jason was a-feedin' the wildcat beef blood to make 'im mean. Never saw a meaner cat in my life! Didn't hardly get old Scout in the cage until the cat sprang on him and laid open his side until you could see a whole panel of his ribs!"

"But that didn't kill 'im?" I said.

"Nope, but the old cat spat 'im with the other paw," Eddie said. "That finished the best dog I ever had! Had to give a man five dollars to take Scout out behind the house and shoot 'im to put 'im outen his misery. Guns barked all the time I was there. Had to take the dogs that fit the cat out behind the house and polish 'em off."

"I'd fight that wildcat myself," I said, as I thought about the poor dogs the cat had mangled. "I'll go in the cage with it!"

"Somebody'd haf to polish you off, too," Eddie said. "Now don't get riled. Don't get worked up and lose your head. If I'd a-knowed it would've upset you like this I wouldn't have told you!"

I stood a minute looking down at the toe of my shoe. I thought about the October night when old Buck put the cat up a tree and the way he ran it, full speed like he's after a fox. That was the way Buck had put many a coon up a tree. And just as soon as he treed, I hurried to the tree, thinking he'd got me a coon. But when I reached the place where he was barkin' up a great saw-timber-sized oak with branches big enough for crossties sprangled out from its bushy top, I knew it wasn't any coon. I hardly had to use my lamp, for the big wagon wheel of an October moon was as bright as day and flooded the fields and woods with light. And the wind had whipped enough of the rich wine-colored leaves from the tree so that I could about see over every limb. I walked around the tree looking up and spied the old cat, stretched out, his belly against a big flat limb. He didn't look worried to me. He looked like a cat that was full of confidence. He was a pretty thing a-layin' up there on the limb with his head a-stickin' over and his eyes shining like wind-whipped embers on a pitch-black night.

"Buck, you won't fight 'im," I said to myself. "I'll take care of him, myself." So I went up the tree with my lasso rope. The old cat didn't mind my climbing up there. He laid perfectly still. He was a-takin' himself a good rest. Buck had crowded him pretty hard in the chase. He didn't let him get to the Artner rock cliffs. That was where the wildcats denned. I climbed up at about the right distance and hung my lamp on a twig. I looked for the right opening to throw my rope so I wouldn't hit a limb and scare the cat and make him jump from the tree. I didn't want Buck to fight this cat; I wanted to take 'im alive. I found the right opening. I steadied myself and I threw my lasso.

Guess I was lucky. It went around his neck and I jerked the slack as the cat jumped. But I had him. The more he jumped the tighter the rope drew around his neck. And when his long red tongue popped outen his mouth, I drew him up to me, some weight at the end of the rope. I took him from the tree and released the lasso enough to give him enough breath to keep him alive. I tied his feet with the cords, good and tight. I kept the lasso tight enough not to give him too much wind. I put the wildcat under my arm and carried him to Blakesburg.

Old Buck wasn't satisfied because he didn't get to fight the cat, and he trailed along at my heels a little disappointed. But

I knew this was a good catch for one night. It was more than a coffee sack full of dead possums, coons, polecats, minks, weasels, and foxes. If you hunt in these woods, fifty dollars for one night is not to be sneezed at. And it made me the most respected hunter in Blake County, for I was the only man that had ever gone up a tree and took a wildcat with my hands and carried him home in my arms. People knew that I did it, for I'd done it many times before. Older hunters than I was had seen me do it. I took the wildcat home, put him in a cage, and when people passed along the street, they'd come to look at him. And it pleased me when they walked over to see what kind of a looking man I was, just a little, slender, beanpole-sized man with a scraggly beard, that could go up a tree and catch a wildcat.

"Eddie, I'm a-tellin' you not to fight old Buck against that cat," Hade said. "If you'd see that thing cut a dog all to pieces once, you'd never go up in the tree and take him down any more. You'd lose your nerve. The way my poor old Scout run to the side of the cage, looked at me, and cried like a baby," Hade's voice changed until I thought he was crying, "I'll never be able to forget."

I couldn't stand to see that, I thought. I love dogs too well. But I didn't say another word to Hade. Thoughts were running through my mind. I walked into the express office and left Hade standing.

"Remember, Eddie, that my dog was the nineteenth dog that cat had kilt," Hade warned me. "Remember, Radnor'll take your money and—"

I didn't hear the rest of his words. I knew what I was going to do. I knew Buck or I, one, would fight the cat. I didn't want it a-killin' any more dogs. And I knew that I'd like to fight Jason Radnor to even up an old score. I didn't care if he did weigh two hundred and ninety. I hardly knew what I was doin' when I expressed my batch of hides. I went to the First and Peoples Bank and drew out every dollar I'd ever saved.

When I got home, I went over to the corner of the house where I had old Buck tied.

"Buck, one of us has to kill a wildcat tonight," I said. "Do you think you can do it?"

Old Buck looked up at me with his big, soft, brown eyes. Then I unsnapped his chin and started across the yard. I was on my way.

"You're not a-goin' a-huntin' this early," Mollie said when she saw me leading Buck across the yard.

"Yep, I am," I said. "There's a wildcat that's a-killin' a lot of dogs and we want to get 'im."

"Do be careful, Eddie," Mollie warned me. "If it's that dangerous and old Buck trees it, don't you go up and take it from the tree."

"I'll promise you I won't take it from a tree," I said.

I wonder if old Jason will remember me, I thought, as I walked toward Auckland, a distance of twelve miles.

When I reached the shack down the hill from the slaughterhouse there was a man ahead of me with a big English bull.

"There's the dog that'll kill that damned wildcat," a beardy-faced man said, pointing to the big broad bulldog.

The beardy-faced man looked at old Buck, then he looked at me. Buck wasn't a big dog. And he looked pinched in two, for I hadn't fed him anything. I didn't want to feed 'em anything before a fight. Buck smelled blood and trouble. He held his tail down as if he were about to spring at something. Then I heard a pistol go off behind the house and I knew another dog was finished. Buck was on his mettle, for he didn't know exactly what was taking place. I pulled my hat down low and got my six-hundred-odd dollars ready.

Soon as the big red-faced man ahead of me had paid the five dollars to fight his bulldog, I stepped up to the entrance.

"Say, feller," said the tall, hatchet-faced man at the door, "you don't aim to fight that old dog against this wildcat, do you? He's not as big as the wildcat!"

"I want to fight the dog or fight the wildcat myself," I said, and then I gave a wild laugh.

The man looked at me with his black, beady eyes like he thought I was crazy. But he let me inside the shack.

It was a big room filled with men and a few dogs. Over at the far end of the room was a big wire cage. And inside the cage lay the same old wildcat that I had taken from the oak tree on Seaton Ridge. He was a-layin' there as peacefullike, just like any cat, with his head across his paws, as if he wanted to sleep and the men and dogs wouldn't let him. He looked just as mean as he did the night I carried him back to Blakesburg. His big tushes hung out over his lips. And his whiskers looked like old Davey Burton's handle-bar mustache. Beardy-faced men, with mean-looking eyes, stood back and looked at the cat. I led Buck up to the cage where he could get a whiff of the cat. I looked down to see what Buck thought. All he did was jerk his tail. He never even growled.

When the big, clean-shaven, well-dressed man led his bulldog up to the cage, the bull tried to break through to the cat. He trembled all over, growled, and scratched the floor. When he barked, the slobbers flew from his big mouth.

"I'm a-puttin' up a hundred dollars on that dog," a man said. "What odds you givin'?"

And then the bets started. I looked over against the wall and there sat big Jason Radnor behind a table, counting out money to cover the bet. Since the cat belonged to Jason, no one but him was allowed to bet on the cat. Jason covered all the money that was bet on the dog, giving three-to-two odds. It was a funny way to bet, and we'd never bet that way at rooster fighting. And I guess that's why everybody wanted to see the cat killed. Jason was raking in the money. But I wanted to see the cat killed because it was killin' the dogs.

"Jason's got a gold mine with that cat," said a tall lantern-jawed man who was standing beside me.

And while the greenbacks were shelled out on top of the

table, for the bulldog was a good bet, Jason pulled money from a drawer and covered each bet. I watched Jason to see if he was looking at me and if he recognized me. But he was too busy betting and making money to recognize anybody. He was sitting there with all that money around him, and I knew this kind of betting was better than playing poker on Sundays or spitting at cracks. Jason was in the money.

"Say, mister, what have you been a-feedin' that bulldog?" asked a short, dark-complexioned man.

"Beef blood and beef bones," the owner said. "I've been a-feedin' 'im that and getting 'im ready for this fight ever since Radnor first brought the cat here!"

"I'll bet a hundred then," the man said.

Jason covered his hundred while the bulldog charged at the chain.

"All bets in?" Jason asked.

There wasn't any answer.

"Let 'im in the gate, Little Man," Jason said.

A little man with a scattered, heavy beard on his weather-beaten face unlocked the cage door. And the big man patted his dog on the back.

He's a good-lookin' bull to be slaughtered by that cat, I thought.

"Take 'im, Buck, and good luck!" the man spoke with a trembling voice as he unsnapped the collar and the bulldog charged full force toward the cat. As the bulldog charged at its throat, the cat leaped high in the air, and when it came down on the dog's back, it raked a paw around his slats, his big claws, longer than a tack hammer, sinking deeper and deeper as the bulldog groaned.

"There goes my money," a man shouted.

"There goes all our money," the tall man said. "Damn, I wish we'd get a dog that could kill that hellcat. I've lost over a thousand dollars in this dang hole."

I didn't listen to all the men said. I looked down at my Buck. He was moving his tail like a cat does when it sees a mouse and gets ready for the crouch. When the poor bulldog got the cat's claws from his ribs, he came over to the wire and cried like a baby. I never heard more pitiful crying. It hurt me through and through to hear it.

"He's through," a man said. "When they do that, they've had enough. Take him from the cage."

He didn't look like he was clawed up too badly until he came from the cage.

"Mister, you'll have to have Sherman to polish 'im off," Little Man said. "He's through. If you don't have 'im finished, he'll die by degrees."

When the well-dressed man led his bulldog out behind the house to have Sherman polish him off, another tall lanky man from Culp Creek came up with a big mountain cur. He was a long dog with a mean black eye.

You might not get to fight the cat, Buck, I thought. If I were betting, I'd bet on this dog.

"What have you been a-feedin' this dog, mister?" a little stooped-shouldered man asked.

"Corndodger," the cur's owner said. "Just what you feed a good dog."

"I was raised on it, mister," another man said. "I'm bettin' fifty on your dog!"

"Looks like a good bet to me," a tall lanky man with fuzzy chin whiskers said. "I like his build. Listen to his growlin' at that cat! Sounds like low thunder!"

But the bets didn't go as high as they did on the English bull. I looked over at Jason's table and I didn't see the stacks of greenbacks like I'd seen there a few minutes before. And just as the last money was in and Jason was covering it, we heard a pistol fire twice. The English bull had been polished off. And the big mountain cur, with his bristles raised on his

back like jutted rocks along the top of a winter-bleak mountain, charged against the chain to get to the cat.

"Ready to go, Little Man," Jason said. "Turn 'im in."

The beard-scant, weathered-looking little man who tended
to the cage unlocked the door, and the tall man let the big
cur inside and unsnapped the collar. When the cat saw this
big black mountain cur, he never rose to his feet but laid flat
on his back as the dog charged, and just as the dog started
over for the cat's throat, he ripped into him from beneath with
both hind feet. The cur whined, fell over, got up again, and
whined as pitifully as a small baby crying. He walked slowly
to a corner of the cage—I couldn't bear to look at him. I wanted
to get into that cage so bad I could hardly stand it.

"It's a shame," one of the men said, "to fight good dogs
against that murdering wildcat. You can feed 'em beef, beef's
blood, corndodger, and anything you want to feed 'em, but that
doesn't make any difference when it comes to a fight. Not one
dog has stayed with that cat three minutes!"

"Lost again," another man said, not paying any attention to
the poor cur that had lost his life. "Lost another fifty bucks."

Sighs went up from among the mean-eyed men when Little
Man pulled the cur through the door. He was awful to look at,
and to think of him now makes me mad. Old Buck looked
at the poor cut-to-pieces cur disgustedly.

"Get 'im to Sherman quick," Little Man said. "Let 'im polish 'im off soon as he can, to put 'im outen his misery."

We saw two more fights. We saw the cat lay on his back
and cut a pretty shepherd to pieces. There wasn't much betting
on this fight, although the shepherd came the nearest getting
to the cat's throat of any of the dogs. And there was a big
brindle bulldog that the cat seemed to hate more than any
dog that had been turned in. That bull never even got close
to the wildcat. He had him cut to pieces before he got halfway
across the cage. What was left of him was dragged outside by
his master, a well-dressed city man from Auckland.

"I'm glad it's over," said a big fat man with a handle-bar mustache. "I'd rather see cockfighting, a boxing bout, or a wrestling match any old time as to see these good-looking dogs go in there and get ripped up."

"Yep, I'd rather go with my wife to the movies as to slip out here to this unlawful place and see this," said the tall man who had bet heavily on every fight against the cat.

"It's a wonder this place ain't raided by the law!"

"But it's not over yet," I said loud enough so the men could hear me.

They were mixing around and intermingling in the crowded room, getting ready to leave. And I couldn't blame them for that. I'd smelled enough and I'd seen enough for one evening. The smell in the shack was awful. The crowd was awful, too.

I couldn't understand how anybody could enjoy seein' dogs cut to pieces by a wildcat.

"But that dog can't do anything," one man said. "That cat'd kill 'im before Little Man got 'im inside."

"Little Man ain't a-puttin' this dog in," I said. "I'm goin' in the cage with 'im myself."

"What's that I hear?" Jason said from over in the corner, as he stacked his money away.

"I'm going to take old Buck in myself," I said.

"Are you crazy, feller?" Jason said. "Don't you know if a man gets ripped up here, we can't have Sherman to polish 'im off, and this place will be raided shore enough."

"I wouldn't be afraid to fight that cat," I said. "Give me a piece of rope fourteen feet long and I'll fight 'im."

"Don't be foolish," Jason said. "You don't seem to know much about the power of a wildcat!"

Then I heard a lot of whispers in the crowd. I heard men saying that I was off in the head.

"How much are you willing to bet that my wildcat won't kill your dog?" Jason said. "You'll be the only one to bet on your dog. No one else will!"

"I think I got about six hundred and fifty-three dollars," I said. "It's my life savings and I don't want to bet it all."

"Well, I've got ten times that," Jason said. "I'll put my pile against yours!"

Then the men who'd been moving toward the door stopped. They were surprised at the money I had. And they were surprised when Jason said he'd put up all he had against what I had. They knew he had a pile, for he had taken their money on twenty-four fights. My dog was Number Twenty-five for the cat to fight. And I knew all the men except Sherman, Little Man, Jason, and the fellow who took our money at the door would be for me. They'd want to see my dog win.

"Mister Radnor, I hate to bet all my money," I said. "If I lose, I won't have a dollar in the world left and my dog will be gone."

"Well, that's what you come here for, to fight that old mongrel, wasn't it?" Jason said gruffly as he put the last roll of bills back in the table drawer. "And I'd as soon have your money as anybody else's."

"Yes, but I didn't know you had sich a big wildcat," I said. "And I can't stand to see it a-killin' all these fine-looking dogs."

"Come on or get out," Jason said. "After all, we bet here. This isn't a playhouse. It's a fightin' house."

"Will you let me take my dog inside? If you will, I'll put my pile up against yours!"

"I'm afraid of it," Jason said.

"Let 'im learn," one of the men shouted. "We've seen about everything now. Let's see something new!"

"I'm willin' to run the risk," Jason said thoughtfully, as he arose from the table and looked me over.

Then I went over to the table and counted out my money. Jason brought his from the drawer and I made him let me look inside to see that the drawer was clean.

"You watch the money, men," I said to the fellows gathered around me. "I want this to be square and honest."

"We'll see to that," said the fellow that had lost the big English bull.

"Sure we will," said the one that had lost the cur.

"Then open the door, Little Man," I said.

Old Buck didn't growl and he didn't charge against the chain. He just looked at the cat and jerked his tail.

"He's a funny dog," said one of the men behind me.

But I didn't look back to see who had said it. I had my eye on the cat. Buck had his eye on the cat. Then I reached down and rubbed his back. I patted his head as I reached midway of the cage. The cat laid perfectly still. He planned to work on Buck like he did the big mountain cur. Then I unsnapped Buck's chain. Buck crouched halfway. But he didn't take his eye off the cat. And he never growled, but he crept slowly toward the cat as I stepped to one side. Men rushed up and stood on their toes around the cage, like something was going to happen.

Buck went close. But he wouldn't go farther.

"Watch 'im, Buck," I said. "Let 'im make the first move."

Buck held like an Irish setter—he didn't go a step. The cat looked at him with his shiny green eyes, and Buck looked back at the cat. Then all at once the cat began to crouch. Buck held his position. Then the cat made a flying charge and Buck flattened on the cage floor. As the cat went over, Buck whirled and sprang from behind like April lightning. He caught the cat across the skull and the sound went plunk. It was a light crash but the cat sprawled senseless on the floor, its legs quivering and drawing up to its body then out again, each time a little weaker.

"What did that dog do?" a man asked me.

"What about that?" another man said.

"Leave that money or there'll be another death," I heard a voice growl.

"That dog knows how to tree wildcats," I said. "And he knows how to kill them. It's been suicide on the dogs to put them in here, dogs that never fought a wildcat. Buck knows that a wildcat's skull is as easy to crush as a rabbit's. It's a little bit easier—a wildcat's skull is thinner."

"Good boy, Buck," I patted his head.

I snapped the chain into his collar and we left the cage. The wildcat had breathed his last.

"There's your cat, Jason Radnor," I said. "He'll never kill another dog. And the money you made by clawin' dogs to pieces won't do you any good."

"Who are you, anyway?" Jason said, his voice trembling. He was shaking all over.

"Jason, I'm the man that caught that wildcat," I said. "My dog treed it and I went up in the tree and brought it down with my hands. I'm Eddie Battlestrife. You remember my dad, don't you—remember, you tried to kill him? Shot 'im not four feet away between the eyes but you didn't kill him. The bullet parted his hair. He was taking a few quarters from you in a poker game that Sunday afternoon. Now don't shake, Jason, I'm not a-goin' to hurt you. I just want all that money. It's good money and I like money and I like to see old Buck kill a wildcat that's kilt twenty-four dogs."

"Easy, Radnor," said the tall man that owned the cur. "Don't move. Keep your hands up! He took your money and he took it fair."

"Fairer than the way you got it from us," the bulldog's owner said.

"Nice bank account now," I said as I picked up the rolls of greenbacks and put them back in my hunting coat.

"It's a fraud," Jason wept. "It's a stick-up!"

"Easy, Mr. Radnor," the tall man said, as I walked from the shack with old Buck. "Keep your hands up!"

"You won't have to polish this dog off, Sherman," I said as I went through the door. "You can bury your cat."

Jesse Stuart,
Biographer

God's Oddling

Author's Introduction

I think the best way I can introduce you to God's Oddling and tell you why and how I wrote it is to repeat the preface from the book:

This is the one book I have wanted most to write all my life. It is about my father, Mitchell Stuart. It is for him, too. Even though my father was unable to read or write anything but his own name, I believe he was a great man. He was great in spirit and great in his influence upon others. There is no other man that I have ever loved or respected more. When I set out to write this book, I discovered that I had already been writing it all my life, for I had written poems and stories and articles about my father from the time I started writing. God's Oddling, then, is the harvest of all my writing seasons. It is the best book I could write, and I hope it is worthy of the man I have tried to portray.

Although my father was named Mitchell after his father, everyone in Greenup County called him Mitch or Mick. Most people, including my mother, called him Mick. That's the way I remember him, too.

The title of this book, God's Oddling, comes from something my father used to call my brother and me. For years he used to call me "oddling" because I had gone away to school and become a writer, and because I didn't smoke the tobacco we grew or drink the mountain liquor brewed nearby. I was recovering from my heart attack when my father died. During those last days he used to come visit me at my house, and he still called me "oddling." It was then, just before he died, that I thought my father was one of God's oddlings, not me. He was a proud, independent man, who always made his own decisions and went his own way. He was a very gentle man, too. He was an oddling, all right.

I have chosen four excerpts from God's Oddling for you to read. From them, I hope you will get a picture of my father, of my mother, and of what life was like for the Stuart family beside the Big Sandy River in the eastern Kentucky mountains long ago.

The Earth Poet

The first excerpt describes my father and his love and appreciation for the land.

W E LIVED by signs or what people now would call superstitions. When I was old enough to learn anything, I learned to respect the peewees. My father and mother loved those birds. And, in the little house where I lived until I was nine, a pair came each spring. My father used to say, "Must be time to plow the garden, our pewees are back." Nothing, no sign or indication, escaped my father. I recall he always told me to expect rain when the leaves spiraled up toward the sky, and so whenever I see oak leaves twisting up from the strong, sturdy boughs, turning over and showing their soapy bellies to the wind and hot sun, I know that a storm is coming and I remember my father.

Nothing ever escaped my father for he was an earth poet who loved the land and everything on it. He liked to watch things grow. From the time I was big enough for him to lead

me by the hand, I went with him over the farm. If I couldn't
walk all the way in those early days, he'd carry me on his back.
I learned to love many of the things he loved.

I went with my father to so many fields over the years and
listened to him talk so often about their beauty that I know
now that he had wonderful thoughts which should have been
written down. Thoughts came to him faster than a hummingbird flits from one blossom to another.

Sometime in the dim past of my boyhood, my father un-
loaded me from his back under some white-oak trees just beginning to leaf. "Look at this hill, son," he said, gesturing
broadly with a sweep of his hand. "Look up that steep hill toward the sky. See how pretty that new-ground corn is."

This was the first field I can remember my father's taking me
to see. The rows of corn curved like dark-green rainbows around
a high slope with a valley and its little tributaries running down
through the center. The corn blades rustled in the wind, and
my father said he could understand what the corn blades were
saying. He told me they whispered to each other, and this was
hard for me to believe. I reasoned that before anything could
speak or make a sound it had to have a mouth. When my father
said the corn could talk, I got down on my knees and I looked
a stalk over.

"This corn hasn't got a mouth," I told my father. "How
can anything talk when it doesn't have a mouth?"

He laughed like the wind in the corn and hugged me to his
knees, and we went on.

On a Sunday, when my mother and sisters were at church,
my father took me by the hand and led me across two valleys
to a cove where once giant beech timber had stood. He was
always restless on Sundays, eager to get back to the fields in
which he worked all week. He had cleared a piece of this land
to raise white corn, which he planned to have ground for meal
to make our bread. He thought this cove was suited to white
corn. He called it Johnson County corn. Someone had brought

the seed from the Big Sandy River, in the county where my father was born and lived until he was sixteen. When he had cleared this cove, set fire to the giant beech tops, and left ash over the new ground, he thought this earth would produce cornfield beans too. In every other hill of corn he had planted beans. Now these beans ran up the cornstalks and weighted them with hanging pods of young, tender beans. Pictures I saw later of Jack and the Beanstalk always reminded me of this tall corn with bean vines winding around the stalks up to the tassels.

But the one thing my father had brought me to see that delighted him most was the pumpkins. I'd never seen so many pumpkins with long necks and small bodies. Pumpkins as big around as the bottom of a flour barrel were sitting in the furrows beneath the tall corn, immovable as rocks. There were pumpkins, and more pumpkins, of all colors—yellow and white, green and brown.

"Look at this, won't you," my father said. "Look what corn, what beans, what pumpkins. Corn ears so big they lean the cornstalks. Beans as thick as honey-locust beans on the honey-locust tree. And pumpkins thicker than the stumps in this new ground. I could walk all over this field on pumpkins and never step on the ground."

He looked upon the beauty of this cove he had cleared and his three crops growing here. He rarely figured a field in dollars and cents. Although he never wasted a dollar, money didn't mean everything to him. He liked to see the beauty of growing things on the land. He carried this beauty in his mind.

Once, when we were walking between cornfields on a rainy Sunday afternoon, he pointed to a redbird on its nest in a locust tree, a redbird with shiny red feathers against the dark background of a nest. It was just another bird's nest to me until he whispered, "Ever see anything as pretty as what the raindrops do to that redbird sitting on her dark nest?" From this day on, I have liked to see birds, especially redbirds, sitting on their nests in the rain. But my father was the first one to make me see the beauty.

"A blacksnake is a pretty thing," he once said to me, "so shiny and black in the spring sun after he sheds his winter skin."

He was the first man I ever heard say a snake was pretty. I never forgot his saying it. I can even remember the sumac thicket where he saw the blacksnake.

He saw more beauty in trees than any man I have ever known. He would walk through a strange forest laying his hand upon the trees, saying this oak or that pine, that beech or poplar, was a beautiful tree. Then he would single out other trees and say they should be cut. He would always give his reasons for cutting a tree: too many trees on a root stool, too thick, one damaged by fire at the butt, one leaning against another, too many on the ground, or the soil not deep enough above a ledge of rocks to support them.

Then there were the hundreds of times my father took me to the hills to see wild flowers. I thought it was silly at first. He would sit on a dead log, maybe one covered with wild moss, somewhere under the tall beech trees, listening to the wind in the canopy of leaves above, looking at a clump of violets of percoon growing beside a rotted log. He could sit there enjoying himself indefinitely. Only when the sun went down would we get up and start for home.

My father wouldn't break the Sabbath by working, except in an emergency. He would follow a cow that was overdue to calve. He would watch over ewes in the same manner. He followed them to the high cliffs and helped them deliver their lambs, saving their lives. He would do such things on Sundays, and he would fight forest fires. But he always said he could make a living working six days in the week. Yet he was restless on Sundays. He just had to walk around and look over his fields and enjoy them.

Sometimes when I went with my father to a field, we'd cross

a stream, and he'd stop the horse, sit down on the bank in the shade, and watch the flow of water. He'd watch minnows in a deep hole. He wouldn't say a word, and I wouldn't either. I'd look all around, wondering what he'd seen to make him stop, but I never would ask him. When he got through looking, he'd tell me why he'd stopped. Sometimes he wouldn't. Then we'd go on to the field together, and he'd work furiously to make up for the time he had lost while he sat beside the stream and watched the clean water flowing over the sand and gravel to some far-off place beyond his little hill world.

My father didn't have to travel over the country searching for something beautiful to see. He didn't have to go away to find beauty, for he found it everywhere around him. He had eyes to find it. He had a mind to know it. He had a heart to appreciate it. He was an uneducated poet of this earth. And if anybody had told him that he was, he wouldn't have understood. He would have turned and walked away without saying anything.

In the winter, when snow was over the ground, and the stars glistened, he'd go to the barn to feed the livestock at four in the morning. I have seen him put corn in the feedboxes for the horses and mules, then go out and stand and look at the morning moon. He once told me he always kept a horse with a flaxen mane and tail because he liked to see one run in the moonlight with his mane arched high and his tail floating on the wind.

I've gone out early in the morning with him, and he's shown me Jack Frost's beautiful architecture, which lasted only until the sun came up. This used to be one of the games my father played with me on a cold morning. He showed me all the designs that I would never have found without him. Today, I cannot look at white fields of frost on early winter mornings and not think of him.

When spring returned, he was always taking me someplace to show me a new tree he had found, or a pretty red mushroom growing on a rotting stump in some deep hollow. He found so many strange and beautiful things that I tried to rival him by making discoveries, too. I looked into the out-of-way and unexpected places to find the beautiful and the unusual.

Once, in autumn, we went to the pasture field to hunt paw-paws. "Look at the golden meat and the big brown seeds like the seeds of melon or a pumpkin," he said. "Did you ever taste a banana in your life that was as good as a pawpaw? Did you ever see anything prettier than the clean sweet golden fruit of a pawpaw?" I never forgot how he described a pawpaw, and I've always liked their taste.

He took me to the first persimmon grove I ever saw. This was after frost, and the persimmons had ripened and had fallen from the trees. "The persimmon is a candy tree," he said. "It really should have been called the gumdrop tree." I was a small boy then, but ever since I've seen ripe persimmons after frost as brown gumdrops.

I didn't get the idea of dead leaves being golden ships on the sea from a storybook. And neither did my father, for he had never read a book in his life. He'd never had a book read to him either. It was in October, and we were sitting on the bank of W-Branch. We were watching the blue autumn water slide swiftly over the slate rocks. My father picked up leaves that were shaped like little ships and dropped them into the water.

"These are ships on swift water," he told me, "going to far-off lands where strangers will see them." He had a special love for autumn leaves, and he'd pick them up when we were out walking and ask me to identify them. He'd talk about how pretty each leaf was and how a leaf was prettier after it was dead than it was alive and growing.

Many people thought my father was just a one-horse farmer who never got much out of life. They saw only a little man, dressed in clean, patched overalls, with callused and brier-scratched hands. They often saw the beard along his face. And they saw him go off and just stand in a field and look at something. They thought he was moody. Well, he was that all right, but when he was standing there and people thought he was looking into space, he was looking at a flower or a mushroom or a new bug he'd discovered for the first time. And when he looked up into a tree, he wasn't searching for a hornet's nest to burn or a bird's nest to rob. He wasn't trying to find a bee tree. He was just looking closely at the beauty in a tree. And among the millions, he always found one different enough to excite him.

No one who really knew him ever felt sorry for my father. Any feeling of pity turned to envy. For my father had a world of his own, larger and richer than the vast earth that world travelers know. He found more beauty in his acres and square miles than poets who have written a half-dozen books. Only my father couldn't write down the words to express his thoughts. He had no common symbols by which to share his wealth. He was a poet who lived his life upon this earth and never left a line of poetry—except to those of us who lived with him.

Sounds on the Wind
In the hills our life was often harsh and brutal. We were very poor and we had to move from one rented farm to another to try to improve our lot.

RENT WAS raised on my father. Twelve dollars in cash was too much to pay a month for the use of one hundred acres of land and pasture for his cattle, and all the land he wanted to cultivate. Again we were ready to go. We had cleared that farm for somebody and we were ready to move on. We were willing to move away from our neighbors. One house was in sight down the creek from us. We were living too close. "This place is too much like town to suit me," said my mother. We were ready to go. Our family had increased three new members while we were living here. It was early January when we were getting ready, but we were delayed. Herbert, the brother next to me, "took down" with pneu- monia. I recall vividly the January day with a little bit of sun when my father sat on a box under a leafless apple tree. He wrung his hands and said: "It is too unbearable to stand. If we could have only had a doctor here in time to have saved him."

I recall seeing the spring wagon with a pine box roped to the bed and two mules hitched to it. And then the short train of buggies and wagons and spring wagons that followed. We had to go five miles to my grandfather's farm for burial. He was there, his white hair tousled by the blowing wind. He called to the driver who drove the leading team, "Right this way." The driver drove out across a little field and all the other teams followed. It was the best way to get to the top of the hill.

Grandfather Hilton had cut the wires of his pasture fence. We saw the fresh dirt thrown up near some pine trees. I re- member the songs they sang, some of the words the preacher said. I remember how cold my feet got standing in the mud, and how the people cried. All of the others in the family cried but I did not. I cried when I went back home and he was gone.

That night at the fireside Mom said: "Well, I feel free in moving on now. Herbert is buried on land that belongs to my father. He will not sell it while he lives. It will be part mine by inheritance at his death and for my part I shall take the place where the grave is. You know I just couldn't stand to move on and leave my son's grave on property owned by other people. It is foolish to be that way but that is the way I feel. We don't own any land to bury him on, but I can rest tonight knowing that his body lies on my father's soil. We have to move now. I can stand this place no longer."

I wanted another brother. I would say to Mom: "Mom, I

want another brother. Herbert is not here any more. Herbert is dead. I have no one to play in the sand with me. I have no one to help me gather the hen eggs from the nests in the woods. I have no one to wade the creek with me and catch the craw-dads."

I can remember how the tears would drop from Mom's eyes while she would be sitting before the fire. She would not speak. She would sit there and darn away on a sock heel. She would knit sweaters. She would cut dresses for the neighborhood women. She would get them to piece on her quilts while she cut their dresses. Mom was skilled that way. She would pattern their quilts. She would wait on their sick. They came to Mom for things.

I would go out into the woods that came down to our door. I would hear the wind rustle the leaves. I would look for my brother Herbert. I didn't see how he could stay away so long. I would hear him in the wind. I could hear him speak. I would call to him. But no answer. Just the empty wind rustling the dead leaves on the ground. Just the wind rustling the green leaves on the tree. Life was so funny. It was strange. I could not understand how the earth could hold Herbert so long and let me live. I didn't think it fair that he should sleep in the ground and I could go on playing in the sand forever—see the spring come with birds, green leaves on the willows, Sweet Williams on the cliffs. Hens cackling. Geese chasing the butterflies. And Herbert not there.

I said to Mom one day: "Why did Herbert have to die? Why does anybody have to die? Why can't we live forever?"

And Mom said: "It is because of God, son. We are like the flowers. We come for a season like the Sweet William. See how it blooms in the spring. See how it turns brown and dies in the fall-time of the year."

And then I said: "God is not a fair man, Mom, or he would have let Herbert play in the sand with me. Herbert sleeps under the ground, Mom. You know how hard that is. I don't want ever to sleep under the ground. I want Herbert back to play with me. I don't like to play doll with Sophia and Mary.

I was the only boy in the Hollow then. I had to swim by myself. I had to live by myself. I didn't like their dolls. I didn't like to do what girls did. One day I saw a man riding up to our house. He rode a big sorrel horse that had its tail twisted up in a knot. Its legs were splashed with mud. The man carried a little leather bag.

I ran to the house to see who the stranger was. We very seldom saw a man pass our house. When we did we ran inside the house and looked out the window. The stranger met me at the door. I remember. He put his hand on my head. He asked me to hug his neck. He said: "You will hug my neck when you see what I brought you." He went on toward the horse that was tied to the fence post. I ran into the house. I heard a cry. I said: "It is another Herbert, isn't it, Mom?"

Mom was there in bed. She smiled. She pulled the sheet back. I saw the baby. "Here is your brother that the doctor fetched you," said Mom. "Dr. Morris brought him."

"Where did he get him?" I said.

"From behind a stump over there on the hill," Mom said.

I looked at him. Then I ran back to the hill where the Sweet Williams grew. I looked behind every stump on the hill. I was hunting for babies. Funny, as many hens' nests as I had found behind those stumps and had never found a baby. I looked every place. I ran wild, hunting for another baby. I ran to the house and told Mom I'd hunted for babies and couldn't find any. Then said Mom: "Only doctors can find babies."

That night Pa said: "I want to call this boy James. It is a name my people have carried for generations. It came from the country across the ocean, I am told. It is a name to be found in the Bible. It is a name I like. I have a brother named James. Four of my brothers have boys named James. I must have a James."

Mom said: "Add Mitchell to it. That is your name, the name of your father, your father's father, and your father's father's father."

So I had a brother James Mitchell. When he cried I put the cat into the bed with him. I remember when he crawled. I called him Rawl. When he started pulling up by steps I called him Awger. He crawled out to the sand-pile with me. Acorns would fall from the tree and hit his head. He would cry. He was little but he crawled under the floor one day. Mom couldn't go under after him. The hole was not big enough for Mom to get back under. I had to take some of the underpinning from under the house to go after him. I pulled him out by his dress-tail.

Mom would say: "I cannot stand to live here any longer, Mick. Herbert died in this house. You must move me out. We must go to another place where none of us died. It seems like I can hear Herbert walking in the dead leaves when the wind blows. I can hear them hit the windowpanes at night and I think of Herbert. He is with me too often here. Sticks he drove in the ground are still out there by the corncrib with the white string he tied to them. I've never pulled them up. I can't bear to."

Pa would say to Mom: "Soon as a house is emptied in the Hollow we'll get it. We'll move to it. I can get rent for the third, maybe, by having my own mule."

The last house in the head of the Hollow was emptied.

Pa rented it for the third. He had found work for himself and his mule at a dollar and a quarter a day, work for me at a quarter a day, and Mom got housework at a quarter a day. "We need the money," Pa said. "I ain't paid for my baby's casket yet. That was fifteen dollars. Butler has waited a long time now on me. I never stole chickens to pay a debt yet. I ain't going to. I aim to pay my jest and honest debts."

The same spring wagon that hauled my brother away took

our furniture on the road again. I led the cows, called the hounds, and later came back for an express-load of chickens. Our new place was the most desolate place I had ever seen. My father "took sick" there. Our corn rotted in the cold wet ground, for spring was late that year. Heavy rains fell on the lowlands we were to cultivate. And the young corn that did get up through the sour earth was cut down by the crayfish. The fruit was killed that year. The cattle took sick. It was a bad season, but we didn't give up; we battled on. My mother would never give up. There was no such phrase in the language for her as "give up."

She picked the scattered berries—gathered a few apples that escaped the spring frost, and made jelly from the wild grapes. We cut the tall grass along creek banks for the cows that winter. We made a supply of baskets from the tall oak timbers. I cut the timber and split it. My mother wove the baskets. I sold them. When I sold them she always requested that I tell the purchaser that my father made the baskets. Some of those baskets were built so endurably that I saw one I sold years later after I had finished college. It had been used as a feed basket too. I had unpleasant thoughts of a hard winter and a woman's hand when I saw it. All the time my mother labored on baskets she would say: "This is going to be a hard winter." This was the winter of 1917. Snow lay on the ground all winter and an icy crust was frozen over its top. Birds died by the hundreds and rabbits shrank to the bone. Cattle became lean. The dark days—the soldier trains passing through on the other side of the bony ridge of hills. Men would shout from the windows: "We are going to get the Kaiser."

I remember the house had blackberry briers growing at the rock doorstep. Owls hooted from the dark timber at midday. We found a house snake on the wall plate. Pa killed it with a corn knife. I remember the dark puddle of blood on the floor. Sophia couldn't scrub up the stain.

Mom said: "This is a God-forsaken place. Two graves under the plum tree in the garden. I can't stand it here. The owls make it lonesome."

We could hear the owls come and get our chickens at night. Pa would run out in the snow barefooted in the winter and fire the shotgun into the night as the big winged bird silently muffled the frosty wind with his wings. We could hear the foxes bark from the hills above the house. We could hear cats meow from the dense dark woods. We could hear the wind break the limbs from the trees and ooze through the brier thickets.

James was four. He would take the spotted hounds down among the dead cornstalks. He would say to the dogs: "Sic 'em." There wasn't anything to hunt there in the open fields but the quails that fed on the corn grains and grass seed. But James followed the hound dogs at four. I hunted with my father at night. I carried the 'possums in a coffee sack, and the coons. I wouldn't carry a skunk. He couldn't hire me to. I didn't like the scent. But there was money in the skunk hides. We sold fur. We went over the hills in early spring and dug roots of mayapple, ginseng, and yellowroot and sold them to Dave Darby. Later, we picked wild strawberries, raspberries, and blackberries and peddled them from door to door in Greenup. We made enough to eat and buy our clothes for winter. We paid for the coffin Herbert was buried in. I worked from before sunup until after sundown for my quarter. I was called Lazybones.

Pa said: "You must have book-learning, son. You must not grow up like a weed. You must not grow up like I have. I can't write my name till you can read it." I remember seeing Pa try to read the words on tobacco pokes. He would spell the word first. Then he would call it something. He would work and work with a word like a dog at a groundhog hole gnawing roots and rocks to get the groundhog.

I walked three miles out of the Hollow with my sister to school after the corn was laid by. We met the foxes in our path many a morning. We saw the squirrels play over our heads in the tall timber. Sawmills had not come to the Hollow yet. We saw the rabbits hop across our path. We met other children. They were strange children or we were strange children, one. I wanted to outlearn the boys I was in class with. I wanted to turn them down in spelling and get the prize for the most headmarks. When I turned one of the boys down I laughed. When one turned me down I cried. My sister and I would hold school before we got to school to see if I had the spelling words down pat. I wanted to outrun anybody in school. I wanted to tell them what to do. I fought with them, whipped and was whipped. It was a great place to be. I loved school—no beans to pick, no corn to cut, no hogs to feed, no wood to get. I learned fast because I worked hard.

My sister learned fast. We were called: "Sal Stuart's youngins. They learn fast. They are mean brats. They fight like mad cats —claw, bite, and scratch. That boy. The girl is clean and pretty always. That boy's knuckles are dirty and tough." It was true I'd met the other boys and played hard knuckles. I'd rake my knuckle-skin against the rough bark on the oak to make it tough and outdo the other boys.

One day in spring, when I was cutting brush and James was piling it and carrying water to the field to me, Sophia hollered to me from the house. She said: "Come to the house and see what is here." I went to the house, I heard the baby cry. It was the weakest crying I'd ever heard. Its crying sounded like the tiny meows of a baby kitten. I knew I didn't have another brother.

"Another brother," said Mom. "But he's so little. So little I'll have to pin him to the pillow. I'm afraid of losing him in the bed. He's so little."

She called him Lee. "I have heard of Lee," Mom would say

when Pa would speak about Grandpa fighting for Grant. "My
people died fighting for Lee."

One day the doctor came to see Lee. He could not give him
new life. He couldn't do anything to save him. He was so small.
Mom had him tied to the pillow. The doctor walked out of
the house. He said to Pa: "Just a matter of hours, Mitch. He's
getting his breath with a gurgling sound now."

Fever killed him. Fever had killed Herbert. James took the
fever. I prayed that he would live. He was sick when the same
express that hauled Herbert away hauled Lee. It was in April,
1918. The roads were muddy. The wind was cold. We followed
Lee to the same hill where Herbert was still sleeping soundly
under the pines and the oaks. Grandpa was there and cut the
barbed-wire fence so that the teams could go up the hill and
dodge the coal-ruts where the wagons had hauled the heavy
loads from the mines and the sulphur water oozed yellow in
the ruts. Lee was planted beside Herbert. I cried. Mom cried
and cried. Pop shed tears down his leaf-brown cheeks. James
was home with the fever. It was late spring before he could get
out of bed. One leg was left lame. He hobbled with a stick.
He would walk awhile and rest awhile.

I had said viciously that I would never return to that pine
grove on my grandfather's farm. I had said I would never go
back where Herbert's grave was. But I had returned. I had
followed for six miles through the mud this time. I drove a
team of black horses. The same preacher was there. He was
the Reverend Oaks. There were two mounds beneath those
pines now. We left the hill. My horses ran away for they were
turned toward home. I let them run. After they were willing
to quit running and became very tired, I made them run more.

Some of you will remember the heavy snow that fell in April
that spring. My father and I were walking to the barn. I refused
to step in his tracks any more, as I had done before when there
came deep snows. I made a path of my own. I said to myself:

"You are a man of the hills. You have let them hold you in. You were born among them—you'll die among them. You'll go to that pine grove where we went less than two months ago. You will lie there forever in that soil. Your night will then have come when man's work is over. Since you have brought us into the world, isn't there some escape from fevers? Can't we move to a place where we can get a doctor easier? Two of my brothers are dead and sleeping over there by that pine grove. Don't they have the same right as I have to be here? Now they are gone. Life for them was a tragedy. They had better not have cost my mother the pain of birth—dying young when it can be prevented. I have had pneumonia twice and typhoid twice. I was able to survive them. It was because I was strong. Now these hills will not always hold me. I shall go beyond them some day."

Again my mother said: "I cannot stand this place any longer. We must move on." We had cleaned this farm up and run some new fences. We had made it possible for other people to live there. So it was time for us to move on. My father rented another place.

The spring wagon was loaded again and we moved to another part of W-Hollow. The house was a log house upon a steep bank. There was a sulphur spring under some beech trees in the front yard and hollyhocks grew all around it. It was a flower garden surrounded by rabbits and sassafras. But we had no time to play with flowers. Spring was on us and we had to get land cleared for spring plowing. We had to get corn and potatoes in the ground. They were the staples and other things mattered less—corn and potatoes mean life in the hills.

The Stuarts and their relatives, the Hiltons, took over W-Hollow. They didn't own any of it at first, but later they managed to win practically the whole valley—all the land owned by the Daughterys, Collinses, and Myerses, and some more. They raised hay, cattle, sorghum cane, and tobacco, some sweet potatoes and strawberries.

They've lived here from 1896 until the present. The Stuarts still remain but I am the last, and leave no sons. It is a half-century valley for any one family, and our time is about up.

My father's plow and my mother's hoe turned over all the pebbles and stones on hill and bottom of this valley. They lived in eight different places in this neighborhood. They planted millions of steps, more than any other couple who ever lived here. But I cannot find one of them now.

Testimony of Trees

Finally in 1920 my father was able to buy some land of his own. He paid $300 for 50 acres of wilderness that nobody wanted. It was uncleared land, without a building or a fence on it. But it was ours. We cleared the land and built our house, and a barn. Then one day trouble came walking down the road.

WE HAD JUST moved onto our farm when Jake Timmins walked down the path to the barn where Pa and I were nailing planks on a barn stall. Pa stood with a nail in one hand and his hatchet in the other while I stood holding the plank. We watched this small man with a beardy face walk toward us. He took short steps and jabbed his sharpened sourwood cane into the ground as he hurried down the path.

"Wonder what he's after?" Pa asked as Jake Timmins came near the barn.

"Don't know," I said.

"Howdy, Mick," Jake said as he leaned on his cane and looked over the new barn that we had built.

"Howdy, Jake," Pa grunted. We had heard how Jake Timmins had taken men's farms. Pa was nervous when he spoke, for I watched the hatchet shake in his hand.

"I see you're still a-putting improve-ments on yer barn," Jake said.

"A-tryin' to get it fixed for winter," Pa told him.

"I'd advise ye to stop now, Mick," he said. "Jist want to be fair with ye so ye won't go ahead and do a lot of work fer me fer nothing."

"How's that, Jake?" Pa asked.

"Ye've built yer barn on my land, Mick," he said with a little laugh.

"Ain't you a-joking, Jake?" Pa asked him.

"Nope, this is my land by rights," he told Pa as he looked our new barn over. "I hate to take this land with this fine barn on it, but it's mine and I'll haf to take it."

"I'm afraid not, Jake," Pa said. "I've been around here since I was a boy. I know where the lines run. I know that ledge of rocks with that row of oak trees a-growing on it is the line!"

"No it hain't, Mick," Jake said. "If it goes to court, ye'll find out. The line runs from that big dead chestnut up there on the knoll straight across this holler to the top of the knoll up there where the twin hickories grow."

"But that takes my barn, my meadow, my garden," Pa said. "That takes ten acres of the best land I have. It almost gets my house!"

The hatchet quivered in Pa's hand and his lips trembled when he spoke.

"Tim Mennix sold ye land that belonged to me," Jake said.

"But you ought to a-said something about it before I built my house and barn on it," Pa told Jake fast as the words would leave his mouth.

"Sorry, Mick," Jake said, "but I must be a-going. I've given ye fair warning that ye air a-building on my land!"

"But I bought this land," Pa told him. "I'm a-goin' to keep it."

"I can't hep that," Jake told Pa as he turned to walk away. "Don't tear this barn down fer it's on my property!"

"Don't worry, Jake," Pa said. "I'm not a-tearing this barn down. I'll be a-feeding my cattle in it this winter!"

Jake Timmins walked slowly up the path the way he had come. Pa and I stood watching him as he stopped and looked our barn over; then he looked at our garden that we had fenced and he looked at the new house that we had built.

"I guess he'll be a-claiming the house too," Pa said.

And just as soon as Jake Timmins crossed the ledge of rocks that separated our farms Pa threw his hatchet to the ground and hurried from the barn.

"Where are you a-going, Pa?" I asked.

"To see Tim Mennix."

"Can I go too?"

"Come along," he said.

We hurried over the mountain path toward Tim Mennix's shack. He lived two miles from us. Pa's brogan shoes rustled the fallen leaves that covered the path. October wind moaned among the leafless treetops. Soon as we reached the shack we found Tim cutting wood near his woodshed.

"What's the hurry, Mick?" Tim asked Pa who stood wiping sweat from his face with his blue bandanna.

"Jake Timmins is a-tryin' to take my land," Pa told Tim.

"Ye don't mean it?"

"I do mean it," Pa said. "He's just been to see me and he said the land where my barn, garden, and meadow were belonged to him. Claims about ten acres of the best land I got. I told him I bought it from you and he said it didn't belong to you to sell."

"That ledge of rocks and the big oak trees that grow along the backbone of the ledge has been the line fer seventy years," Tim said. "But lissen, Mick, when Jake Timmins wants a piece of land, he takes it."

"People told me he's like that," Pa said. "I was warned against buying my farm because he's like that. People said he'd steal all my land if I lived beside him ten years."

"He'll have it before then, Mick," Tim Mennix told Pa in a trembling voice. "He didn't have but an acre to start from. That acre was a bluff where three farms jined and no one fenced it in because it was worthless and they didn't want it. He had a deed made fer this acre and he's had forty lawsuits when he set his fences over on other people's farms and took their land, but he goes to court and wins every time."

"I'll have the County Surveyor, Finn Madden, to survey my lines," Pa said.

"That won't hep any," Tim told Pa. "There's been more people kilt over the line fences that he's surveyed than has been kilt over any other one thing in this county. Surveyor Finn Madden's a good friend to Jake."

"But he's County Surveyor," Pa said. "I'll haf to have him."

"Jake Timmins is a dangerous man," Tim Mennix warned Pa. "He's dangerous as a loaded double-barrel shotgun with both hammers cocked."

"I've heard that," Pa said. "I don't want any trouble. I'm a married man with a family."

When we reached home, we saw Jake upon the knoll at the big chestnut tree sighting across the hollow to the twin hickories on the knoll above our house. And as he sighted across the hollow, he walked along and drove stakes into the ground. He set one stake in our front yard, about five feet from the corner of our house. Pa started out on him once but Mom wouldn't let him go. Mom said let the law settle the dispute over the land.

And that night Pa couldn't go to sleep. I was awake and heard him a-walking the floor. I knew that Pa was worried, for Jake was the most feared man among our hills. He had started with one acre and now had over four hundred acres that he had taken from other people.

Next day Surveyor Finn Madden and Jake ran a line across the hollow just about on the same line that Jake had surveyed with his own eyes. And while Surveyor Finn Madden looked through the instrument, he had Jake set the stakes and drive them into the ground with a poleax. They worked at the line all day. And when they had finished surveying the line, Pa went up on the knoll at the twin hickories behind our house and asked Surveyor Finn Madden if his line was right.

"Surveyed it right with the deed," he told Pa. "Tim Mennix sold you land that didn't belong to him."

"Looks like this line would've been surveyed before I built my barn," Pa said.

"Can't see why it wasn't," he told Pa. "Looks like you're a-losing the best part of your farm, Mick."

Then Surveyor Finn Madden, a tall man with a white beard, and Jake Timmins went down the hill together.

"I'm not so sure that I'm a-losing the best part of my farm," Pa said. "I'm not a-goin' to sit down and take it! I know Jake's a land thief and it's time his stealing land is stopped."

"What are you a-goin' to do, Pa?" I asked.

"Don't know," he said.

"You're not a-goin' to hurt Jake over the land, are you?"

He didn't say anything but he looked at the two men as they turned over the ledge of rocks and out of sight.

"You know Mom said the land wasn't worth hurting anybody over," I said.

"But it's my land," Pa said.

That night Pa walked the floor, and Mom got out of bed and talked to him and made him go to bed. The next day Sheriff Eif Whiteapple served a notice on Pa to keep his cattle out of the barn that we had built. The notice said that the barn belonged to Jake Timmins. Jake ordered us to put our chickens up, to keep them off his garden when it was our garden. He told us not to let anything trespass on his land and his land was on the other side of the stakes. We couldn't even walk in part of our yard.

"He'll have the house next if we don't do something about it," Pa said.

Pa walked around our house in a deep study. He was trying to think of something to do about it. Mom talked to him. She told him to get a lawyer and fight the case in court. But Pa said something had to be done to prove that the land belonged to us, though we had a deed for our land in our trunk. And before Sunday came, Pa dressed in his best clothes.

"Where're you a-going, Mick?" Mom asked.

"A-goin' to see Uncle Mel," he said. "He's been in a lot of line-fence fights and he could give me some good advice!"

"We hate to stay here and you gone, Mick," Mom said.

"Just don't step on property Jake laid claim to until I get back," Pa said. "I'll be back soon as I can. Some time next week you can look for me."

Pa went to West Virginia to get Uncle Mel. And while he was gone, Jake Timmins hauled wagonloads of hay and corn to the barn that we had built. He had taken over as if it were his own and as if he would always have it. We didn't step beyond the stakes where Surveyor Finn Madden had surveyed. We waited for Pa to come. And when Pa came, Uncle Mel came with him carrying a long-handled double-bitted ax and a turkey of clothes across his shoulder. Before they reached the house, Pa showed Uncle Mel the land Jake Timmins had taken.

"Land hogs air pizen as copperhead snakes," Uncle Mel said, then he fondled his long white beard in his hand. Uncle Mel was eighty-two years old, but his eyes were keen as sharp-pointed briers and his shoulders were broad and his hands were big and rough. He had been a timber cutter all his days and he was still a-cuttin' timber in West Virginia at the age of eighty-two. "He can't do this to ye, Mick!"

Uncle Mel was madder than Pa when he looked over the new line that they had surveyed from the dead chestnut on one knoll to the twin hickories on the other knoll.

"Anybody would know the line wouldn't go like that," Uncle Mel said. "The line would follow the ridge."

"Looks that way to me too," Pa said.

"He's a-stealin' yer land, Mick," Uncle Mel said. "I'll hep ye get yer land back. He'll never beat me. I've had to fight too many squatters a-tryin' to take my land. I know how to fight 'em with the law."

That night Pa and Uncle Mel sat before the fire and Uncle Mel looked over Pa's deed. Uncle Mel couldn't read very well and when he came to a word he couldn't read, I told him what it was.

"We'll haf to have a court order first, Mick," Uncle Mel said. "When we get the court order, I'll find the line."

I didn't know what Uncle Mel wanted with a court order, but I found out after he got it. He couldn't chop on a line tree until he got an order from the court. And soon as Pa got the court order and gathered a group of men for witnesses, Uncle Mel started work on the line fence.

"Sixteen rods from the dead chestnut due north," Uncle Mel said, and we started measuring sixteen rods due north.

"That's the oak tree, there," Uncle Mel said. It measured exactly sixteen rods from the dead chestnut to the black oak tree.

"Deed said the oak was blazed," Uncle Mel said, for he'd gone over the deed until he'd memorized it. "See the scar, men," Uncle Mel said.

"But that was done seventy years ago," Pa said.

"Funny about the testimony of trees," Uncle Mel told Pa. Tim Mennix, Orbie Dorton, and Dave Sperry were there too. "The scar will allus stay on the outside of a tree well as on the inside. The silent trees will keep their secrets."

Uncle Mel started chopping into the tree. He swung his ax over his shoulder and bit out a slice of wood every time he struck. He cut a neat block into the tree until he found a dark place deep inside the tree.

"Come, men, and look," Uncle Mel said. "Look at that scar. It's as pretty a scar as I ever seen in the heart of a tree!"

And while Uncle Mel wiped sweat with his blue bandanna from his white beard, we looked at the scar.

"It's a scar, all right," Tim Mennix said, since he had been a timber cutter most of his life and knew a scar on a tree.

"Think that was cut seventy years ago," Orbie Dorton said. "That's when the deed was made and the old survey was run."

"We'll see if it's been seventy years ago," Uncle Mel said as he started counting the rings in the tree. "Each ring is a year's growth."

We watched Uncle Mel pull his knife from his pocket, open the blade, and touch each ring with his knife-blade point as he counted the rings across the square he had chopped into the tree. Uncle Mel counted exactly seventy rings from the bark to the scar.

"Ain't it the line tree, boys?" Uncle Mel asked.

"Can't be anything else," Dave Sperry said.

And then Uncle Mel read the deed, which called for a mulberry thirteen rods due north from the black oak. We measured to the mulberry and Uncle Mel cut his notch to the scar and counted the rings. It was seventy rings from the bark to the scar. Ten more rods we came to the poplar the deed called for, and he found the scar on the outer bark and inside the tree. We found every tree the deed called for but one, and we found its stump. We surveyed the land from the dead chestnut to the twin hickories. We followed it around the ledge.

"We have the evidence to take to court," Uncle Mel said. "I'd like to bring the jurymen right here to this line fence to show 'em."

"I'll go right to town and put this thing in court," Pa said.

"I'll go around and see the men that have lost land to Jake Timmins," Uncle Mel said. "I want 'em to be at the trial."

Before our case got to court, Uncle Mel had shown seven

of our neighbors how to trace their lines and get their land back from Jake Timmins. And when our trial was called, the courthouse was filled with people who had lost land and who had disputes with their neighbors over line fences, attending the trial to see if we won. Jake Timmins, Surveyor Finn Madden, and their lawyer, Henson Stapleton, had produced their side of the question before the jurors and we had lawyer Sherman Stone and our witnesses to present our side, while all the landowners Jake Timmins had stolen land from listened to the trial. The foreman of the jury asked that the members of the jury be taken to the line fence.

"Now here's the way to tell where a line was blazed on saplings seventy years ago," Uncle Mel said, as he showed them the inner mark on the line oak; then he showed them the outward scar. Uncle Mel took them along the line fence and showed them each tree that the deed called for, all but the one that had fallen.

"It's plain as the nose on your face," Uncle Mel would say every time he explained each line tree. "Too many land thieves in this county and a county surveyor the Devil won't have in hell."

After Uncle Mel had explained the line fence to the jurors, they followed Sheriff Whiteapple and his deputies back to the courtroom. Pa went with them to get the decision. Uncle Mel waited at our house for Pa to return.

"That land will belong to Mick," Uncle Mel told us. "And the hay and corn in that barn will belong to him."

When Pa came home, there was a smile on his face.

"It's yer land, ain't it, Mick?" Uncle Mel asked.

"It's still my land," Pa said, "and sixteen men are now filing suits to recover their land. Jake Timmins won't have but an acre left."

"Remember the hay and corn he put in yer barn is yourn," Uncle Mel said. Uncle Mel got up from his chair, stretched his arms. Then he said, "I must be a-gettin' back to West Virginia to cut timber. If ye have any more land troubles, write me."

We tried to get Uncle Mel to stay longer. But he wouldn't stay. He left with his turkey of clothes and his long-handled, double-bitted ax across his shoulder. We waved good-by to him as he walked slowly down the path and out of sight on his way to West Virginia.

Clearing in the Sky

This last excerpt tells of something that happened after I was a grown man, married and living with my wife and daughter in a house of my own, near my parents' farm. One day my father insisted I take a long walk with him because he had something to show me. What he showed me that day made me realize once again that he was truly one of God's oddlings.

"THIS IS the way, Jess," said my father, pointing with his cane across the deep valley below us. "I want to show you something you've not seen for many years!"

"Isn't it too hot for you to do much walking?" I wiped the streams of sweat from my face to keep them from stinging my eyes.

I didn't want to go with him. I had just finished walking a half mile uphill from my home to his. I had carried a basket of dishes to Mom. There were two slips in the road and I couldn't drive my car. And I knew how hot it was. It was 97 in the shade. I knew from that January until April my father had gone to eight different doctors. One of the doctors had told him not to walk the length of a city block. He told my father to get a taxi to take him home. But my father walked home five miles across the mountain and told Mom what the doctor had said. Forty years ago a doctor had told him the same thing. And he had lived to raise a family of five children. He had done as much hard work in those years as any man.

I could not protest to him now. He had made up his mind. When he made up his mind to do a thing, he would do it if he had to crawl. He didn't care if it was 97 in the shade or 16 below zero. I wiped more sweat from my face as I followed him down the little path between the pasture and the meadow.

Suddenly he stopped at the edge of the meadow, took his pocketknife from his pocket, and cut a wisp of alfalfa. He held it up between him and the sun.

"Look at this, Jess!" he bragged. "Did you ever see better alfalfa grow out of the earth?"

"It's the best looking hay I've seen any place," I said. "I've not seen better looking alfalfa even in the Little Sandy River bottoms!"

"When I bought this little farm everybody around here said I'd end up with my family at the county poor farm if I tried to make a living here," he bragged again. "It took me thirty years to improve these old worn-out acres to make them do this!

"But this is not what I want to show you, Jess," he said as he threw the wisp of alfalfa to the ground. "Come on. Follow me!"

I followed him through the pasture gate. Then down a little narrow cattle path into the deep hollow.

"Where are we going?" I asked when we started to walk a log across the creek toward a steep, timbered bluff.

"Not up or down the hollow," he laughed. "But there." He pointed toward a wooded mountaintop. "That's the way we are goin'!"

"But there's not even a path leading up there," I said.

"There's a path up there now," he said. "I've made one."

I followed him across the foot log he had made by chopping

down a white-oak, felling it over the deep-channeled stream. It was a foot log a flash flood couldn't carry away because its top branches rested on the far side of the channel behind a big tree. He hadn't chopped the white-oak all the way off at the trunk. He had left a little of the tree to hold it at the stump. His doctors had told him not to use an ax. But he had cut this white-oak to make a foot log across the stream so he could reach the rugged mountain slope.

Now I followed my father up the winding footpath under the tall hickory trees, a place where I used to come with him when I was a little boy to hunt for squirrels. We would shoot squirrels from the tall scaly-bark hickories and black walnuts with our long rifles. But that had been nearly thirty years ago. And through the years, from time to time, I had walked over this rugged mountain slope and there was never a path on it until my father had made this one. It was a pretty little foot-path under the high canopy of hickory, walnut, and oak leaves. We couldn't see the sky above our heads. Our eyes could not find an opening among the leaves.

In front of me walked the little man who once walked so fast I had to run to follow him. But it wasn't that way now. Time had slowed him. The passing of the years and much hard labor had bent his shoulders. His right shoulder, the one he used to carry his loads, sagged three inches below the left one. His breath didn't come as easy as it used to come. For he stopped twice, and leaned on his cane to rest, before we reached the top of the first bluff. Then we came to a flat where the ground wasn't so steep.

"I like these woods, Jess," my father said. "Remember when we used to come here to hunt for squirrels? Remember when we sat beneath these hickories and the squirrels threw green hickory shells down at us? The morning wind just at the break of day in August was so good to breathe. I can't forget those days. And in October when the rabbits were ripe and the frosts had come and the hickory leaves had turned yellow and when the October winds blew they rustled the big leaves from the trees and they fell like yellow raindrops to the ground! Remember," he said, looking at me with his pale blue eyes, "how our hounds would make the rabbits circle! Those were good days, Jess! That's why I remember this mountain."

"Is that what you wanted to show me?" I asked.

"Oh, no, no," he said as he began to climb the second bluff that lifted abruptly from the flat toward the sky. The pines on top of the mountain above us looked as if the fingers of their long boughs were fondling the substance of a white cloud. Whatever my father wanted me to see was on top of the highest point on my farm. And with the exception of the last three years, I had been over this point many times. I had never seen anything extraordinary upon this high point of rugged land. I had seen the beauty of many wild flowers, a few rock cliffs, and many species of hardwood and softwood trees.

"Why do you take the path straight up the point?" I asked. "Look at these other paths! What are they doing here?"

Within the distance of a few yards, several paths left the main path and circled around the slope, gradually climbing the mountain.

"All paths go to the same place," he answered.

"Then why take the steep one?" I asked.

"I'll explain later," he spoke with half-breaths.

He rested a minute to catch his second wind while I managed to stand on the path by holding to a little sapling, because it was too steep for my feet to hold unless I braced myself.

Then my father started to move slowly up the path again, supporting himself with his cane. I followed at his heels. Just a few steps in front of him a fox squirrel crossed the path and ran up a hickory tree.

"See that, Jess!" he shouted.

"Yes, I do," I answered.

"That brings back something to me," he said. "Brings back the old days to see a fox squirrel. But this won't bring back as much as something I'm goin' to show you."

My curiosity was aroused. I thought he had found a new kind of wild grass, or an unfamiliar herb, or a new kind of tree.

Only twice did my father stop to wipe the sweat from his eyes as he climbed the second steep bluff toward the fingers of the pines. We reached the limbless trunks of these tall straight pines whose branches reached toward the blue depth of sky, for the white cloud was now gone. I saw a clearing, a small clearing of not more than three-fourths of an acre in the heart of this wilderness right on the mountaintop.

"Now, you're comin' to something, son," he said as he pushed down the top wire so he could cross the fence. "This is something I want you to see!"

"Who did this?" I asked. "Who cleared this land and fenced it? Fenced it against what?"

"Stray cattle if they ever get out of the pasture," he answered me curtly. "I cleared this land. And I fenced it!"

"But why did you ever climb to this mountaintop and do this?" I asked him. "Look at the fertile land we have in the valley!"

"Fertile," he laughed as he reached down and picked up a double handful of leaf-rot loam. "This is the land, son! This is it. I've tried all kinds of land!"

Then he smelled of the dirt. He whiffed and whiffed the smell of this wild dirt into his nostrils.

"Just like fresh air," he said as he let the dirt run between his fingers. "It's pleasant to touch, too," he added.

"But, Pa—" I said.

"I know what you think," he interrupted. "Your mother thinks the same thing. She wonders why I ever climbed to this mountaintop to raise my potatoes, yams, and tomatoes! But, Jess," he almost whispered, "anything grown in new ground

like this has a better flavor. Wait until my tomatoes are ripe!
You'll never taste sweeter tomatoes in your life!"

"They'll soon be ripe, too," I said as I looked at the dozen or
more rows of tomatoes on the lower side of the patch.

Then above the tomatoes were a half-dozen rows of yams.
Above the yams were, perhaps, three dozen rows of potatoes.

"I don't see a weed in this patch," I laughed. "Won't they
grow here?"

"I won't let 'em," he said. "Now this is what I've been wanting you to see!"

"This is the cleanest patch I've ever seen," I bragged. "But
I still don't see why you climbed to the top of this mountain
to clear this patch. And you did all this against your doctor's
orders!"

"Which one?" he asked, laughing.

Then he sat down on a big oak stump and I sat down on
a small black-gum stump near him. This was the only place
on the mountain where the sun could shine to the ground.
And on the lower side of the clearing there was a rim of shadow
over the rows of dark stalwart plants loaded with green tomatoes.

"What is the reason for your planting this patch up here?"
I asked.

"Twenty times in my life," he said, "a doctor has told me
to go home and be with my family as long as I could. Told
me not to work. Not to do anything but to live and enjoy the
few days I had left me. If the doctors have been right," he said,
winking at me, "I have cheated death many times! Now, I've
reached the years the Good Book allows to man in his lifetime
upon this earth! Threescore years and ten!"

He got up from the stump and wiped the raindrops of sweat
from his red-wrinkled face with his big blue bandanna.

"And something else, Jess," he said, motioning for me to
follow him to the upper edge of the clearing, "you won't under-

stand until you reach threescore and ten! After these years your time is borrowed. And when you live on that kind of time, then something goes back. Something I cannot explain. You go back to the places you knew and loved. See this steep hill slope." He pointed down from the upper rim of the clearing toward the deep valley below. "Your mother and I, when she was nineteen and I was twenty-two, cleared this mountain slope together. We raised corn, beans, and pumpkins here," he continued, his voice rising with excitement—he talked with his hands, too. "Those were the days. This wasn't land one had to build up. It was already here as God had made it and all we had to do was clear the trees and burn the brush. I plowed this mountain with cattle the first time it was ever plowed. And we raised more than a barrel of corn to the shock. That's why I came back up here. I went back to our youth. And this was the only land left like that was.

"And Jess," he bragged, "regardless of my threescore years and ten, I plowed it. Plowed it with a mule! I have, with just a little help, done all the work. It's like the land your mother and I used to farm here when I brought my gun to the field and took home a mess of fox squirrels every evening!"

I looked at the vast mountain slope below where my mother and father had farmed. And I could remember, years later, when they farmed this land. It was on this steep slope that my father once made me a little wooden plow. That was when I was six years old and they brought me to the field to thin corn. I lost my little plow in a furrow and I cried and cried until he made me another plow. But I never loved the second plow as I did the first one.

Now, to look at the mountain slope, grown up with tall trees, many of them big enough to have sawed into lumber at the mill, it was hard to believe that my father and mother had cleared this mountain slope and had farmed it for many years. For many of the trees were sixty feet tall and the wild vines had matted their tops together.

"And, Jess," he almost whispered, "the doctors told me to sit still and to take life easy. I couldn't do it. I had to work. I had to go back. I had to smell this rich loam again. This land is not like the land I had to build to grow alfalfa. This is real land. It's the land that God left. I had to come back and dig in it. I had to smell it, sift it through my fingers again. And I wanted to taste yams, tomatoes, and potatoes grown in this land."

From the mountaintop I looked far in every direction over the rugged hills my father and mother had cleared and farmed in corn, tobacco, and cane. The one slope they hadn't cleared was the one from which my father had cleared his last, small patch.

I followed him from his clearing in the sky, down a new path, toward the deep valley below.

"But why do you have so many paths coming from the flat up the steep second bluff?" I asked, since he had promised that he would explain this to me later.

"Oh, yes," he said. "Early last spring, I couldn't climb straight up the steep path. That was when the doctor didn't give me a week to live. I made a longer, easier path so I wouldn't have to do so much climbing. Then, as I got better," he explained, "I made another path that was a little steeper. And as I continued to get better, I made steeper paths. That was one way of knowing I was getting better all the time!"

I followed him down the path, that wound this way and that, three times the length of the path we had climbed.

The Thread That Runs So True

Author's Introduction

This book is about the joys, the sorrows, the sweet and the bitter, of my years as a teacher. It is a book that some of my friends tried to dissuade me from writing. But I had to write it.

When I began writing The Thread That Runs So True, I said teaching was the greatest profession in the world. Not too many people agreed with me then, but, as the years have passed, many have changed their minds until they are in full accord with this statement.

When I began teaching, the schoolroom was not supposed to be a very interesting place, and this great profession was looked upon by many as being something of secondary importance. Now, the interest of all America is focused upon America's schools and their importance to our survival as a nation.

No one can ever tell me that education, rightly directed without propaganda, cannot change the individual, community, county, state, and the world for the better. It can. There must be health, science, technology, the arts, and conservation of all worthwhile things that aid humanity upon this earth. And there must, above all, be character education.

As a teacher in a one-room school, where I taught all

eight grades, and then high school, as a principal of
rural and city high schools and superintendent of city
and county school systems, I learned by experience that
teaching is the greatest profession there is, and that the
classroom can be made one of the most exciting places
on earth for young, middle-aged, and older people to
improve themselves for more useful and richer living.

I left teaching, the profession I loved, because I
thought I couldn't make enough to live. I raised sheep,
lectured, wrote novels and made money, but my heart
was always in the schoolroom. And it still is.

The two excerpts I've chosen from The Thread That
Runs So True will give you an idea of the range of my
experiences as a teacher. The first incident happened
when I was seventeen years old and teaching in my first
school, a one-room schoolhouse. Since that day I have
had many difficult problems as a teacher and admin-
istrator but none so tough as this one. You will see why.

The Fight with Guy Hawkins

THE FOLLOWING Monday I had stayed at the
schoolhouse to do some work on my school records, and Don
Conway had gone home with his sister and brothers. This was
the first afternoon I had stayed at school after all my pupils had
gone. The room was very silent and I was busy working when
I heard soft footsteps walking around the building. I looked
through the window on my left and I saw Guy Hawkins' head.
His uncombed, tousled hair was ruffled by the Lonesome Valley
wind.

I wondered why he was coming back. I wondered if he had
forgotten something.

Then I realized this was the first time he had been able to catch me by myself. And I remembered a few other incidents in Greenwood County's rural schools where a pupil had come back to the school when the teacher was there alone, and had beaten heck out of him. I could recall three or four such incidents. But I didn't have time to think about them. Not now. Guy came in the door with his cap in his hand. I didn't want him to see me looking up at him, but I did see him coming down the broad middle aisle, taking long steps and swinging his big arms. He looked madder than any man or animal I had ever seen. He walked up to my desk and stood silently before me.

"Did you forget something, Guy?" I asked.

"Naw, I've never forgot nothin'," he reminded me.

"Then what do you want?" I asked.

"Whip you," he said.

"Why do you want to fight me?" I asked him. I dropped my pencil and stood up facing him.

"I don't like you," he said. "I don't like teachers. I said never another person with your name would teach this school. Not as long as I'm here."

"It's too bad you don't like me or my name," I said, my temper rising.

"I won't be satisfied until I've whipped you," he said.

"Can you go to another school?" I asked him. "The Valley School is not too far from where you live."

"Naw, naw," he shouted, "if anybody leaves, you'll leave. I was in Lonesome Valley first. And I ain't a-goin' to no other school because of you!"

"Then there's nothing left for us to do but fight," I said. "I've come to teach this school and I'm going to teach it!"

"Maybe you will," he snarled. "I have you penned in this schoolhouse. I have you where I want you. You can't get away! You can't run! I aim to whip you right where you stand! It's the same place where I whipped your sister!"

I looked at his face. It was red as a sliced beet. Fire danced in his pale-blue, elongated eyes. I knew Guy Hawkins meant every word he said. I knew I had to face him and to fight. There was no other way around. I had to think quickly. How would I fight him?

"Will you let me take my necktie off?" I said, remembering I'd been choked by a fellow pulling my necktie once in a fight.

"Yep, take off that purty tie," he said. "You might get it dirty by the time I'm through with you."

I slowly took off my tie.

"Roll up the sleeves of your white shirt too," he said. "But they'll be dirty by the time I sweep this floor up with you."

"Sweep the floor up with me," I said.

He shot out his long arm but I ducked. I felt the wind from his thrust against my ear.

I mustn't let him clinch me, I thought.

Then he came back with another right and I ducked his second lick. I came around with my first lick—a right—and planted it on his jaw, not a good lick but just enough to jar him and make him madder. When he rushed at me, I side-stepped. He missed. By the time he had turned around, I caught him a haymaker on the chin that reeled him. Then I followed up with another lick as hard as I had ever hit a man. Yet I didn't bring him down. He came back for more. But he didn't reach me this time. He was right. I did get my shirt dirty. I dove through the air with a flying tackle. I hit him beneath the knees. I'd tackled like this in football. I'd tackled hard. And I never tackled anybody harder than Guy. His feet went from under him, and I scooted past on the pine floor. I'd tackled him so quickly when he had expected me to come back at him with my fists, that he went down so fast he couldn't catch with his hands. His face hit flat against the floor and his nose was flattened. The blood spurted as he started to get up.

I let him get to his feet. I wondered if I should. For I knew it was either him or me. One of us had to whip. When he did get to his feet after that terrible fall, I waded into him. I hit fast and I hit hard. He swung wild. His fingernail took a streak of hide from my neck and left a red mark that smarted and the blood oozed through. I pounded his chin. I caught him on the beardy jaw. I reeled him back and followed up. I gave him a left to the short ribs while my right in a split second caught his mouth. Blood spurted again. Yet he was not through. But I knew I had him.

"Had enough?" I panted.

He didn't answer. I didn't ask him a second time. I hit him hard enough to knock two men down. I reeled him back against a seat. I followed up. I caught him with a haymaker under the chin and laid him across the desk. Then he rolled to the floor. He lay there with blood running from his nose and mouth. His eyes were rolled back. I was nearly out of breath. My hand ached. My heart pounded. If this is teaching school! I thought. If this goes with it! Then I remembered vaguely I had asked for it. I'd asked for this school. I would take no other.

Guy Hawkins lay there sprawled on the unswept floor. His blood was mingled with the yellow dirt carried into the school-room by seventy bare feet. I went back and got the water bucket. With a clean handkerchief, I washed blood from his mouth and nose. I couldn't wash it from his shirt. I put cool water to his forehead.

I worked over a pupil—trying to bring him back to his senses —who only a few hours before I had stood beside and tried to teach how to pronounce words when he read. "Don't stumble over them like a horse stumbles over frozen ground," I told him, putting it in a language he would understand. I had pro-moted him. I'd sent Guy and Ova after water when other pupils had wanted to go. On their way to get water, I knew they chewed tobacco and thought they were putting something over on me. I had known I couldn't allow them to use tobacco at school. I had known the time would eventually come. But I wanted to put it off as long as I could. Now I had whipped him and I wondered as I looked at him stretched on the floor how I'd done it. He was really knocked out for the count. I knew the place where we had fought would always be marked. It was difficult to remove bloodstain from pine wood. It would always be there, this reminder, as long as I taught school at Lonesome Valley.

When Guy Hawkins came to his senses, he looked up at me. I was applying the wet cool handkerchief to his head. When he started to get up, I helped him to his feet.

"Mr. Stuart, I really got it poured on me," he admitted. "You're some fighter."

This was the first time he had ever called me "Mr. Stuart." I had heard, but had pretended not to hear, him call me "Old Jess" every time my back was turned. He had never before, when he had spoken directly to me, called me anything.

"I'm not much of a fighter until I have to fight, Guy," I said. "You asked for it. There was no way around. I had to fight you."

"I know it," he said. "I've had in mind to whip you ever since I heard you's a-goin' to teach this school. But you win. You winned fair too," he honestly admitted. "I didn't think you could hit like that."

Guy was still weak. His nose and mouth kept bleeding. He didn't have a handkerchief and I gave him a clean one.

"Think you can make it home all right, Guy?"

"I think so," he said.

He walked slower from the schoolhouse than he had walked in. I was too upset to do any more work on my recordbook. I stood by the window and watched him walk across the school-yard, then across the foot log and down the Lonesome Creek Road until he went around the bend and was out of sight. Something told me to watch for Ova Salyers. He might return to attack me. I waited several minutes and Ova didn't come. Guy had come to do the job alone.

I felt better now that the fight was over, and I got the broom and swept the floor. I had quickly learned that the rural teacher was janitor as well, and that his janitor work was one of the important things in his school. I believed, after my brief experience, that the schoolhouse should be made a place of beauty, prettier and cleaner than any of the homes the pupils came from so they would love the house and the surroundings, and would think of it as a place of beauty and would want to keep it that way.

The floor was easy to sweep. But it was difficult to clean blood from the floor. I carried a coal bucket of sand and poured it on the blood and then shoveled up the sand and carried it out. I had the blood from the floor. Then I scrubbed the place but the stain was there. I could not get it from the oily, soft pine wood. I knew this was one day in my teaching career I would never forget.

The Contest with Landsburgh High School

Here is the story of another unforgettable day in my teaching career. It also concerns a battle but not the kind I fought with Guy Hawkins. The battle here is a battle of minds; the combatants are the student body of Winston High School, 14 pupils strong, with me as the sole teacher, versus the student body of Landsburgh High School, 400 pupils strong.

WHEN I told my pupils about a scholastic contest with Landsburgh High School, I watched their expressions. They were willing and ready for the challenge. The competitive spirit was in them.

"We must review everything we have covered in our textbooks," I told them. "We must cover more territory in our textbooks too. Hold up your right hands if you are willing!"

Every pupil raised his hand.

Right then we started to work. In addition to regular assignments, my pupils began reviewing all of the old assignments we had covered.

Despite the challenge ahead and all the reviewing and study we planned to do, we never stopped play. The Tiber River was frozen over. The ring of skates and merry laughter broke the stillness of the winter nights. We skated on the white winding ribbon of ice beneath the high, cold winter moon. Often we'd skate until midnight. We'd hear the wind blow mournfully over the great white silence that surrounded us and sing lonesome songs without words in the barren branches of the bankside trees. And we'd hear the foxes' barking, high upon the walls of sheltering cliffs, mocking the music of our ringing skates.

Over the week ends we'd go to Tiber where we'd cut holes in the ice and gig fish. The boys and I would rabbit-hunt up and down the Tiber Valley in the old stubble fields now covered with snow and swept by wind. We'd track minks, possums, raccoons, weasels, and foxes to their dens. We'd climb the mountains and get spills over the rocks into the deep snow. This took our minds from books and taught us another kind of education. It was as much fun as reading books. Now that a big contest was before us, we needed diversion. And we got it. Our state was not usually cold enough for winter sports. This winter was an exception, and we took full advantage of it.

When we hunted the girls didn't go with us, but when we skated, fished, and rode sleighs they went along. There was a long gentle slope not far from the schoolhouse, we found ideal for our sleighs. It was almost a mile to the end of our sleigh run. We went over the riverbank and downstream for many yards on the Tiber ice. We rode sleighs during the noon hour, before and after school.

On winter days when the snow had melted, leaving the dark earth a sea of sloppy mud, we designed floor games for our little one-room school. They were simple games such as throwing bolts in small boxes. And we played darts. We also played a game called "fox and goose." We made our fox-and-goose boards and we played with white, yellow, and red grains of corn. We had to make our own recreation. I never saw a distracted look on a pupil's face. I never heard one complain that the short, dark winter days were boresome because there wasn't anything to do. I think each pupil silently prayed for the days to be longer. We were a united little group. We were small but we were powerful. We played hard, and we studied hard. We studied and played while the December days passed.

When the big day came, early January, we dismissed school. This was the first time we had dismissed for anything. We had never lost an hour. I had actually taught more hours than was required. This was the big day for us. It was too bad that another blizzard had swept our rugged land and that a stinging wind was smiting the valleys and the hills. But this didn't stop the boys and me from going. Leona Maddox, my best Latin pupil, couldn't go along. Her father, Alex Maddox, wouldn't let her ride a mule seventeen miles to Landsburgh to compete in a contest on a day like this. I couldn't persuade him to let her go.

On that cold blizzardy morning, Budge Waters rode his mule to school very early and built a fire in the potbellied stove. When the rest of us arrived on our mules at approximately seven o'clock, Budge had the schoolroom warm. We tied our mules to the fence, stood before the fire, and warmed ourselves before we started on our journey. Then we unhitched our mules from the fence and climbed into the saddles. Little clouds of frozen snow in powdery puffs arose from the mules' hoofs as six pupils and their teacher rode down the road.

Though the force of wind in the Tiber Valley was powerful,

it was at our backs. The wind was strong enough to give our mules more momentum. We made good time until we left the valley and climbed the big hill. Here, we faced the wind. It was a whipping wind—stinging, biting wind on this mountain—that made the water run from our eyes and our mules' eyes, but for us there was no turning back. We were going to Landsburgh High School. That was that. We were determined to meet this big school; big to us, for they outnumbered us twenty-six to one. Soon we were down in Hinton Valley. Then we rode to the top of the Raccoon Hill, where we faced the stinging wind again.

"Mr. Stuart, I have been thinking," Budge Waters said, as we rode along together, "if you can sleep in a fodder shock when it's twelve degrees below zero, we can take this contest from Landsburgh High School! I've not forgotten how you walked seventeen miles to carry us books. All of your pupils remember. We'll never let you down!"

Budge Waters thought of this because we were riding down the mountain where I had slept that night. Then we rode down into the Raccoon Valley, and Billie Leonard, only thirteen years old, complained of numbness in his hands, feet, and lips. He said he felt as if he was going to sleep. I knew what he was talking about. I had had the same feeling the day Ottis Baylor had put my hands and feet in cold water. We stopped at a home, tied our mules to the fence, and went in and asked to warm. Bert Patton, a stranger to us, piled more wood on the open fire until we were as warm as when we had left the schoolhouse. We told him who we were and where we were going.

"On a day like this!" he said, shaking his head sadly.

We climbed into the saddles again. We were over halfway now. The second hitch would put us at Landsburgh High School. We had valley all the way to Landsburgh, with walls of rugged hills on each side for windbreaks.

At eleven o'clock we rode across the Landsburgh High School

yard, and hitched our mules to the fence around the athletic field. There were faces against the windowpanes watching us. Then we walked inside the high school, where Principal Ernest Charters met and welcomed us. He told us that he was surprised we had come on a day like this and that we had been able to arrive so soon.

In the Principal's office my pupils and I huddled around the gas stove while we heard much laughter in the high-school corridors. The Landsburgh High School pupils thought we were a strange-looking lot. Many came inside their Principal's office to take a look at us. We were regarded with curiosity, strangeness, and wonder. Never before had these pupils seen seven mules hitched to their schoolyard fence. Never before had they competed scholastically with so few in number—competitors who had reached them by muleback. The Landsburgh High School Principal didn't feel about the contest the way we felt. To him, this was just a "setup" to test his pupils for the district contest which would soon be held. He told me this when he went after the sealed envelopes that held the questions. We warmed before the gas stove while he made arrangements for the contest.

"Those questions were made out by the state department of education," he said when he returned. "I don't know how hard they are."

My pupils stood silently by the stove and looked at each other. We were asked to go to one of the largest classrooms. A Landsburgh High School teacher had charge of giving the tests. When the Landsburgh High School pupils came through the door to compete against my pupils, we knew why Principal Charters had selected this large classroom. My pupils looked at each other, then at their competitors.

I entered redheaded Jesse Jarvis to compete with ten of their plane-geometry pupils. I entered Billie Leonard against twenty-one of their selected algebra pupils.

"Budge, you'll have to represent us in grammar, English literature, and history," I said. "And I believe I'll put you in civil government. Is that all right?"

"Yes," he agreed. Budge had never had a course in civil government. All he knew about it was what he had read in connection with history.

"Robert Batson, you enter in history and grammar.

"Robin Baylor, you enter in algebra.

"Snookie Baylor, you enter in algebra and plane geometry.

"Sorry, Mr. Charters," I said, "we don't have anyone to enter in Latin. My best Latin pupil, Leona Maddox, couldn't make this trip."

After the contest had begun, I left the room. Miss Bertha Madden was in charge. I took our mules to Walter Scott's barn on the east end of Landsburgh, where I fed and watered them.

With the exception of an interval when the contestants ate a quick lunch, the contest lasted until 2:30 P.M. I had one pupil, Budge Waters, in four contests. I had planned to enter him in two. Just as soon as Budge had finished with civil government, we started grading the papers. All the pupils were requested to leave the room.

We graded the papers with keys. Mr. Charters, Miss Madden, and two other teachers, and I did the grading. Mr. Charters read the answers on the keys, and we checked the answers. Once or twice we stopped long enough to discuss what stiff questions these were. We wondered how far we would have gotten if we —all of us, college graduates—had taken the same test. One of the teachers asked me, while we graded these papers, if Budge Waters had ever seen these questions before.

When we were through grading the papers, Mr. Charters called the contestants into the classroom.

"I want to read you the scores of this contest," Principal Charters said. His voice was nervous.

"Budge Waters, winner in English literature.

"Budge Waters, winner in grammar.

"Budge Waters, winner in history with almost a perfect score.

"Budge Waters, winner in civil government.

"Why didn't you bring just this one boy?" Principal Charters asked me.

"Because I've got other good pupils," I quickly retorted.

"Billie Leonard, winner in algebra, with plenty of points to spare.

"Jesse Jarvis, second in plane geometry, lost by one point.

"Snookie Baylor and Robin Baylor tied for second place in algebra.

"Congratulations," said Principal Charters, "to your pupils and to you, on your success. It looks as though Winston High will represent this county in the district scholastic contest. I've never heard of such a remarkable thing."

When we left the Landsburgh High School we heard defeated pupils crying because "a little mudhole in the road like Winston beat us."

In a few minutes our mule cavalcade passed the Landsburgh High School. Faces were against the windowpanes and many pupils waved jubilantly to us as we rode by, our coattails riding the wind behind our saddles, and the ends of our scarfs bright banners on the wind. We rode victoriously down the main street of Landsburgh on our way home.

The Year of My Rebirth

Author's Introduction

This is a book about life—or, more specifically, about the life I almost lost on October 8, 1954. On that day, as I was leaving the auditorium at Murray State College in Kentucky after giving a lecture, it happened—a heart attack. At the time I didn't understand; it was only much later that I realized that, rather than being an end, October 8, 1954, was a beginning.

I was confined in Room 223 in the Murray Hospital. I learned later that I was given one chance out of a thousand to live. For seven days my clothes were not removed for fear the least movement of my body would finish me. I was in an oxygen tent for twenty-one days and in the hospital forty days before I could be moved.

It took five days to take me 500 miles to my home in W-Hollow in eastern Kentucky. I was permitted to travel only a few hours each day. Most everyone thought my life's work was finished.

At my home on my farm in W-Hollow, I was put to bed. I was not permitted visitors except my wife and daughter and a few of my relatives. But in my room there was a window where I could see out on a walk in our backyard. Here my wife, Naomi, fed small grain to the birds. She fed carrots and lettuce to the wild rabbits, corn to the gray squirrels, and bread to the possums. I watched many species of wild birds fly in over the white fields of snow and pick up the grain

263

from the walk. I watched the two possums who came from under our floor, where they slept by the hot water pipes, and ate the bread. I watched the wild rabbits hop in from their nesting places under the ferns and in the sedge to eat the carrots and lettuce leaves. And I watched the gray squirrels come down the hill, from a giant white oak which was their winter home, to eat the corn she had left for them upon the picnic table. Then, I watched the little ground squirrels come in and gather loads of small grain into their mouths and scamper away. They denned in holes behind the rock walls on either side of a stream that flowed through our yard and through a large tile under our house. All of the different species of birds and animals ate together. Although I wasn't permitted to have company, I wasn't lonely. I could see so much through my window.

It was now three months that I had been confined to bed. I was beginning to wonder if I would ever be well again. And then something happened that gave me new courage. On January 1, 1955, the year and I started out together, brand new: I began writing a daily journal. I was writing this journal for two reasons. As a result of my heart attack my hands had become stiff and sore. Dr. Vidt suggested that I gently squeeze and fondle a rubber ball to loosen them up. That sounded like nonsense to me. I'd rather gently tap the keys of my typewriter and maybe write a few stories and poems as a by-product.

That's what they were afraid of. They'd taken my old friend, the typewriter, and stowed it in the attic, where I couldn't see it and be reminded of my beloved trade. But they allowed me a pen and a sheet or two of paper a day. So I decided to work the stiffness and soreness out of my fingers by writing a journal.

The second reason was my wife, Noami Deane. She

urged me to write it. Later she told my why. For weeks she had watched me lying in bed, staring at the ceiling, sometimes refusing to talk, examining my bleak future and wondering if it wouldn't have been better if my heart had stopped beating altogether. Naomi is a wise woman and, like other lucky men's wives, she knows me inside and out. She knew that, with me, it was write or die. She started me writing this journal.

"I want to keep a journal," I said to Dr. Vidt. "How much writing will I be permitted to do?"

"No more than one page a day," he told me. "If you feel the least bit tired, don't write that much."

"If I don't feel tired, can I do one page with each hand?" I asked.

He told me this would be all right. So, while lying in bed in January, I was allowed to write two pages of longhand per day. My hands were so stiff I could hardly hold a fountain pen. My writing was terrible, but readable. But as the days passed, I added a little more writing each day. And later, I was allowed to sit on the side of the bed and put my feet down on the floor. As strength returned to me, my wife Naomi and our daughter Jane helped me learn to walk again.

Soon I was walking across the room by myself. And very soon after I had taken my first steps, I was walking over the house and looking out the windows. My world from the windows of our house was a new one. Everything had a new meaning and life was greater than it had ever been. My world was expanding. Before the grass greened in our yard and the Easter lilies bloomed I had walked from our front door down the walk, about 100 feet, to the road. Everything I did was so exciting I recorded it in my journal. Each day the pages of my journal expanded. My hands were losing their stiffness slowly, and I was walking slowly. One day I walked over a hundred yards up the valley to the tool shed. By April I had walked a mile. I recorded all these things.

During the year I continued to write more each day, walk farther, and make friends with more animals and birds. Yet, I had to spend most of each day in bed. After I had taken my walk, I would lie in bed and write down my experiences. I wondered why I hadn't observed all of those things before in my valley where I was born and where I had lived all my life. The only reason I knew was that while I was well and strong, I had taken life for granted. I did not realize its value. I knew its value now. I knew what it was to struggle to live. I felt deeply for all the living things of this earth, human and animal. And then I found the words for the dedication to my journal, The Year of My Rebirth: "For all those who have the will to live."

I Will Not Die

In order for you to understand the full implication of what that dedication means to me, I want you to read the following excerpt from the book's Prologue which describes my heart attack and what it did to me and for me.

ONE DAY in April of 1955, I found myself in pursuit of the first butterfly of spring. He was a large fellow, yellow with black trimmings on the wings, and flying against a stiff, cool morning wind. I didn't chase him, but I walked briskly to see where he was going. Why was I following a butterfly? I stopped in the front yard and started thinking.

When I was a small boy and played along the W-Hollow stream, I used to sit for hours, back a safe distance, where I could watch them drink the sun-warmed water from the sand bar. Wild honeybees often came to the same sand bar for a load of warm water. Loaded, they'd take off like a plane, get higher and higher, and then level off on their proper course. They went straight toward a wild-bee tree somewhere in the woods and I would course them until I found the tree. It was a lot of fun to sit for hours and watch the wild bees and the multicolored butterflies. I often scared the butterflies up from the sand into a brilliant cloud in the sunlight.

In those days I'd never seen a movie. Radio and television were unheard of then. I'd never read a novel, and we didn't take any magazines. My only recreation was observing the wild-life of bees, birds, and animals that lived around me. And I found more than bees and butterflies watering on sand bars along the streams. I found turtles' nests with white, tough-shelled eggs where the sun would heat the sand someday and hatch little turtles. I found terrapins' nests in the sand and water snakes sunning on logs and rocks above the stream. I watched silver minnows darting up and down the deep holes of blue water, waiting for some insect to drop from the air.

I read the landscapes, the streams, the air, and the skies. I took my time about doing it. I had plenty of time to live and to think. I had plenty of time to grow up in a world that I loved more and more as I grew older. I didn't know then how good a world it was to grow up in. I didn't know how fortunate I was until later, when I saw other American children in the big cities who had to play ball in a street and dodge automobiles. They always had to be on the lookout for something that might hurt them. I had never seen a car until I was seven years old.

I had so many good, carefree, lazy days as I was growing up. I never rushed at anything, unless we had a field to finish plowing before a rain came. And in "case of a pinch"—my father used to call it—I could do as much work as two or three my age. But normally I'd sit under the hickory trees and watch the gray squirrels eat, and never kill them. I liked to sit on a hilltop and listen to my hounds, Rags and Scout, chase a fox. I never got in a hurry up there unless I ran to a crossing to see the fox in the moonlight. When I possum-hunted, I never got in a hurry unless Sir Robert or Jerry-B-Boneyard, Don or Trusty-Red-Rusty caught something on the ground or was barking very fast at something in a small tree or in a shallow hole.

This was the kind of life I knew until I finished high school. Then I went to the steel mills. When the whistle blew in the morning, I had to be there. At noon, when it blew, I dropped whatever I was doing and ran to my boardinghouse, for I had only thirty minutes to eat and be back at work. When the whistle sounded at four, I could take my time walking to my boardinghouse, for the day was done. But at the steel mills I learned about whistles and what they meant. The sound of the whistle was a way of life. My way of life was changing.

I had tremendous strength and power. The strongest man I worked with in the blacksmith shop I once laid down in the dust. I got this strength by growing up slowly. I didn't have a balanced diet and all the vitamins. I had biscuits, fat pork, ham and red gravy, fried apples, and sometimes fried chicken for breakfast. And in season we often had squirrel for breakfast.

Now I was eating different food. I didn't get biscuits. I was eating toast. And lean hamburger instead of fat pork. But it wasn't the food that made the difference. It was the time that bothered me, and it bothered others. There was that eternal tension of keeping up with time. It was harder than the work. It geared one up until he lost his slow stride. I lost a part of the way I had lived on the farm. I watched people walking in cities. First it was very strange to watch everybody walking in a hurry, and I laughed. Even the city dogs, I thought, walked sidewise to keep from flying.

At a later date, in college, I didn't have any money, but had a will to work and a lot of confidence. So I started working my way through college. In one year I set a record at Lincoln Memorial University, for I never missed a meal in 365 days. I had to be there to wash the pots and pans. I thought the dining room couldn't open unless I was there. I was really getting into the swing of things. I went out for the cross-country, the two-mile, the quarter-mile, and low hurdles. I became editor of the college paper. When I went to read proofs of my paper, I walked from Harrogate, Tennessee, to Middlesboro, Kentucky, a distance of five miles, and through a long tunnel under Cumberland Gap. There were signs up saying, "Dangerous. Keep Out!" I disregarded the signs, for it saved time to walk through the hill and not over it. I was getting to be a keyed-up man. I had to make every minute count.

After graduating from college, I taught school and walked home seventeen miles—one way—on the weekends. I carried books to my pupils, not the state-prescribed list, but my list— good books I'd read. I saw the need of education, and I wasn't going to let anyone in a class of mine escape an education if I could help it. I'd teach him and I'd get him books. I didn't have time now to watch butterflies, and I had forgotten how to course bees.

Life had changed for me. I didn't have time to fool with people who were slow. I was kind to weakly people, but impatient with them. When I carried 100-pound sacks to or from a truck on our farm, I first carried one, then two, and I got up to three. Why lose all that time carrying 100 pounds at a time? Besides, there was something wrong with a man who couldn't carry twice his own weight. Insects and small animals could. There were insects that could lift forty times their own weight. I cut eighty-eight shocks of corn, twelve hills square on a steep hillside, in one day when two men my age, working on the opposite hill in corn the same size, cut thirty-nine. When two men strained to lift a tile—and this on my fortieth birthday—I told them to stand back. I lifted the 400-pound concrete tile, reinforced with steel, up into the wheelbarrow. Yet this wasn't twice my weight. That would have been 444 pounds.

I was really getting out of the rut now. The boys I knew and liked were the huskies who wouldn't take no for an answer. I liked these doers. I was one. Time would run out one of these days. Even if I lived to be ninety, there was not time enough. My mother's father, uncles, and aunts had averaged ninety-two years. Dad's hadn't been so fortunate. Many of them had died younger because they'd got tangled up with unfriendly mountain neighbors. But I had the years ahead of me. And schools all over America needed plenty done for them. In one year I made eighty-nine talks in thirty-nine states. That year I had two books published, as well as a few short stories and articles. I didn't have time to write poems any more, except in airports and railway and bus stations.

No longer did I work a day on my farm and then walk slowly five miles to the post office and back, stopping to sit along the way by wild phlox or on the bank of a quiet stream and write poems. I'd lost that good feel of earth, its beauty and sounds, I once had. I didn't have time now. I'd made a road and owned a car, and I couldn't waste time walking five miles. I'd once heard a friend of mine say, "America is my lemon. Brother, how I love its juice." This was the way I felt too. I was teaching, writing, buying more hill acres and trying to farm them, and I was sought after as a lecturer. One night was long enough in any city where I lectured. I used every spare minute to see more of America. Drive, drive, like the drive wheels on a big Mallet engine. Once I liked the train rides across the Midwest, the fast trains that thundered across America. But these trains got too slow for me. I had to save time. I needed more time. I liked to take nonstop flights between Chicago and Dallas, and Chicago and New York, and Miami and Boston. I liked that world above the skies. I liked the company of hurrying people.

One night we landed in New Orleans and the limousine from the airport got behind some slowpoke. The fellow next to me started talking to the driver about our Louisiana hayride. I chimed in about the slow ride. We passed a wreck on the way, but so what! Wrecks were for other people. Not for a limousine on its way to distribute important folks like us to our hotels. This stranger and I made the driver mad, and we didn't tip him. He made us mad, too.

Another time, it took the limousine as long to get from the airport to downtown Chicago as it had taken me to fly from Huntington, West Virginia, to Chicago. I let the driver know I didn't like slow service. If he got me to Chicago in a hurry, he always got a good tip. I liked speed. I was a speedy American. I was getting into the swing of a life that had crept up on me so gradually I took it to be normal.

My wife, Naomi, was the first one to meddle with me. She said, "Why are you always in a hurry? You're even in a hurry to eat. You'd better slow down."

She's the only one who ever tried to halt me. I told her I was pushing on only three fronts now: writing, lecturing, and farming—tree farming, for I'd set 22,000 trees the last two years. I'd be too old to reap the benefit of those trees. But somebody would. I'd never been a selfish guy. Naomi shouldn't comment. I was forty-seven, but Mom's ancestors averaged ninety-two. I reminded Naomi of that. And she said, "Yes, but their world was different. It was a quiet country world, like you were born and grew up in."

I was glad it was different. I liked my day and time better. I wanted to live long enough to ride on a plane powered by cosmic rays. I'd been reading a lot in the papers about it. That would be the way to travel—fast!

But I had seen a few things I couldn't forget. Once I was in a hurry in Manhattan, so I rushed into a self-service place, where I would not have to starve while I waited on the slow waiters. As I was getting a piece of pie, I looked at a large heavy man with a small mustache, tired eyes, and a bow tie. He toppled over and almost took me with him. He fell like a sawed-down tree, but I jumped back and he missed me. There was a doctor inside and he made the people stand back. An ambulance was called, and the man was carried out, moaning and groaning, on the stretcher. I bought four or five papers that evening to see if he was important enough to be mentioned. He wasn't. He might have been just another small businessman. But I wanted to know what had happened to him. That was a strange thing to do, just fall over like that.

Another strange thing happened in Chicago. I was trying to pass a man, walking fast, on the sidewalk. I was already abreast of him, when he pitched forward. A cop saw him fall, and came running. Then he called an ambulance. But this man died while the cop and I stood there. Others gathered around to look. The ambulance and a doctor came, but it was too late. After they put him in the ambulance, someone said, "Well, we've all got to go. That's a nice way. He went in a hurry!"

That happened to this man all right. But each one gathered there was sure he wouldn't be next. Stress and strain. People always in a hurry. Death on the street. I knew this wasn't for me. I had almost a half century before me yet. This quick death was for others. But I did have worries. I didn't know exactly why. My debts were paid. I had money ahead. I had a home, a checking account, and a car. I had an agreeable wife, except she was always after me for hurrying. Sometimes she actually nagged at me about it. But I still held onto my male independence. Once she told me I might topple over if I didn't slow down. That was when I was telling her how to drive the car to beat the scoundrel that tried to hog the road. I told her to ram him. That was after the doctor gave me some little green pills to slow me down. His green pills didn't slow me down, because I slowed them down the drain.

Then, one day in September of 1954, I had some sort of pain

in my chest. Nothing I took relieved me. I'd never had a pain like this one. I didn't think I could get my breath much longer. Finally, Naomi dragged me to the young doctor in my home town, and he laid me down on a table and put a pill under my tongue about the size of a No. 3 shot. Then I began to feel a little easier. The doctor told me to go to a heart specialist.

"Can't be my ticker, doc," I said. "For five generations on either side there has never been a heart attack."

"But you're living in a different age," he said.

Somebody had said that before.

I didn't want to go to the hospital, but they made me. I told the specialist exactly what had happened. Before I was through with him he called in a second specialist—a specialist's specialist, I guess—and I was in the hospital two nights and three days and had every test in the doctors' books thrown at me. But I was happy when they looked at this chest of mine and finally smiled and said, "Your trouble is muscular. Chest muscles, that's what's wrong."

No man ever left a hospital happier than I. America was my lemon again. In less than two weeks I was on a plane flying across Kentucky. Train was too slow. I had with me three books to read, four stories, and a dozen poems to revise. The following day I was to give two major talks, one in the morning to the teachers of Kentucky's First Educational District at Murray and one at Flora, Illinois, in the afternoon. A chartered plane would be at Murray to take me to Flora. This was nothing special. I had made three major talks in a day, shuttling from talk to talk by chartered plane. I'd done it once in Illinois, flying in a little chartered plane across a part of Chicago to the big airport. I loved it.

In the Murray State College auditorium I had a full house. The balcony was filled, and at the back they were standing. I was scheduled to speak an hour. I spoke over an hour for good measure. When I finished, several were in the aisles to meet me.

I didn't have time to meet them. I had to hurry. The chartered plane was waiting. I had to be on my way to carry the ball for the schoolteachers of America. More than a hundred had come from the auditorium, and they watched from the side lines when the Opposition to Life broke through my imaginary defenses and brought me down with a shoestring tackle prettier than any ever made on a football field. My feet went higher than my head. *I will not die, I will not die,* I said to myself as I went down. I knew now what had happened to the man in the restaurant in Manhattan and what had stopped the man on the street in Chicago.

I never knew when or how I got to the hospital. Later, I learned I was blue and gasping for breath, that my crippled heart was beating over 250 times a minute trying to pump blood past the clot to save my life. Edith Meeker McDougall, who was to become my day nurse, met the ambulance when it arrived. She placed a resuscitator over my mouth and nose to give me extra oxygen. This might have been the split-second action that saved my life. I remember the kind face of this wonderful nurse when I awoke to consciousness.

After my wife arrived in Murray and realized the seriousness of my attack, she phoned our family physician, Dr. Charles E. Vidt, of Ironton, Ohio, who, with Dr. Hugh Houston of Murray, decided to call Dr. Woodford Troutman, a specialist from Louisville, to see me. I barely remember Dr. Troutman's visit. For, at that time, it was a matter of life and death with me. A heart attack wasn't anything like what I had a few times imagined one would be. I have never suffered any kind of pain, and never will again, comparable to the pain of a heart attack.

At this very minute two people are dying somewhere in America of heart attacks. Out of every 160 people in the United States, one person will die of a heart attack this year. And this victim can as well be you as the other fellow. Approximately three heart-attack victims out of every four survive, thanks to medical science and our skilled heart specialists and our heart associations and the great work they are doing. But of every five Americans who will die this year, approximately three will die of heart trouble.

I was lying helpless when I awoke to consciousness on a narrow hospital bed under an oxygen tent. The cool wind I had taken to be that of home was the good cool oxygen blowing over me from the tank. And the sound of the winds and the hissing snakes I had heard in dreams was the sound of the oxygen blowing from the tanks that was making the difference between life and death for me. I knew what had happened to me. I couldn't think very clearly, but I could remember vaguely the pain and the falling. I was among strangers until my wife walked into the room.

"What's this all about?" I whispered. "Where am I? In what hospital? When did you get here?"

Then I learned from Naomi Deane and my day nurse, Mrs. McDougall, that I was brought by ambulance from Marvin Wrather's home in a hurry the previous Friday at noon. Naomi and our daughter, Jane, had left home as soon as Mr. Wrather phoned the news to Greenup, Kentucky. Since we didn't have a phone, the message was relayed to Naomi, by her parents. She and Jane, along with my brother-in-law, Herbert Liles, my sister Glennis, and my brother James, drove that afternoon and all night, 500 miles to Murray, and arrived at four Saturday morning.

Others had come and gone—my father and my oldest sister, Mrs. Henry Keeney; Mr. and Mrs. Orin Nelson; another sister and brother-in-law; and two nieces and their husbands. All I could remember was a red shirt someone had worn. No visitors were supposed to be allowed in my room, but after they had driven this far, they were allowed in. They looked at me under the oxygen tent and then went away. My father had pushed three automobile loads of people relentlessly across the length of the state to get to me. This was the farthest distance he had ever been away from home. I felt very deeply about their making this long trip, and Naomi said I spoke to them and called them by name. This I do not recollect, for I was busy in my dreams, working with my parents on the land we loved. Say what one will, I believe that when the end is close one will go back, in dreams at least, to his beginning.

I told Naomi where I had been and what I had been doing. I was still tired. And somewhere close to my heart, my chest felt as if a hole had been torn in it. I could not lift my arms. I could not write, but I asked Naomi to take down a letter to Milton Eisenhower. I was sure I had seen Mrs. Milton Eisenhower. To this day I have never forgotten any detail of our meeting. Weeks after Naomi had sent the letter, it occurred to me that she had been dead for some time. Months before, I had read about her death in our local paper.

Then I dictated a second letter, to Glen Hilton, telling him to put lime on my ground to kill the broomsedge. My wife tried to stop me, but after the realistic dream I had of working with Glen Hilton, I insisted she send the letter. I wasn't thinking clearly when I did all this. But no one could have told me I wasn't. Dad was back home now trying to see that my orders for spreading lime, disking, and sowing were carried out as I had seen it done in my dream.

Living under this oxygen tent was a strange existence. I felt as if the sky had fallen in, that I was in my grave. I felt so powerless, so listless, I didn't want to move. Although my body was slow to come back, my mind came back more quickly. And when I was able to think, I was depressed to the extent that if there had been a weapon near and if I could have used my hands to reach it, I might have finished myself. This was not my way of thinking. Something had gone terribly wrong with me. Something had happened I couldn't help. Vaguely, I could remember harshly criticizing people for finishing their own lives when they were deeply afflicted by some incurable disease. Now I reasoned that they had been justified. Why come so near and not go all the way?

In these black days of depression, while I lay under the oxygen tent and saw only the faces of my wife, doctor, and nurses, I grew tired of each one. They were the dear people fighting the hardest to save my life. Yet the ones who did the most for me I cared for the least. I didn't have anything personal against them, but I couldn't warm up to them, couldn't feel thankful for their efforts. I reasoned very passively and calmly that they should let me die, let me get out from under that tent where the sky had come down and the grave had enclosed me.

They should let me die, let me have the second part of life, I thought. I had thoroughly enjoyed the first, up until now. But I was ready for the second half, the unknown. I was stirred by curiosity about the long journey. Even in my drugged state of body and mind, I could get a little excited about going. I would close my eyes and pretend that I was going, and sleep.

I entered a beautiful world long past, with sun I could not hold in the sky, flowers I could not keep fresh on their stems, and sumac leaves I could not keep from coloring and dying in an autumn season and blowing away on the wind of 1916.

The sudden flight of a pheasant from the cluster of sawbriers at my feet startled me. I stopped to watch the big bird rise up on its whirring wings to go over and down beyond the brush fence that enclosed our pasture field. I had scared this rooster pheasant up, and often his mate with him, many times before. But I had never found him in this part of the pasture where there was a grove of pine seedlings. Sawbrier clusters, growing among these young pines, made me careful where I stepped, since I was barefooted.

The sun was getting high in the blue sky, and I had not

found the cows yet. Gypsy was hiding. I had been down in the deep Byrnes Hollow where the tall beeches grew. I always went there first in the mornings to see the gray squirrels. They fed early and went into their hollow dens in the giant beeches long before the morning sun had dried the dew. But I was up early, too, and I sat under the den trees and watched the young squirrels come out of the holes and play on the big leafy branches.

I also knew where the wild birds' nests were—redbird, ground sparrow, song sparrow, and thrush. I had found a whippoorwill's nest once on a big leaf under an oak, and I had found a hummingbird's nest, too. I knew the crows had their nest in a tall pine and the chicken hawks had theirs in the bushy top of a giant whiteoak.

I could find all these birds' nests, and I was usually able to see snakes before they saw me. But Gypsy was hard to find in this forty-acre pasture, and that's why I always came out before my mother. There was a place where I drove Gypsy for her to milk. That was under the big, bushy-topped whiteoak that didn't shade anybody but Gypsy, my mother, and me.

"Jesse! Oh, Jesse!" Mom called. "What's keepin' you so?"

Mom's voice wasn't so pleasant. I'd know her voice anywhere and any time. I had been a little slow this morning, watching squirrels, listening to young hawks and crows as their parents fed them. I liked to stand under the trees and just listen.

"Jesse, Jesse, do you hear me?" Mom's familiar voice was louder and closer this time. "Answer me, Jesse! Have you found the cow?"

"No, Mom," I replied. "Gypsy's hidin' someplace."

"You've had time enough to have been over all the pasture two or three times," she said. "I'll find the cow myself."

I put my feet down carefully between the clusters of sawbriers, for I was ever mindful of snakes. Often a dark stick on the ground made me stop suddenly and jump back.

As I stepped between the sawbrier clusters, I touched the small pines with my hands. There were dewdrops on the pine-tree needles. These dewdrops weighted them like little lumps of polished silver until the sun lifted them skyward in white ribbons of mist. There were dewdrops on the red-tinted saw-brier leaves, the hard stems of the sawbriers, the milkweed and silkweed leaves, which were shaped like stiff hog's ears, only they were green. And the bright wind above me was filled with streamers of mist riding from the wild flowers, leaves, buds, briers, and pines. This pasture world was filled with the music of wild birds' singing and the soft blowing of the June wind through the pine needles and sumac leaves.

I knew my mother was hunting impatiently for Gypsy. But I could not help but stand there, bareheaded and barefooted, and breathe the fresh white mists into my lungs. In two springs and summers of hunting Gypsy here, I had never seen the pasture prettier. I hated to end it all by finding Gypsy and taking her to the whiteoak to be milked.

If only I could command the sun to stop where it was in the sky and hold all the white mists where they were in the air. If I could keep the pasture daisies as white and the wild roses as pink as they were now. If I could keep the sawbriers in clusters with their red-tinted leaves. If I could make this pasture and time stand still, I'd do it! I'd keep this world just as it was.

My father was thirty-five years old, my mother thirty-three, and they were very old and very wise to me. I was nine in this year of 1916, and I loved everything about it.

I stepped from the grove of miniature pines into the narrow little path made by Gypsy's tracks. Where the path made a sharp U-turn around a sweet-apple tree, I almost walked into Gypsy. Here she stood munching on the blighted sweet apples that had fallen to the ground. She was a big bony cow with a pair of horns fox hunters had already spoken for at her death. My father had often said the reason she was bony was because her horns were so big it sapped her strength to carry them. I *often wondered how she got through the brush and briers with such big horns. "Go on there, Gypsy," I scolded her loud enough for Mom to hear. "What are you doin' hidin' from me?"*

Gypsy had moved under a patch of alders. She was a smart cow all right. There the biting flies would leave her alone. They couldn't stand alder leaves when the sun dried the dew and the leaves began to wilt.

"So, you've finally found her," Mom said. She had come up from the Byrnes Hollow and into the path behind me.

"She was back there in the alder bushes," I said, surprised to see my mother pleased and smiling. Mom was tall, just an inch under six feet, and her hair was black as the crows' wings. Mom's eyes were gray as the bark on the poplar tree, and her teeth between her smiling lips were as white as the daisy petals in the pasture.

"Come, Jesse," she said. "We must get the milking done."

Gypsy trotted on ahead of Mom and me, knowing there would be something special for her under the tree. Mom never missed bringing Gypsy something extra to eat while she milked her. Fresh-cut grass from the yard, apple peelings, sweet corn, corn shucks, or salt. This morning there was some salt under the tree.

When we reached the bushy-topped whiteoak where Mom milked, a gray squirrel ran out one of the long branches, jumped to the ground, and hopped over the hill toward the beech grove. My mother didn't even look up. She sat on a stool and milked with both hands. The streams of milk hitting the bottom of the big zinc bucket beat a rhythm all their own.

I stretched out upon the ground to look up into the whiteoak leaves. When the wind rustled the leaves I could see the blue sky. I half shut my eyes and looked through my eyelashes at the changing leaf pictures. I thought there might be another squirrel hidden among the trembling leaves.

I couldn't keep the pine seedlings from growing into saw-log timber. I couldn't stay the hunters' guns from pheasants, crows, hawks, and squirrels. I couldn't hold the wild rose and the blooming daisy beyond their seasons. I couldn't keep the young spring wind blowing over me. I suddenly wanted Mom to finish milking. I listened to hear her say, "Jesse, let's be goin'." For I was waking from this dream world I couldn't hold.

Instead of a warm June wind and green leaves above me, there was the hiss of oxygen in a cool tent. That wasn't my mother standing there. It was a nurse. My mother no longer milked Gypsy under the whiteoak. Mom rested at Plum Grove. And this wasn't 1916, it was 1954. But dream world or real, there was one thing I was certain of. I had been with an angel in that pasture.

The Summing-up

This next excerpt tells you about one of the happiest days of my life—as a writer, a teacher, and a Kentuckian.

ALL MY LIFE important things have happened to me in October, the middle part of October particularly. Naomi Deane and I were married by a (retired) Methodist minister on October 14—actually at 12:05 in the morning, so as to avoid getting married on Friday the thirteenth. We were that superstitious. Then my first book, *Man with a Bull-tongue Plow*, was published on October 14, 1934. For one reason or another—I never asked for it—eight of my books have been published on October 14. When one of my books became the selection of a book club, my publisher gave me a big party in New York on October 14. We ended up at the Stork Club at three o'clock in the morning. That was the only time I was ever in the Stork Club.

This year a group of my friends, citizens of Riverton and Greenup, and some civic groups chose October 14 on which to pay me a great honor. Then they changed it to October 15, a Saturday, so that schoolteachers could come from around the state.

I don't know exactly how to describe this occasion. They had the Governor proclaim it Jesse Stuart Day. The president of the University of Kentucky came down to speak. Hundreds of my friends, hundreds of other people I'd never set eyes on, newspaper reporters, and radio people came here to wish me well. They unveiled a stone marker set on the green in front of the courthouse in Greenup with my name and face and a few kind words on it. It turned out that my friends around here had been planning this occasion for a long time, ever since I was so sick that they didn't know if I was going to pull through.

I gave a short speech today, the first one I've been allowed to give in a year and a week. Maybe it's the last one I'll ever give. And it wasn't much of a speech because my doctors said I had to write it all out beforehand and then read it very slowly. I'd rather speak spontaneously, and in the old days I would use hardly a note. But this is what I said today:

My friends, I've spoken to many audiences over America, but this is the greatest audience I have ever faced. This is the highest honor that has ever come to me, to stand here on this spot in the courthouse yard and speak to you. All along this has seemed like a dream, but now I know this is reality.

It is a fine tribute to anyone to be so honored in his home town. And it is most unusual for a writer. When you travel over America, you see but few markers up for writers. Those few you find were erected after their deaths. What makes this occasion unique is the fact that this tribute is being paid to me in my lifetime. I have not always been a good boy in my home town. But I never was at any time in my life without ambitions and dreams. Because this is my country that I know so well. I've written so much about this town, changed its name three times, on paper that is, to Greenwood, Blakesburg, and Honeywell.

The Tussies and Bushmans, Didway Hargis, Sparkie, Arn and Peg Sparks, Shan, Finn, and Mick Powderjay, Old Op and Lucretia Acres, Doshie, Hootbird and Ben Hammertight, Alf and Julia Pruitt, the Beatinest Boy, Scrappie Lykins III, and Red Mule—all are my children. There are a whole host of lesser-known children, too. Maybe because my friends here know these people so well is why I am honored today.

Perhaps another reason why this has happened is that I have dared to dream of lifting the education of our youth to a higher level and of doing something for the teaching profession. I have learned that sound teaching, tolerance, and love are the greatest things on earth. I know I've had teachers who have influenced my life.

You who visit Greenup, Kentucky, today, see the jackets of my books enlarged and displayed over the street intersections. When each of these was published, I always had two fears. I wondered what the repercussions would be on my people and my friends, and I used to think there would never be another book of mine published. But there have been more published. There will always be more published as long as I live. I am not boasting when I say this. I have too much to say, too many stories to tell, to quit now. This forces me to consider the time I have left.

Regardless of what has already or ever will happen to me, I have never felt sorry for myself. Now, I rejoice that I am living. Look today what I would have missed if those scales, holding life on one side and death on the other, so evenly balanced for so many days, had been tilted in death's favor. I wouldn't have been here speaking to you, standing before an audience for the first time since last October 8, when I spoke at Murray State College right before my attack. I am happy just to be alive. To be here to receive this honor in my home town from my neighbors, my near and faraway friends, makes me rejoice. I have so many things to be thankful for, of which the greatest is life.

Each day, I make myself believe this day will be the finest. Yesterdays are gone forever, and tomorrows never come. I feel just as surely as I am standing here that I have reached on this day the middle milestone of my life. I expect and hope to do as many more books as you see jackets displayed over the streets. I might even do more if I am given more time. This rests not only in the hands of my good physicians but in the hands of the Great Physician over all.

You know, my friends, people must have courage. The young, middle-aged, and old alike must be courageous. We must have the will to live forever. We must have the will to do forever. We must have the will to dream forever. We cannot turn back. We have to live now, in the present, rejoice, dream, and lay plans for those tomorrows that may never come.

If you read my earlier books, you will find they are now dated. I based those stories upon real incidents, real people. But things changed here. The people are still very much independent individuals. But when I first started writing, I used dialect. Dialect isn't spoken here very much any more. People's speech, dress, and way of life here have changed, and they continue to change at such a rapid rate it makes one's head swim. How can we remain isolated when our youth have fought all over the world, when they are practically all finished high school, and a solid minority of them are going to college? I am only forty-eight now, but I can remember when there were only six automobiles in this county. I've seen every foot of hardroad come. I worked here, doing a man's work, helping to pave the streets in this town before I entered high school.

As times have changed and people have progressed, my stories have changed. I seldom go back into history for a story. I have written of the present because I have found it interesting. I like to write of life that is being lived around me. I like to write about something I know and can see or have seen. And in the future I shall pursue the same course. People live dramas so strange and incredible they often have to be changed to be made plausible; then, they become fiction. I like to think I was born in the right place at the right time.

Here today among my many friends are people who have helped me when I needed help. Here in this group are people who have given me food when I was hungry. They have loaned me shirts and socks. They have given me a bed to sleep in on cold, rainy winter nights when I was walking to and from high school. Among my friends here today are four former teachers who helped shape my life: my first- and second-grade teacher, who taught me to read and write, Calvin Clarke, now a businessman in Portsmouth, Ohio; Mrs. Nora Riggs Scott of Flatwoods, Kentucky, who taught me in the sixth grade; Mrs. Earl Kotcamp of Greenup, who taught me in the seventh; and Mrs. W. A. Voiers of Vanceburg, Kentucky, who gave me extra of her time in high school to teach me algebra and who has remained interested in my work ever since.

I wish it were possible for two others to be here today. They have left many footprints on this spot of earth since the turn of this century, never dreaming a marker would be erected here to one of their children. This was their home town, too. I wish I could, in some way, turn back the clock and have them here for today. But this is impossible. They gave all their children good training and strong family ties. They encouraged us in our small but worthy endeavors. Our family was all for one and one for all. We learned to work, sweat, and live together. My home was the strong springboard from which I dove into the waters of life, believing firmly it was my duty to amount to something.

It can never be truthfully said that you in my home town haven't been good to me. You and my fictional children are becoming chummier all the time. Minor reforms in education which seemed radical twenty years ago, when I advocated them, have come to pass. Because I have followed my profession diligently, whether I have pleased or displeased you, I am thus honored by you. And for this honor I am grateful from the depths of my heart.

Reporters asked me yesterday how I felt about the celebration. I couldn't tell them, for the story was too long to tell. Only the people who have lived here know and remember. But I felt the way the Duke of Wellington must have felt after the Battle of Waterloo. Though he had won, his allied forces had taken a lot of punishment and there was great suffering. I felt the way General Meade must have felt after the Battle of Gettysburg. He had repelled General Lee's invasion of the North, but his losses were great and his forces were battered terribly. I felt victorious, but battered, too.

My battle lasted longer than the Duke's or the General's. I was never relieved of my command like Meade. My battle started on October 14, 1934, when I shocked this community with a big volume of verse. A few critics and reviewers called *Man with a Bull-tongue Plow* poetry. But only a few people here called it anything that was repeatable. These few were enlisted as my scouts. If they had not rallied around me, I couldn't have made it. They remained my true friends over the troubled years. They rejoiced yesterday when the marker was unveiled on the courthouse square in Greenup. Many of the older ones actually wept. But I didn't. I didn't shed a tear. I wouldn't let myself. To keep from doing so, all I had to do was to think back over the years.

My war actually started before October 14, 1934, when my first book was published. It started about 1929, when I did my first high-school teaching here, though there were clashes even back in 1924, when I was barely seventeen and did my first rural school teaching. The condition of our schools, and education generally, at that time was just miserable. Kentucky youth wasn't being given the chance, in these schools, to develop into an enlightened citizenry. It didn't take a smart man to see these obvious injustices, but it took a stubborn one to do something about them. After my first taste of teaching, I vowed to escape it forever. I hadn't planned any war, I liked to laugh a lot and have fun with my friends in town. I was not a radical. I was a hill-country Republican who voted and lost.

But in 1929, 1931, and from 1933 to 1937, I got into a series of violent school fights. I made more enemies than I'd ever believed a man could make in such a short time. I wrote article after article about schools and teachers, stupidities and abuses in education, and my beliefs—they never got published. Finally, I burned all these articles no one would accept. But I couldn't burn away my ideas.

The ideas and changes I fought so hard for in those days seem like only common sense today. Most of them have been accepted, bills passed, legislative action taken. I fought for consolidation of the schools, even though I lived and taught in a small backwoods school district, because I knew that bigger schools would bring finer facilities and better education to the outlying districts. I fought to do away with local district trustees. In my early years of teaching, each local school district (and there was only one school to a district and one teacher to a school) had three trustees, five members of the county board of education, and a superintendent. That meant that a single teacher had nine bosses to report to. She didn't know which way to turn.

I fought the school board when it passed a rule that married women couldn't teach. As early as 1932, I fought for old-age and retirement pensions for teachers. I fought the parents who wanted to keep their young children home from school during planting and harvesting seasons to work on the farm. I drummed it into their heads over and over again: school comes first, school comes first. I struggled to open up McKell High School to everyone, no matter what his age, and I had pupils from eleven to sixty-seven. I attacked and tried to have changed the unfair system of taxation by which schools were supported and which injured the schools in rural areas. I insisted that even in the lower grades the school term should last for nine months, that the thorough education of the very young was the most important of all.

I wrote articles, I made speeches, I pestered and plagued people. I fought hard, maybe too hard, anyway hard enough to make a lot of enemies.

When I was superintendent of Greenup County schools, two years before my first book was published, I finally had to go armed. I received threatening letters. I had fist fights. The people in certain county districts rose up against me. Many times my mother sent brother James to warn me not to walk on a certain road on my way home. We had friends who reported what they heard to my parents. My brother or one of my sisters, sometimes both, got a message through to me wherever I was and regardless of what I was doing, even if I was in a meeting with my school board. Certain people my secretary always let in to see me. They came only only for one purpose. To warn me of danger.

Next I was elected principal of McKell High School in Western Greenup County. There I worked under a friendly county-school superintendent and helped to build one of the finest high schools in this state. Though I still received threatening letters, I disregarded them. I was a happy man, writing and teaching, buying discarded acres, setting trees, dating Naomi Deane Norris. But people still disliked me at home. My brother had an old car, for which he paid fifty dollars, and he used to drive to the house where I boarded to tell me when to come home and when to stay away.

After I went to England on a Guggenheim Fellowship, I thought that, when I returned, everything would be all right. I started a newspaper, since I couldn't get back my principalship of McKell High School. In fact I couldn't get a place to teach anywhere in Kentucky, near or far. So I crossed the river to Portsmouth, Ohio, where I had a most successful teaching year and continued to edit my paper. But once too often I went home.

The day before, my brother drove all the way to Portsmouth in his old car to tell me to stay out of my home town, that the feeling was still high there. I disregarded this warning. I wanted to see my parents, and I wanted to see Naomi Deane Norris. Besides, I wasn't afraid. I got the worse end of the fracas. On a side street in Greenup I was slugged from behind with a blackjack. I bled profusely, blood filling my shoes from the three scalp wounds, two of which laid open my skull.

There followed two attempts to bring my assailant to trial. People on both sides went armed. The feeling was so high for the first trial that it was postponed. It was postponed again for a similar reason. Although this man had tried to kill me, the indictment against him was for assault and battery rather than for a felony. I'm glad at least that I wasn't armed that night. When finally brought to trial, he was fined two hundred dollars. I understand he never paid the fine. If it was ever paid, his friends paid it. I don't know. I don't like to think about this. I don't even care to remember him.

But I had shaped my life. Angry men with blackjacks couldn't change that. I knew what I wanted to do. I wanted to teach, write, conserve land, and work with American youth. I believe that educators, with their way-over-the-head theories, were missing the point. We must start from the practical bottom and work up, instead of starting at the theoretical top and, perhaps, tumbling down. It didn't take a deep thinker and a smart man to observe what I had. I wasn't either of these. I was a country schoolteacher with a little experience and a dream.

My parents begged me to leave the progress of schools to others and to get out while I was alive. One school-board member, my best friend, told me not to reapply for county superintendency, for if I served again, I would be killed. He said I had done more in one year with the scarce dollars than others had done in twenty-five. But he said I went too fast. I should leave it to others now to consolidate my gains.

Writing and World War II took me away from teaching, and I never returned, at least not full time. Now all that could cause my unpopularity at home was the sensitivity of people when they read one of my books. These books were admittedly about them. People declared I had hurt my part of America, my state, home town, and friends. They claimed my books were not true pictures. The criticism that hurt me most was of *Foretaste of Glory*, which appeared early in 1946, shortly after I was released from service. This book was so unpopular I almost gave up. I wondered if my writing life was worth constantly taking these insults and angry attacks. And I knew that

I could write only of home, my valley, these people.

My wife and I sat down one day and discussed if we would leave here and where we would go. And when I got to thinking about leaving my country, not fighting for this land and these schools and these people I loved, I got my fighting clothes on again. The result was an article, "I Made My Home Town Mad." And I wrote another, "An Author in His Home Town." Both articles were published. I wouldn't leave now. I determined to stay and fight. The fighting had diminished to words. There wasn't any violence. There were no more near riots. I was gaining ground. Many of the people who disliked me personally at least respected my opinions now.

Also, I had a new group coming on. These were the young people I had taught. They were my friends. Had all remained close to home, I soon would have had the majority on my side. But many left here for other parts of this country for economic reasons. But things were changing for me. I was given honorary degrees by four institutions in four different states, one of which was 1,700 miles away. My stories, poems, parts of my books were published in a hundred high school and college textbooks. If the children of my enemies went through high school, studied their English textbooks, they would probably run across my name. A succession of mayors of our little town got letters of inquiry about me. The last one got so many he couldn't answer them in his nonsalaried office. He asked me to write a pamphlet about myself answering a number of stock questions so he could send it out. Slowly the people in town, almost all of them, came around.

How did I feel to end this twenty-one-year-old war, this series of battles that had lasted from October 14, 1934, to October 15, 1955? I never had such a wonderful feeling. It ended better than any book I have ever written. I wanted to be loved by the people of my town, for I loved them. What on earth could make a man happier than to be honored by his neighbors?

Jesse Stuart,
Poet

Poetry

Author's Introduction

Writing poems is a part of my living almost as essential as breathing or eating. Whether my way of creating poems is the right way or not, it is the right way for me. Whether my subject matter for verse is right or not, it is right for me. I like to write them my way. I like to select the raw material and weave a poetic fabric of my own.

It is impossible for me to belong to a school of poetry unless it would be built around me or over me. My poetry has to be my way. I hardly expect others, and do not even wish them to come my way. Let them be free to write any way they wish or any way they can.

I have written poems as far back as I can remember. I am not, however, a machine, capable of writing a poem every day. I cannot write until the mood occurs; but when it does I have to write the same as I have to breathe. I have to write or die.

By the time I graduated from college, I had written many, many poems. But I didn't keep them all; some I lost, some I gave to friends, and some I threw away. Of all the poems I had written, I had saved 500.

In the next eleven months, I wrote 703 poems and called them Man with a Bull-tongue Plow. In the meantime I had lived a lot. I had done other things besides write poems. I had farmed during the summer and had failed, due to a disastrous drought. I was now superintendent of Greenup County schools in Kentucky. Since a depression was on and I couldn't get my pay for being superintendent, I sent sheafs of these poems to magazines. They sold and I received money —not much but enough to buy stamps and pay some long-overdue bills. Soon after the poems were printed in these magazines, a book publisher offered to publish them as a book. A few critics called that book, Man with a Bull-tongue Plow, a great book.

In the years that followed, regardless of whatever else I did, I continued to write poems. The words came like April showers. I wrote short stories as well and novels. They too were published.

Turning through an old family album, I got the idea for a second book of poems that I called Album of Destiny. I put 444 poems in this book. I was eleven years writing it. For each poem I kept I discarded five others. I put more time and effort on this book than any other I've written.

Album of Destiny was published in 1944, ten years after the appearance of Man with a Bull-tongue Plow. In two books 1,147 of my poems had been published.

After the war I continued writing poems. Now, instead of putting a large collection of poems together, I published a thin book of verse, Kentucky Is My Land, containing 87 poems.

After having published 1,234 poems in three books, I still couldn't stop writing poems. Ideas came to me on trains, in railway stations, in the schoolroom when I was teaching, and in the fields when I was farming.

After Kentucky Is My Land was published and during the decade from 1950 to 1960, many of the magazines that had published single poems of mine no longer existed. Many of the editors who had accepted my poems were now retired or were dead. Only a few editors would use my poems in their magazines. I couldn't get any publisher interested in a new collection of my poems. Although my three volumes had sold much better than the average poetry collection, I was sure I would never have another book of poems published. I was ready to accept the fact that I would never again achieve wide acceptance as a poet.

In 1960 I went to the American University of Cairo, Egypt, as visiting professor to teach courses in English and education. I was teaching in a school where there were twenty-nine nationalities among the students, and where eighteen languages and twelve dialects were spoken. All the while I was teaching, I kept up my own writing, including poems, although I was sure that, even though I'd never be through with poetry, poetry was through with me.

On February 2, 1961, Mr. Socrates Patsilides, Egyptian by birth but of Greek nationality, phoned me from his office at American University. We lived in an apartment on Gezirah Island which was in the heart of Cairo and was surrounded by the Nile.

"I have a cablegram for you," Socrates Patsilides said.

"Read it for me," I said.

And here is what he read over the phone to me: Delighted to advise the 1960 $5000 Fellowship of the Academy of American Poets awarded you by majority vote of twelve chancellors. Letter follows. Signed, Mrs. Hugh Bullock, President.

After I caught my second breath, I said: "Read it again. There must be some mistake."

"There is no mistake," he spoke positively. "I have read the cablegram correctly."

"I'll be right over," I told him. "Hold everything."

Our daughter Jane and a fellow teacher, Dr. Carl Leiden, and his daughter Leisa, who were in our apartment when I got this phone call, went with me by taxi

over to American University. In less than three minutes
we had covered the distance from our apartment to the
University, which in a round-about way was almost two
miles. I paid the driver 25 piastres for a 9-piastre fee
and told him to keep the change. We rushed through
the gate and to Socrates Patsilides' office.

"Five thousand dollars," Mr. Patsilides exclaimed.

Five thousand dollars was a fortune in Egypt. And it
was a fortune to me, too, for my salary at American
University didn't pay our expenses. Dr. Leiden, Jane,
and I read the cablegram at the same time.

"It looks authentic to me," Dr. Leiden said.

I wondered who was on the Board of Chancellors
that had chosen me for this honor. I didn't have long
to wait. Mrs. Hugh Bullock's letter, which followed
the cablegram said: "You may be interested to know
members of the Board of Chancellors who selected
you: J. Donald Adams, W. H. Auden, Witter Bynner,
Henry S. Canby, Max Eastman, Robert Hillyer, Ran-
dall Jarrell, Marianne Moore, Robert Nathan, John G.
Neihardt, Frederick A. Pottle, and John H. Wheelock."

Always before when I had received some honor, I
had rejoiced. Now, when I read the well-known names
on this list of authors, scholars, editors, and one publisher, names familiar to millions of Americans and
among them better-known authors than I, I wept. The
caliber of the men and women who had voted this
award to me was a greater honor than the financial
remuneration. This made up for all the losses, heart-
aches, and rejections I had received with poetry from
my high school days to the present. In 1962 I had another volume of poetry published called Hold April.

In this section I have selected twenty-six poems, from
Hold April, Kentucky Is My Land, and Man with a
Bull-tongue Plow.

A FARMER SINGING

Sir:

I am a farmer singing at the plow
And as I take my time to plow along
A steep Kentucky hill, I sing my song—
A one-horse farmer singing at the plow!
I do not sing the songs you love to hear;
My basket songs are woven from the words
Of corn and crickets, trees and men and birds.
I sing the strains I know and love to sing.
And I can sing my lays like singing corn,
And flute them like a fluting gray corn-bird;
And I can pipe them like a hunter's horn—
All of my life these are the songs I've heard.
And these crude strains no critic can call art,
Yours very respectively, Jesse Stuart.

TIME FOR A RHYME

Now I shall take the chance to spin a rhyme
And I shall let the fences go unmended,
I shall not dream of any future time
When strength of hand and power of brain are ended.
I shall consider not the fallow field
But I shall leave it for others to plow.
It is not time to think of plowing now,
For others can do work upon the field—
Now let them do it while I write a rhyme.
I speak of them and color of the clay,
I speak of men that live in my lifetime,
And I speak of the men of yesterday.
I do not care to know if this is art—
These common words born in a common heart.

LAND SCROLL

Across the empty fields winter retreats,
Releasing his high mortgage on the weather—
Then wary Spring trips back on airy feet
And buds and grass and wind all laugh together:
"Where is the mortgage winter held on weather—
Where is the winter desolate and gray?
Gone—Gone—and gone we hope forever."
The wind-flowers nod: "Yes, gone forever,
And gone we hope forever and a day—"
And that is all the white wind-flowers said,
Standing by last year's stems so cold and dead.
The land is left a scroll for winds to read—
The gray-starved land is used to birth and growth.
The gray-starved land is left to Spring and youth.

THIS LAND IS MINE

My land is fair for any eyes to see—
Now look, my friends—look to the east and west!
You see the purple hills far in the west—
Hills lined with pine and gum and black-oak tree—
Now to the east you see the fertile valley!
This land is mine, I sing of it to you—
My land beneath the skies of white and blue.
This land is mine, for I am part of it.
I am the land, for it is part of me—
We are akin and thus our kinship be!
It would make me a brother to the tree!
And far as eyes can see this land is mine.
Not for one foot of it I have a deed—
To own this land I do not need a deed—
They all belong to me—gum, oak, and pine.

UPON THIS HIGH HILL

Upon this high hill where the rain clouds nestle,
Where snow is last to fade beneath the sun,
Is home of sawbriar, wild rose, Scottish thistle
And bracken flourishing where freshets run.
Upon this hill infertile land is thin
Among ravines, recessions, folded rocks
Where there's incessant blowing of the wind,
But it is home to possum, hawk and fox.
Tough-butted white oaks easily survive;
Persimmon, dogwood and the sourwood cling
Tenaciously to these rock ribs to live
And leaf and blossom for an unseen spring.
This land gives fresher beauty to the rose,
Land in the wind near sky and sun and star;
Gives autumn colors unsurpassed by those
Rich valleys where the soil and seasons are.

OUR HERITAGE

We are a part of this rough land
Deep-rooted like the tree.
We've plowed this dirt with calloused hand
More than a century.

We know each cowbell's ringing here
Which tells the time of day.
We know the slopes to plant each year,
What our folks do and say.

We know the signals of each horn
And the messages they send
At set of sun or early morn
Upon a blowing wind.

When we lie down in bed at night
And hear a foxhorn blow,
We often rise, take lantern light,
Untie our hounds and go.

We like to follow hounds that chase
The fox until the morn
Then go back home with sleepy face
And on to plow the corn.

There is not one who does not love
A field and farming ground,
With sky and stars a roof above
And a companion hound!

We love this land we've always known
That holds us and our dead—
The rugged slopes with scattered stone
That grow our daily bread.

We love the lyric barking hound
And a piping horn that trills.
We love our high upheavaled ground,
Our heritage of hills.

RETURN

I shall be going soon where no one knows:
I shall go to my pine pole mountain shack.
Before the autumn comes and summer goes
Before the leaves fall—I must be going back.
I was not made to walk on streets of stone
And breathe into my lungs the City smoke;
I must go to the highland world I own
Where I can breathe the air of pine and oak.
I shall go back to where the jar flies sing,
Back to brown hills that shoulder to the sky.
I want to see shikepokes on whirring wings,
I want to hear the bittern's lonely cry,
I want to hear the beetles sing at night,
I want to see the owl fly in the gray starlight.

EARLY AUTUMN

The multi-colored leaves are dying now,
Some hang like golden jewels to the bough,
And with the wind the pretty leaves go flying,
Over fields empty and forgotten now.
And in the wind the bare tree-tops are sighing,
Rabbits have found new drifts for sleeping now
Where briars have caught the leaves and held them **down**,
Cattle sleep now beneath the green pine bough
When there is not room in the stack and mow,
And cattle bed on dead leaves drifted down
In briars— And overhead day-drifting skies
Are filled with flying leaves and wild-bird cries.
The birds at night sleep in the shocks of fodder
On rugged hills beside the Sandy water.

GO, DANCE TONIGHT

Tomorrow may be bitter, who can tell.
Oh, listen to that call: "Move Children, Move!"
Tomorrow may be bitter, who can tell,
So spend this night a-dancing with your Love.
Oh, can't you hear that lonesome violin,
And can't you hear the strumming of guitars?
Better than listening to a lonesome violin
Out by oneself beneath the winter stars.
Now listen to that call: "Move Children, Move!"
First couple out—waltz up and down the hall,
"Move Children, Move!" Step lightly with your Love.
"Move Children, Move!" Oh, don't you hear that call!
"Move Children, Move!" That lonesome violin!
You see the bird flies out—the crow hops in.
"Move Children, Move!" Too slow that step you're in.

KYON MURRAY

"Stuart, when you came cross the hill today
Did growing corn and tall trees talk with you?
Last year when I was well it was that way—
I heard them talking when the wind blew through
The leaves and blades— And do the crickets and
The jar-flies sing out on the pasture hill?
Stuart, I do wish you could understand
How hard it is to lie against the will.
For fourteen months I've lain here on my back
And listened to the Spring and winter rain
Beat on the board roof of this mountain shack,
Knowing that I shall not be well again—
To walk upon the grass about the place,
To see the trees and feel the wind on my face."

HARD LUCK

I know he made cross-ties to earn his bread.
I know his crops burned in last summer's drouths,
And this is all he finds to buy the food
That goes to fill ten hungry children's mouths.
He gets eight cents to make a standard tie
Of hardwood tree— I think a man can make
Fifteen of these—a dollar twenty-cents per day—
Keeps his children from starving in a way.
Better to work on just a little pay.
It's all because the summer fields stayed dry,
Crops failed, and there was nothing left to do
But make cross-ties for men that pay so little;
Go home and eat corn-bread and play the fiddle.
They say the rich are having hard-luck too.

WHO BUILT AMERICA?

Who built America?—now I ask you.
Who cut the forest, plowed the rooty hills?
Who spanned the rivers and who built the towns?
America—the pioneers built you!
They made of you a nation. Their stubborn wills
Help conquer you, help cut your forest down.
The oxen and the horse help conquer you,
And they sleep with their masters under clay.
And no one dreams that they lived yesterday.
These conquerors now are dust—they are all dust,
And tall beech trees grow where their dusts are lain;
Tall nettles grow above and die again
In white caressing of the autumn rain.
Dust of these pioneers now did their shares;
Blue Dreamers now—America's "Conquerors!"

THEIR ANCIENT LOVE IS WRITTEN IN THIS DUST

Their ancient love is written in this dust
Of Flying Cloud and Princess Morning Star;
At last the plow has reached their final tryst
And sandbriar roots have sapped the dust they are.
He sleeps, a broken arrow in his skull,
In the cornfield by the waters of Siloam;
Her beads and bracelets are still beautiful,
Their bones preserved and bleached by sands of home.
Where did pursuit of happiness take these
When sunlit Siloam waters lapped the shore
And young spring winds sang in the willow leaves?
On red-moon nights what Gods did they implore?
And by some rival chieftain was he slain?
Was she once lovely? How did she meet harm?
Her face upturned to roots and summer rain,
She's found, through time, assurance on his arm.

GONE TODAY

It's hard for me to think that Hughes is dead
Since full of life I saw him yesterday—
Short of stature, grumbling, brown curly head;
So short among the careless boys at play:
And that was when the college grounds were green
And clouds went floating over lazily,
With apple blossoms white among soft-green;
In the twilight Spring-time of east Tennessee.
It's hard for me to think that Hughes knows night.
When very young we talked far in the night
About the glorious life ahead for us,
And how we dreamed of things that we would write.
Now Worley Hughes is sleeping on the hill,
And I am here—I'm plowing on the hill.

FREE RIDE

When he implaned in Dallas
A pestering airways guest
To ride the constellation
I queried why this pest
Should be Chicago bound.

Whom did he plan to see?
Why he chose the skyway?
And why his ride was free?

Before the perfect landing
Our guest approached the door
Ignoring signs and manners
And those he rushed before.

Soon as the door was opened
And steps for us let down
This Texas fly was greeting
A fly whom he was meeting
In big Chicago town.

SCHOOL MASTER, ONCE

It is most painful now as I
School master once return to this;
Master of learning, all they had
Until they grew and went beyond.
This barn was dear to them and me.
Only the skeleton remains;
Parts of the roof, windows and doors
And master's desk and window panes
Are gone into oblivion.

The birds and bats now carry on,
Where elm trees have reached new heights;
Young winds blow over greened-up fields
That lie in all directions here
Where fields of grass run with the winds.
These friendly winds have not erased
The memories of what has been
From those who caught fire here that spread
The flame of learning to the world.

SONG

Hard knuckles of the wind knock on my door.
The clock strikes twelve.
                            Another year has ended.
I stop my work with papers on the floor
And put away the books that have befriended
Me on so many nights before the fire.
Time at my heels has never brought me fears.
Someday Time will catch me.
                            I shall retire
Since mortal flesh cannot outlast the years.
Time cannot make me tremble like the leaf!
I look into the empty night and stare,
Midnight is lonely and is filled with grief;
Out there tonight is the ghost of yesteryear.
High in the midnight sky the bright stars glisten
While I begin my New Year with a song—
A melody to make the people listen.
I'll sing for all—the poor, the weak, the strong!

THE LAST LEAVE HOME

To see these rugged hills of home again
Before uncertain flight through troubled skies,
To be where autumn wind sends down red rain
Has brought me moods and hot tears to my eyes.
These are the jutted hills that nurtured me,
That gave me substance since my life began;
Within whose bounds I have known liberty
As much as any mortal on earth can.
I have stood here when other winds have blown
In seasons past to watch rain-dropping leaves;
Now I recount with pleasure days I've known
Before a change to scenes beyond the seas.
Upon this earth, beneath these clouds of fleece,
I wish I could command this time to stop
That I may know again these hills of peace
Where only leaf-blood trickles drop by drop.

A SONG FOR NAOMI

Time has been good that you and I have known
 Since poetry paid for your wedding ring;
And we bemoan Time has so quickly flown
 Between our summer and beginning spring.

We were so eager in our springtime hour
 To build a little house against the cold,
To plant our yard with native shrub and flower
 And watch their springtime blossoms first unfold.

We work to fill our cellar and our bins,
   We work from spring until the freeze and frost;
We work against lean hungry mountain winds;
   We work to find our labor is not lost.

To know we have a home upon this earth,
   To have a little fire to sit before
And hear the crickets singing on the hearth ...
   To have this much and still to work for more.

PARENT TIES

While we keep vigil of this infant daughter
Through lightning and cannonading thunder,
Through lamentations of the wind and water,
I think of families now torn asunder,
Scattered and lost on roads with evil turning
While we sit safely here behind log walls
In warmth reflected from our wood fire's burning,
Safe from the wind and rain that sadly falls.
I think of quails that nest among the sedges
Hovering their fledglings through the storm;
I think of parent foxes guarding ledges
To keep their wayward young from hunter's harm.
Never before have I felt parent ties,
That comforts of a home can mean this much;
When not a parent, my roof was the skies
And homes were houses without living touch.

ADMONITION TO A CHILD

Ah, sleep, you child, and let the wind howl round you.
You are too young to listen to the howls.
Lie still my child and sleep where winds have found you,
Lie there and do not wake to threatening scowls.
Heed not for heavens often threaten rain,
The thunder peals and yet no rain will fall,
And from a peaceful heaven comes a sudden rain
When one has not dreamed of a rain at all.
What does it matter what will happen, child?
When you are old as I you'll understand.
But while you can lie there and sleep, my child,
And let men strong as I furrow the land,
Then do not open once your sleep-closed eyes,
You'll find the world will take you by surprise!

TIME PASSES

An empty house can soon deteriorate
And birds take over eave and chimney stone,
And hinges red with rust on door and gate
Are signs to show that time has come and gone.
The golden wasps will find a way to enter
After one pulls the shades and bolts the door
To gallivant and die in cool midwinter
On windowpanes, in beds and on the floor.
The flimsy furtive moth will not be kind
To take the best one has to suit his taste;
The mice will enter, multiply and find
Books, manuscripts and everything to waste.
The sturdy walls one builds cannot shut out
Collective dampness and night-colored gloom
Where uninvited guests have brought about
Destruction to each nicely furnished room.

HOLD APRIL

Hold on to April; never let her pass!
Another year before she comes again
To bring us wind as clean as polished glass
And apple blossoms in soft, silver rain.
Hold April when there's music in the air,
When life is resurrected like a dream,
When wild birds sing up flights of windy stair
And bees love alder blossoms by the stream.
Hold April's face close yours and look afar,
Hold April in your arms in dear romance;
While holding her look to the sun and star
And with her in her faerie dreamland dance.
Do not let April go but hold her tight,
Month of eternal beauty and delight.

LULLABY

Rest now, young brain, for dreams will break too soon
And shatter on your world like slivered glass;
These dreams will be as mists beneath the moon
And lonely as winds muffling autumn grass.
I speak to you of dreams since I've known dreams
And blood that flows in you has flowed in me;
I must warn you that dreams are dead flower stems
And sap that comes each season with the tree.
Rest now, for you have years of life to face
And many paths to walk beneath the sun;
You'll know the joy and sting of love's embrace
Before your travail on this earth is done.
Rest now, young brain, in tender brittle growth!
Be still, small hands, do not clutch for the wind!
Rest now, for many dreams will come with youth!
Be frugal with the life you have to spend!

LAND WHERE THE HONEY–COLORED WIND IS FAIR

Give them leaf-laundered wind to breathe again,
Land where the honey-colored wind is fair,
Fondling the yellow stems of dying grain,
Combing the broomsedge fields' long, golden hair.
Give them a land of melancholy wind
To stir music in them eternally;
They would want sight if they were going blind,
And if tone-deaf, they would like melody.
They have breathed carbon on too many roads
And choking smoke in cities near and far;
They have been too submissive to strange fads,
Now let them wear the wind and sun and star.
The lonesome water's wordless, soothing songs
Are great for them beneath their bluer skies;
Nature's mistakes are better than man's wrongs,
Give them love language of the wild birds' cries.

WHY EVER GRIEVE?

Why ever grieve for blighted bloom and leaf
When Winter fought the Spring to keep his crown;
His second coming was a time so brief,
But long enough to sow his death-seeds down.
Why ever grieve for all this bitter strife
Since Spring returns with certainty and pride
To frozen Earth with promise of new life
With Nature her assistant and her guide.
The flowers that Winter killed will grow again
And cloaks of green adorn each naked tree
With Nature's healing sun and soothing rain.
With wordless blueprints from eternity.

COMMENTARY AND STUDY QUESTIONS

What are you after when you read literature? Is it enjoyment —enjoyment of what you are experiencing? Is it an appreciation of the reading experience? Yes, these are fundamental goals, but *enjoyment* and *appreciation* are slippery words. What do they mean? How, exactly, do you come by them? If you are already a seasoned spectator at football games, can you imagine enjoying the game without knowing the rules? Perhaps football became meaningful to you so long ago that you cannot remember when you first picked up the mental tools of analysis and evaluation that mean so much to your Saturday afternoon experience. The enjoyment of literature comes about in much the same way, with analysis and evaluation going on constantly as you read. For a genuine appreciation of literature, the more you know about the basic problem which a writer faces, the more fully realized your reading experience will be.

The word *experience* has been used often in the paragraph above. It is a key word to understanding, for the reading of literature *is* an experience, a mental experience, an experience in language. Certainly you will want to know something about the nature of this experience. Not only is it important to be able to analyze the plan for action which an author sets up in order to get his idea across to you, but it is also genuinely rewarding to be able to judge responsibly *why* he succeeded or failed. The serious student of literature knows that he has more than action, humor, or verse before him as he reads. The literature that you have read has a meaning that goes beyond the story line. Even when Jesse Stuart has, seemingly, no other purpose than to spin a good yarn, even as his old friends have entertained him with story after story around an open fire, the stories add up to a meaningful whole. You can tell that the author is a man with a serious purpose in literature. There are, then, two basic questions that you need to keep in mind in order to discover the author's meaning:

1. What is Jesse Stuart's purpose in writing?
2. How well has he succeeded in accomplishing his purpose?

This is the double-barreled challenge you should put to all literature. In fact, it is not a bad test for any work of art.

The questions which follow try to help you toward an evaluation of this sort. They aim also to give you some of the vocabulary and a few of the tools of analysis with which you may
set about forming opinions about what you have read. Since
you like to deal with ideas, the questions have been planned in
such a way that you can identify the basic ideas which go to
make up the meaning of Jesse Stuart's writing. For example,
what does this man have to say about good and evil? About
man and nature? About the purpose of life? Insofar as it is
possible, the questions encourage you, as you go along, to build
up your reactions and conclusions for a final judgment. If you
can come to feel responsible for what you say about the stories
and poems of Jesse Stuart and if you can tell clearly why you
feel as you do, you will have become a thinking reader.

Of course, the questions recognize the regional character of
Mr. Stuart's accomplishment. Jesse Stuart without Kentucky
seems impossible. Nevertheless, it would be profitable for you
to imagine his having lived somewhere else. Would we have
heard from him? In spite of his strong attachment to his part
of the world, however, some of the questions have been planned
to lead you away from his regionalism toward your own evaluation of Jesse Stuart as an individual writer. This is the goal
in a reading experience that is primarily literary. It is well to
remember as you read A Jesse Stuart Reader that you are not
doing so merely to learn more about life in the mountains of
eastern Kentucky, for literature goes beyond life. When Jesse
Stuart writes in his introductions that he has written some
stories exactly as they happened, they are not "life." They are
his interpretations of life, and the interpretations are his indi-
vidually, his alone. And that's exactly what makes the entire
experience of reading and evaluation an exciting discovery.

Finally, the study questions ask you to go back to the exact
words of a story or a poem to quote direct proof when you
offer an opinion or make a judgment. Often, too, in order to
sharpen your sensitivity to language, the study section suggests
that you reread or think about certain lines or passages. It is
a man's way with words that concerns you here. For one thing,
Jesse Stuart has been praised by experts for his accurate in-

terpretation of the hill dialect. A careful attention to the dialect used in the selections will make your reading a much more interesting experience in language.

The second reason for your close attention to the printed page is, of course, obvious. Jesse Stuart, poet, and Jesse Stuart, teller of tales, are one and the same. The beautiful poetic passages in the stories and biographies deserve to be reread. Go back, therefore, when you find such a passage, and reread it.

Art, it has been said, is not an end in itself but a means of addressing humanity. Jesse Stuart has spoken to you, and he has had something to say. The more thoughtfully you delve into what he has had to say, and into how he has said it, the more you will discover about what *you* have to say—about yourself and your world.

ELLA DeMERS
LONG LOTS JUNIOR HIGH SCHOOL
WESTPORT, CONNECTICUT

Nest Egg

Jesse Stuart's introduction suggests a profitable approach to a discussion of this first story. It was a school theme, winning A's at every try. Imagine the young Jesse as a contemporary of yours and try to discover why teachers on every academic level recognized its exceptional merit as a school theme.

1. Write Out of Your Knowledge

First, consider Mrs. Hatton's weekly practice: "Since our teacher Mrs. R. E. Hatton said we would write better about the things we knew, she let us choose our own subject." Do you think Mrs. Hatton's methods were sound? Why? Do you have other ideas? How much of Jesse Stuart's success do you think depends upon this philosophy?

2. Reader Interest

How does Jesse hold his reader's interest in this biography of a young rooster?

3. Good Beginning

Your composition teacher has a great deal to say about good beginnings. Reread Jesse's. Why is it effective? Note also the young writer's skillful transition, or shift, from opening conversation to narration. How does he accomplish this smoothly?

4. Foreshadowing

Pa's feeling of trouble ahead is an example of foreshadowing, hinting, on the author's part, as to what will happen. Note how many times Pa predicts doom. What purpose do the repeated predictions serve the storyteller?

5. Tenderness and Violence

The shrewd Ohio River showman and the intense, cock-fighting neighbors are a part of the vanishing frontier that needs to be recorded. Frontier life has always been a strange contrast of tenderness and violence. Can you find evidence of this contrast in Jesse's early composition?

The Thing You Love

1. Paradox

If you were asked to list the qualities which you would include in a characterization of the hill people you have met in the *Reader*, you would certainly include *tenderness* after having read this story. Some of the other stories in this collection will also point out the violence of spirit that seems to accompany man's living so close to nature. How do you explain this paradox of mountain temperament? A paradox is a true statement that seems to contradict itself.

2. Adolescence

Although we are concerned here with three people and their love for animals, this, you will agree, is Finn's story. Finn is an adolescent. Why is the emotional impact stronger for the reader as he watches a young boy put to the test?

3. Trial by Ordeal

Do you know Marjorie Kinnan Rawlings' regional novel *The Yearling*? Both Mr. Stuart and Mrs. Rawlings give us the moment when young boys pass from adolescence to manhood through the ordeal of "killing the thing you love." Do you accept the sacrifice the boys make as a legitimate part of growing up?

4. Animal Natures

The animals in this story are brave, too. How do cat and dog live up to the best within them, according to their natures?

5. Man's Relationship with Animals

Man's relationship with animals, as Mr. Stuart has pointed out, has always been a timeless theme. The bond between the two remains as mysterious as it ever has been since the days of early man. Only a genuine lover of animals can understand another man's attachment to his animal friend. So, for animal lovers only: does Finn's love for Sweetgum seem real to you? Will a cat follow its master as Sweetgum did?

Uncle Jeff Had a Way

1. Character Contest

Mr. Stuart's introduction makes it clear that he was interested in using the contrast between two characters to shape his story here. Notice that the story centers around the question: Who had the right answers at our home? Characterize Uncle Jeff and Pa in answer to that question.

2. Reader Respect

How does the author build respect for Pa's ways?

3. Reader Sympathy

It is important to the success of the story that we like Uncle Jeff and that we accept his solution with the same good humor Pa does. How does the author accomplish this? Use references.

4. Emphasis

In the animal half of the story the mules are named while the horses remain anonymous. Why?

5. Author Understanding

As you read further in the *Reader*, find other characters that show the author's understanding of both kinds of characters: the steady and the shiftless, the worker and the drone.

No Hero

1. Suspense

The element of suspense is important to this story. Make note of the ways in which the author builds tension for the reader from the opening paragraph to the surprise ending.

2. Dramatic Pause

What is the dramatic effect of Hester's pausing to survey the bright lights of Landsburg from the ridgetop? Why are these lines of lights, with their one "real bright" light, a particularly telling image?

3. Concept of Courage

Hester says he isn't brave. Does the fact that he admits to fear tell you anything about him? Does a man who does not fear danger (there are such!) go through the same ordeal as the ordinary man when he meets physical danger? Which man is more courageous?

4. Reader Sympathy

How does the author build up reader sympathy for Hester King?

5. Audience Gullibility

Consider the ways of the street carnival. What insights do you get into the way the carnival people in this story work upon the gullibility of their audiences?

Rain on Tanyard Hollow

1. Frontier Tale

Here is a story that belongs in the tradition of the American frontier tale. Although it is as harsh and as real as the life it portrays, it can be terribly funny and wonderfully shrewd in what it reveals about human weakness and folly. Try to recall stories by other authors, such as Mark Twain, that are in the same great tradition. Be sure you can justify your selection.

2. Folk Poetry

Read Pappy's prayer for rain aloud. Do you agree that this can be called a sort of folk poetry? Why?

3. Motivation

Examine the motivations, or reasons characters act as they do, in this story: Why was Pappy "a man of much misery"? Does his wife understand that it is more than the great drought that has been bothering him? Does his son?

4. Narrator

Mr. Stuart is particularly effective when he lets a hill character tell the story. Notice that this time it is not the protagonist, the chief character, who tells his own story; rather, the "I" is his son, a participant in the action. What advantages does this choice of narrator give Mr. Stuart in what he wants to say about human nature?

5. Dialect

One scholar of American English, Dr. Raven I. McDavid, Jr., has noted that a writer has at least three ways in which he can create a dialect effect. These are:

a. Spelling. He can use a special spelling to get closer to the actual pronunciation, as *hep* for *help*. He does not, however, need to give all the pronunciations. Why should just a suggestive few do the trick more effectively?

b. Vocabulary. He can include a selection of local vocabulary items, such as *quiled* for *coiled*.

c. Grammar. He can use one or two interesting examples of differing grammatical structures like "it's a sight at 'em that'll come out alive" for "it's a sight how many of them will come out alive."

Make a list of examples for all three devices as you read further in the stories.

Battle with the Bees

1. Inner Conflict

Every short story needs a conflict; without a problem we have little reader interest. In this story, the "inner" conflict is between Pa's way of life and the life his family would have chosen. Find references to support this observation.

2. Physical Conflict

In stories, physical conflicts, like battles with bees, very often reflect the inner conflicts of the principal characters. Show that this is true in "Battle with the Bees."

3. Character Contrast

Big Drone is as authentic a frontier figure as is his opposite, the hard-working pioneer. What are Big Drone's characteristics? How is Little Drone's character effective in contrast? Why does he resent his name?

4. Foreshadowing

Every conflict, of course, must be resolved, or settled. You wait for something to happen to Pa as soon as the story begins. How has the author prepared you early in the tale with hints that foreshadow the conflict to come?

5. Surprise Ending

The conflict, of course, is resolved in Mom's victory over her drone. Is the last paragraph a surprise to you? Does the fact that the battle was planned make the resolution more believable for you? Less believable?

Ezra Alcorn and April

1. Frontier Image

Jesse Stuart writes that, in his imagination, Fairlington was "like a small frontier town in the Old West." The word *frontier* has come to mean a great deal to American readers and television audiences. In fact, most Americans have an imagined set of ideas which they associate with the West: life is simpler and happier on the frontier; a person from the city, or from the East, is rarely to be trusted; men should be strong, silent, and brave; family insults must be avenged. What can you add to this list of values which make up our "frontier image"?

2. Folk Legend

As we read, we watch the author write Ezra Alcorn into folk legend. Notice Ezra's little rituals. What does Ezra "never" do? What does he "always" do? How does his April behavior contrast with his disposition in May?

3. Frontier Humor

Although the humor in this story is more gentle than the strain of laughter that runs through many frontier tales, Uncle Ezra's characterization is part of a tradition in literature known as "frontier humor." It is a tradition known by its exaggeration, superstition, boasting, and by the use of dialect. Find examples from the story that make Ezra a part of this literary heritage.

4. Fact and Fiction

Would the story have gained in strength had Uncle Ezra been lying as usual to Aunt Lillie? Is the half-lie just as effective? Support your answer carefully by giving reasons for your opinion. Remember a writer does not need to give the facts as they actually happened. He selects and shapes incidents in order to give the impression he feels his readers must have.

5. Characterization Clues

What do Uncle Ezra's two final wishes tell you about him?

Wild Plums

1. Jesse Stuart, Poet

Jesse Stuart, author, is almost inseparable from Jesse Stuart, poet. Point out details to show that the poet as well as the storyteller is at work in this story.

2. Relationships

"This day has slipped by like a dream." This is a beautiful line, aptly characterizing the entire experience. Show that Jason Stringer knows from the beginning that this day will be a significant one.

3. Poetic Vision

"The Tygart River bank is a million miles away from here today, Eustacia." Explain this line in the light of that which has been said above.

4. Change and Renewal

Not all of this story is on a poetic level; there is here also a practical schoolman's touch: Mason High School will get a spring vacation. Experts in educational administration insist upon vacations for students at intervals of eight or nine weeks for a renewal, a recharging of mind and spirit. Compare the tone of your school on a day in the middle of a long semester with a day soon after a week's holiday.

5. Themes in the *Reader*

If you agree with the idea suggested in question one, would you further concede that "Wild Plums" represents many of the ideas which go to make up the "message" of Jesse Stuart? The story, then, concerns the promise of youth, of man's joy in the annual renewal of life in the spring, and of Mr. Stuart's constant affirmation that life is good—especially in Kentucky. Before you have finished all of the stories, begin a list of the themes, such as those just listed, that you have found in Jesse Stuart's stories and poems.

The Great Cherokee Bill

1. Changing Patterns

Jesse Stuart's stories are a record of the great change that has come to the Kentucky hill country in our time. The stories he writes of his grandfather's or his father's day are frontier stories, while the tales of his own manhood reflect the transition to a modern, more urban, or city, culture. Some of the other stories in the *Reader* also reflect this transition. What contrasts can you point out between the old and the new ways of life?

2. The Entertainer as a Symbol

The Great Cherokee Bill, symbol, too, of another lost frontier, is an entertainer on a stage in a large, modern regional high school. Is he a sad picture for you? Is he a comic picture? an intensely human picture? a touch of Hollywood? a noble picture? Decide upon your reaction and tell why you feel as you do.

3. Mountain Laughter

Principal Stuart notes the difference in the intensity of the approval of the mountain men and in the strength of their laughter as compared to the audience reaction of the young people. The old squirrel hunters slapped each other on the shoulders and jabbed each other in the ribs with their boney hands. Do you think that the day will come when we shall no longer be able to hear that special kind of "mountain laughter" for which this vanishing frontier is famous? Can it be preserved for us in stories?

4. Group Psychology

Do you think that the Great Cherokee Bill was unusually gifted in his ability to identify the three troublemakers? Have you seen other people who have seemed as sensitive to the presence of problems in a group? Do you think you would have noticed them as quickly had you been prepared to look? What are the characteristics of their behavior in an auditorium group?

The Moon Child from Wolfe Creek

1. Comparison
Mr. Stuart compares the gentling of a wild, lonely mountain boy with the taming of cattle which have gone wild. Notice when the comparison is first made and how it is sustained throughout the story. Does it seem like a sound comparison to you?

2. Loneliness
Reread the last four sentences. Had you thought before of the basic need in every person for play and for human companionship? Why is a lonely child an especially moving figure?

3. Patience
Consider the importance of time in the story. Why was it important for Mr. Stuart to move slowly, to seem to ignore all of Don's moves?

4. Dignity of the Individual
Over and over in the literature of the Western world, stories repeat the theme we have come to characterize as the dignity of the individual. You'll find it in the Bible, in Greek poetry, in every conceivable type of story, old and new. Show how Jesse Stuart in his sympathetic portrayal of the people he knew so well is a part of this Western tradition.

This Farm for Sale

1. Narrator
Rarely has there been a more natural, made-to-order story idea than this for an author who loves with an equal passion his land and the words with which he can describe his land. Since Mr. Stuart's purpose obviously is to have us share these feelings, why is his choice of Shan as a narrator effective? Does his being a nephew rather than a son, a visitor rather than a permanent resident, help further the emotional impact that Mr. Stuart wants us to feel?

2. Emotive Force of Words

Uncle Dick's family needed words to make them see what they had. Consider the advertisement. To what emotions in his readers did Mr. Spencer appeal?

3. Protagonists and Antagonists

The advertisement, powerful as it is, does not move Aunt Emma or the cousins. Look up the meanings of the literary terms *antagonist* and *protagonist*. Can we call Uncle Dick the protagonist? the rest of the family antagonists? Why? Why not? Think here of "inner" conflicts these people represent.

4. Conflict of Values

Mr. Stuart's conflict is one that occurs often in American literature: the "unspoiled" values of life one finds in the "wilderness" against the sophisticated standards of living associated with the city. Reread and point out the parts of the story that clearly establish this conflict.

5. Theme

The theme of the story, in fact, of all of Mr. Stuart's writing, says that the wilderness way of life helped to root America's greatness in frontier virtues. "Go see a way of life, a richness and fulfillment that make America great, that put solid foundation stones under America!" Do you think this is true? Support your answer with carefully considered reasons.

As Ye Sow, So Shall Ye Reap

The title to this story comes from a passage in the Apostle Paul's letter to the Galatians, whom he has been scolding. In the 1961 New English Bible the line reads, "Make no mistake about this: God is not to be fooled; a man reaps what he sows."

1. Meaning: Figurative and Literal

What does this mean? How does this quotation from the New Testament apply to the two boys? Does it have two meanings—one figurative, the words used out of their actual sense, the other literal, the words used in their real meaning?

2. Imagination: Pictures

Your imagination has a good time flashing pictures across the screen of your mind as you read this story. Notice how quickly one hilarious scene follows the other. Beginning with Martha's pappy sitting under the peach tree pretending to read his Bible, describe the scenes which tickled your funny bone the most.

3. Restraint

The scene of reckoning with Shan's father, coming as it does so swiftly after the frantic run, is very nearly perfect. Notice the restraint, or calmness, with which Pa's devastating question is handled. What is the effect of restraint in a climax like this?

4. Motivation

Shan's love for Martha, "so pretty that she hurt his eyes," provides motivation for his actions and ties this well-told story together. Why is it fitting that the last sentence should end wistfully with a reference to her?

No Petty Thief

1. Believability

Mr. Stuart tells us, in his introduction, that he had always recognized this story's built-in handicap—who would believe it? Whether or not it had actually happened is beside the point, for no one expects the author to be a literal reporter. Rather, the story must *seem* to be true. Does your imagination accept the story as Jesse Stuart has imagined it might have happened, given this character, this motivation, and this setting? Why? Be able to back up your answers with proof from the story.

2. Narrator

The author tells us that he "let the man who stole the steam shovel tell the story." Much of the story gets to the reader *over* his naive misinterpretation of the facts, as in his remarks about Kentucky justice toward the end. Why is this a powerful method of narration in this case?

3. Clues to Motivation

Reread the third paragraph in the story. What reasons can you offer for the author's use of the three sentences about sleds in the third paragraph? What, then, motivates the theft?

4. Conclusion

Every author dreams of the perfect last sentence—a sentence that not only says with finality that this is indeed the end, but sums up also in one telling stroke the theme, the character, and his motivation. What does Mr. Stuart's technically beautiful last sentence tell you about this repentant man who will regret what he's done to his "dying day just because of Ma and Pa."

Miss Anna's Asleep

1. Message

Once again, Mr. Stuart's introduction gives the reader an opportunity to consider the art of fiction. Although a writer uses the events of the real world about him, the meaning of a story comes from within the writer. This was a story he had to create in order to get his message across. What is it?

2. Setting

This imagined incident takes place in April. Why did the author choose this month for his setting?

3. Mood

The wind also has a symbolic significance in the story. How is it used to get the mood and meaning across?

4. Unity of Place

Edgar Allan Poe claimed that a short story must have unity. One kind of unity is that of place. By centering all the immediate activity in the schoolroom, Mr. Stuart is able to range freely from the present to the past and back again in order to develop his idea. Find the places in the story where he does this. Show how he makes his transitions in time.

5. A Heritage from the Past

Jesse Stuart has said often that his life is dedicated to education. A real teacher feels his commitment to a teaching heritage that stretches back into the past. Quote from the story to show that Mr. Stuart is especially sensitive to this great tradition.

6. Universality of Theme

A teacher feels also that he is a part of a teaching fellowship that stretches around the world. What do you suppose the editors of the *National Education Association Journal* liked about this story for their million teacher readers?

Old Op and the Devil

1. A Universal Devil

The devil tale is found in literatures all over the world. It comes, of course, in many guises. Most often, however, in folk tales such as this, the devil assumes physical characteristics which are identifiable the world over. Describe the recognizable characteristics of Op's devil. Do you know any other devil tales?

2. A Regional Devil

What physical characteristics or what personal traits give Op's devil local color? In other words, what about him makes him particularly a Kentucky devil?

3. Good and Evil

Man's imagination has always been interested in explaining the existence of evil. In the standard devil tale, the hero has to make a choice between good and evil. Does this happen to Op? What line tells you his decision? What happens as soon as he has made his decision?

4. Reaction

It is the devil's threat to kick the growling dog that brings out the real strength of Op's character. How does Op react? Is the devil's answer satirical or does he mean what he says? Support your answer by referring to the devil's character.

5. Understanding

What does Jesse Stuart tell us about how he feels concerning the goodness or badness of the solitary, wild mountain men? How do you know how Mr. Stuart feels? Does he succeed in making you feel as he does? Refer back to the actual story to tell how he does this.

A Ribbon for Baldy

1. Paradox

Obviously, poverty experienced in boyhood is considered a handicap in our culture. What are some of the other "handicaps" you recognize in the living of an American life? Is it just possible that there is a paradox here, that some of our obstacles may prove to be blessings in disguise? In what way?

2. Education

The actual events recorded in this story took place more than a quarter century ago, yet the reader will note the progressive methods of Professor Herbert. Does your school compete in science fairs? How would you judge Jesse's project?

3. The Land

As you read Mr. Stuart's stories, you can become genuinely interested in the actual geography of the land which he describes with such affection. If you are a city dweller, do these first fifty acres which the Stuarts owned seem like a great deal of land to you? How was it possible for people who owned this much land to be too poor to buy a boy shoes?

4. Reverence for Life

Mr. Stuart wrote "A Ribbon for Baldy" after a serious illness. Like everyone who has been close to death, he found life "more precious than ever before." Find at least one passage that reflects the new intensity of his observation and appreciation.

Tradelast

1. Characterization

As you read this story, it will become clear that Mr. Stuart is shaping the impression he wants you to have through characterization and that several people are being presented rather carefully. The "tradelast" idea is Big Aaron's. What makes him the leader of the group?

2. Author Speaking

Shan's character is even more important, for he is the author speaking. Big Aaron tells Miss Dovie the truth at the end; Shan does not. Which of the two actions does the author lead you to prefer? How?

3. Resistance to Change

Because he is not of the old pioneering generation, nor yet one of the new as are the boys, Old Cief resists change with a great personal unhappiness. What reasons does the author give for Cief's embittered behavior? Do they seem reasonable to you? Why? Why not?

4. Change in Character

A writer must make sure that any change he contemplates in the personalities he has described will seem probable to the reader. Human personalities change only rarely. Does the change in Cief seem real to you? Explain.

5. Local Color in Language

Although Mr. Stuart does not use dialect when he writes about the younger generations, his language still reflects the speech of his part of Kentucky. What words and expressions do you find that give this story local color?

6. Theme

This is a gentle, happy story. What truth about life—as it is lived in the Kentucky hills and in your own home town—are you able to bring away from the reading of it?

Fight Number Twenty-five

1. Sensitivity to Surroundings
How important to the story is the author's sensitivity to his surroundings?

2. Reader Sympathy
An author is successful as an artist if he can make his reader *care* about what happens to his protagonist. Has Jesse Stuart been able to do this? Go back over the story to find how he has won your sympathy for Eddie and his dog.

3. Characterization
Characters in stories are revealed through action, dialogue, and description. In this story the emphasis on character revelation is through action. What does the action in this story tell you about Eddie and his dog?

4. Inner Thoughts and Feelings
Think of other stories in this collection in which you learn *less* about the characters from action than you do from their inner thoughts and feelings.

5. Animal Characters
A famous English critic, E. M. Foster, has observed that most animals are "flat" characters. Flat characters are constructed around one quality. They are types, usually, not growing or changing as the story progresses; they have no depth. Think of the animals in this story and characterize them. Are they flat or do they reveal more than one quality?

6. Technique
Usually we can classify a story in one of several areas of artistic achievement; for power of characterization, for significance of theme, for skill in the structuring of plot, for significant use of setting. In what areas does this story excel? Be sure that you can support your answer.

God's Oddling

God's Oddling is a tribute to Jesse Stuart's father; it is an explanation of the ways in which Mitch Stuart was "great in spirit and great in his influence upon others." Note how the author's plan of presentation, his "pattern of organization," exerts a selective force on the material that follows. For each of the excerpts, answer this question: How does this episode in Mitch Stuart's life reveal his influence upon others?

THE EARTH POET

1. What Makes a Poet?

A basic question for every serious reader to consider at one time or other is: What makes a poet? In what way is he like each of us? In what significant ways does he differ from the average man? Mitch Stuart is an "earth poet," without the "common symbols by which to share his wealth." In what ways was Jesse Stuart's father a poet?

2. Time

What do you learn about the relationship between the father and his young son in this essay? How important a factor is time in the significance of this relationship? How important is time in any father and son relationship? Do you feel that a more modern civilization strains at these ties? Explain your answers.

SOUNDS ON THE WIND

1. Mood

Reread the section on page 229 in which Mom says, "This is a God-forsaken place." The paragraph which follows is an example of Jesse's ability to create atmosphere and mood by the use of strongly emotional details. Find other passages in which he does this effectively. Identify with an adjective the mood he creates.

2. Significant Observation

There is scarcely a selection in the biographical section that does not bring home to the reader Jesse's attachment to the land and his overwhelming desire to possess as much of it as he can. Consider carefully, however, the significant last sentence in the paragraph next to the last. "It is a half-century valley for any one family, and our time is about up." Do you find this an unexpected observation? Why? Why not? What does it tell you about Jesse Stuart?

TESTIMONY OF TREES

1. Line Fights
In order to savor the full sweetness of Pa's victory, you must realize that this land-starved man had just bought his first fifty acres of land after having spent his strength on other men's land. Notice, however, that trouble did not come from an unexpected source. Jake Timmins' reputation was common knowledge. Point out references in the story that prove that line fights and squatter trouble were recognized evils in the hills. Why do you suppose this was so?

2. The Silent Trees
"Funny about the testimony of the trees," Uncle Mel tells Pa. "The silent trees will keep their secrets." What, exactly, does he mean? Explain carefully how Uncle Mel was able to prove that the land was Pa's.

CLEARING IN THE SKY

1. Dialogue and Character
"But there's not even a path leading up there," I said. "There's a path up there now," he said. "I've made one." This dialogue suggests more than the actual words seem to mean. What is the author suggesting to you about Mitch Stuart, American pioneer?

2. Symbolic Meaning—"Pioneer"
It is not enough for Mitch Stuart to find the land as God made it; we learn that it is important for him to improve worn-out acres when he finds them. Find the lines that say this. The dictionary defines *pioneer* as one who first enters or settles a region. Does the character of Mitch Stuart, pioneer, give a new meaning to the word?

3. Folk Learning

Jesse's father found a coffee tree (the Kentucky coffee tree) in his woods. How was he, uneducated in the science of botany, able to identify this? What examples do you know of folk learning in nature? What other examples do you find of this in the *Reader*?

4. The Larger Meaning

As Jesse and his father begin to climb the second bluff, Jesse notices the many other circling paths. "All paths go to the same place," his father explains. "Then why take the steep one?" asks Jesse. You are given the answer, with a physical background, at the end of the essay. Does the answer have a larger, more spiritual meaning? What is it?

The Thread That Runs So True

The Thread That Runs So True is Mr. Stuart's chronicle of his years as a teacher. The excerpts he has chosen give a fascinating picture of the variety of his experiences.

THE FIGHT WITH GUY HAWKINS

1. Human Dignity

This story is a great favorite of Jesse's young readers all over the country. The meeting of teacher and pupil repeats itself every September; both enjoy the challenge. Every teacher knows that the challenge must be met on an individual to individual basis. The key to the situation, of course, is mutual respect for the essential human dignity of the other. In the terms outlined above, explain what Guy thought of Mr. Stuart and why? Why did Mr. Stuart decide to fight? How did Guy react to the fight?

2. Discipline

While Jesse broods over the fallen Guy, he regrets having put off the moment of reckoning with Guy and Ova, for he let them think they were putting something over on him by chewing tobacco. Why do you suppose Guy and Ova acted like this? Should Jesse have acted sooner?

THE CONTEST WITH LANDSBURGH HIGH SCHOOL

1. Dramatic Ride

This 17-mile ride over a mountain in a blizzard on muleback will be as famous in the history of our culture and its values as the long walks of Abraham Lincoln for books and of Booker T. Washington's 500-mile hitch to enroll at Hampton Institute. What about the ride makes it especially dramatic and meaningful?

2. Paradox

This excerpt contains that paradox we see so often in life and in literature. A handicap, again, is actually a blessing. Can you explain the paradox?

The Year of My Rebirth

In this book Mr. Stuart has written his thoughts, his reminiscences, and his trials during the long recovery period following his heart attack.

I WILL NOT DIE

A Search for Values

Mr. Stuart writes with such sensitivity of the past that we are apt to think of him chiefly as an interpreter of a vanishing tradition. As this prologue, however, makes clear he *is* the modern man, a man of the jet age, a writer in America. The essay gives you a fascinating glimpse of an artist in search for meaningful values, of Jesse's Stuart's seeking to define, or to redefine, his philosophy of life. In what way was Jesse Stuart's philosophy of life changed by his heart attack?

THE SUMMING-UP

Interpretation

In autobiography, the reader's interest is centered in the story of the man who interprets the meaning of his life for us. Why do you suppose Mr. Stuart chose this journal entry as the conclusion of the selections?

A Farmer Singing

1. Self Appraisal

"Leaves from a Plum Grove Oak," or "A Farmer Singing," as it is called here, is the first poem in Jesse's first volume of poetry, *Man with a Bull-tongue Plow*. Read it as a letter to the editor and then reread it as a revelation of that search for self-identification and self-appraisal mentioned above. Why is this opening sonnet especially effective in letter form? (All of the poems in his first book are sonnets. A sonnet, you will remember, is a poem of fourteen lines, each of which has five beats. The stress pattern is known by the old Greek adjective *iambic*: unstressed, stressed. There is a set rhyme scheme, and the entire poem is concerned with a single thought or sentiment.) The young poet tells us what his "content" will be. What will be the sources for the images in the poems that follow?

2. His Credo

A credo is a statement of one's beliefs. In what way can we say that "A Farmer Singing" clearly expresses Jesse Stuart's own poetical credo?

Time for a Rhyme

1. Purpose

In this sonnet the young Jesse states his life purpose. What word pictures does he use to make his purpose clear?

2. Decision

Why can you say that his purpose was a "lonely" decision?

Land Scroll

1. Personification

Speaking of an inanimate object or an idea as if it were a person is called "personification." Explain the figure of speech used in the first two lines. Why is it a good personification for a Kentucky hill poem?

2. Lyric Promise

Is the rest of the poem as good as the first two lines? Why? Why not? Refer to specific lines in the poem for proof.

This Land Is Mine

Kinship to the Land

> I am the land, for it is part of me—
> We are akin and thus our kinship be!
> It would make me brother to the tree!

Much has been written in answer to the puzzling question: What makes a poet? Among the mountain folk Jesse was one who was different, and he celebrates this difference in poem after poem. What, then, *does* make a poet? The quotation may help you to get started. What about Jesse Stuart sets him aside from, and yet makes him at the same time more a part of, his land and his people?

Upon This High Hill

1. Detail

This poem is a contrast between the rich valleys and Jesse's own infertile hills. List the details that go to make up the picture of the hill country.

2. Contrast

In what way are the valleys "better" than the hills? Yet the poet seems to prefer the hills to the valleys. Why?

Our Heritage

Emotional Appeal

One more lyric tribute to his "rough land"! List the words and pictures that make for the emotional appeal of the poem.

Return

1. Cumulative Effect
Jesse Stuart is always emphatic when he returns to one of his strongest themes, that of the contrast between life in the hills and life in the city. Notice the last six lines. Have you realized what has been done structurally to establish emotional intensity? The composition principle used here is that of cumulative effect. Explain what the term means by analyzing what Mr. Stuart has done in these last six lines.

2. Shakespearean Sonnet
Here Mr. Stuart was careful to follow the rhyme scheme of the Shakespearean sonnet (ab ab cd cd ef ef gg). See if you can trace this rhyme pattern.

Early Autumn

1. Poem of Description
Just as we can distinguish among different types of prose composition, so can we identify types in poetry. How can you tell that this is a poem of description?

2. Word Clues
Note that the key to an understanding of the poet's description is given in the first line, in the word *dying*. What details does the poet supply to fill in the picture?

Go, Dance Tonight

1. Dance and Characterization
You can try to know the mountain people through their arts, through their songs, through their stories—and through their dances. What do you learn about Kentucky men and women from this poem?

2. Dance and the Physical World
How has the poet tried to recreate the physical aspect of the square dance?

Kyon Murray

1. Poem of Characterization
The title shows the reader that the poet intended this sonnet as a poem of characterization. What are the dominant character traits revealed about Kyon Murray?

2. Poet Himself
What do you learn about the poet in the poem?

Hard Luck

Mood
A singing optimism based on gratitude for everything that has been given him is a dominant characteristic of Jesse Stuart's writing. Usually when he cannot praise, he laughs. Note, however, that this poem is written in a different mood. Use an adjective to characterize the mood of the poem.

Who Built America?

Direct Emotion
For most readers the image of the pioneer as the builder of America relates to a world that belongs well into the past. Jesse Stuart, however, has helped his father and his grandfather "plow the rooty hills"; he has lived the life of a pioneer. Can you feel that his is a direct emotion? What does this do to establish the sincerity of the poem?

Their Ancient Love Is Written in This Dust

Place and People
Jesse Stuart writes of the people who belonged to the land before his ancestors claimed the hill country—the Indians; the place is the same. Do the Indian lovers fit into the landscape Jesse creates as easily as do his hill people? Prove your answer with references to the poem.

Gone Today

Characterization and Description
Elements of both characterization and description combine in this poem. Identify details for each type of writing.

Free Ride

Light Verse
This is the only purely comic poem in this volume. Explain the sources of the humor.

School Master, Once

Relationship
A poet is what he is because his mind deals with relationships. From a contemplation of a deserted schoolhouse, it is not difficult for him to feel a significance that transcends mountains and in one poem encompasses the world. This feat, of course, he accomplishes by the use of symbols. Point out how Jesse Stuart does this in "School Master, Once."

Song

1. Stanza
Study the form of this lyric. Each stanza, or division of the poem, has something different to say. Point this out.

2. Contrast
Show how the poet has used contrast.

3. Theme
What is Jesse Stuart saying to you in this poem? Try to have your statement of the theme go beyond the limits of this one New Year's Eve.

The Last Leave Home

1. Impact
Understanding of this poem is increased if you will consider the historical background. How does the poet tell you what that background is?

2. Telling Words
Keeping the background in mind, what effect is achieved by the use of the words *command* and *blood* in lines 14 and 16?

A Song for Naomi and Parent Ties

Paraphrase
Both poems give the reader a glimpse into Mr. Stuart's family life. One of the surest ways to learn whether or not you have caught the meaning that the poet wants you to have is to write a paraphrase, a statement of the meaning, of the poem in two or three sentences. Paraphrase the meaning in each of these poems.

Admonition to a Child

Paraphrase
Write a paraphrase of this poem. Compare your paraphrase with others written in class.

Time Passes

Emotion
A descriptive poem can be thought of as a painting. In art, too, the painter wants to give more than a photographic representation of what he has seen. What is the *feeling* that Jesse Stuart communicates to you in this poem? What word gives you the first clue as to his purpose?

Hold April

1. Symbol

April, as has been noted before, is one of Mr. Stuart's most productive symbols. Recall its meaning in other poems and stories. See "Ezra Alcorn and April" and "Wild Plums."

2. Suggested Meaning

Note especially the symbol value in the phrase "in dear romance." The word *romance,* too has more than one meaning. Ordinarily the word is used to denote a love affair, but it has a literary meaning, too, suggesting an appeal to imagination and fancy. What other words in the poem hold the same meaning for the reader? (Example, "faerie dreamland.")

3. Power with Words

This is a poem written in the poet's middle years. What lines show you his growing ability to capture beauty in words?

Lullaby

1. Person Addressed

In this sonnet an older person speaks to a young child. To whom do you think the poem is addressed? What clues in the poem lead you to think so?

2. Simile

What does the poet tell us about his own dreams when he uses the expression "shatter on your world like slivered glass"? Find the simile in the line. Is it a good comparison? Why? Why not? A simile is a figure of speech which expresses a direct comparison between two things which belong to different classes. The prepositions *like* or *as* are the grammatical link between the two things being compared.

3. Suggestion
In the same vein he speaks of a young brain's "brittle" growth. Why is this a good adjective for this poem?

4. Theme
The theme of the poem is its essential meaning. The poet sometimes condenses his meaning in a line or phrase as Mr. Stuart has done in this sonnet. What is the theme, in his words?

Land Where the Honey-colored Wind Is Fair

1. Reference
To what do the pronouns "they" and "them" refer?

2. Contrast
The poem is organized around a contrast. What has been contrasted?

3. Concern for an Inner World
Usually the reader does not expect objectivity from a poet. Since Jesse Stuart's concern is for the inner world of feeling, it is his own personal understanding of the truth as he sees it that you should look for. Is this, then, a "true" poem? Support your answer with references to the poem.

Why Ever Grieve?

1. A Special Use of Words
What does the expression "winter kill" mean? What is its significance in this poem?

2. Theme
Repeat the lines which can serve as the theme, not only of the poem, but also of Jesse Stuart's philosophy.

JESSE STUART

JESSE STUART (1906–1984), Kentucky poet, short story writer, and novelist, was one of America's best-known and best-loved authors. A natural-born storyteller, Stuart was the first real poet, according to one critic, to come out of the Appalachian mountain region. During his lifetime he published 2,000 poems, 460 short stories, and more than 60 major books which have immortalized his native Kentucky hill country.

Jesse Stuart was Kentucky's most prolific writer and the state's poet laureate from 1954 until his death. His poetry and prose won high critical praise and innumerable awards, prizes, and fellowships, including the Thomas Jefferson Southern Award, and the Award of the Academy of American Poets. His novel *Taps for Private Tussie* was a Book-of-the-Month Club selection. Also among Stuart's volumes celebrating his native land, people, and their traditions are: *Man With a Bull-Tongue Plow* (poems), *Men of the Mountains* (stories), *To Teach, To Love* (essays), and *Kentucky Is My Land* (poems).